HUNTING ARKANSAS

Hunting Arkansas

The Sportsman's Guide to Natural State Game

by KEITH SUTTON

The University of Arkansas Press
Fayetteville
2002

Copyright © 2002 by Keith Sutton

All rights reserved
Manufactured in Korea

ISBN: 978-1-55728-719-9
eISBN: 978-1-61075-194-0

26 25 24 23 22   5 4 3 2

Designed by Liz Lester

Library of Congress Cataloging-in-Publication Data

Sutton, Keith B.
    Hunting Arkansas : the sportsman's guide to natural state game /
by Keith Sutton.
      p.   cm.
   ISBN 1-55728-719-8 (pbk. : alk. paper)
  1. Hunting—Arkansas. I. Title.
SK53 .S87 2002
799.29767—dc21   2001005408

*To Lewis Peeler,
my constant hunting companion,
whose friendship means more than I can ever express.*

Contents

List of Illustrations	ix
Acknowledgments	xi
Introduction	xiii

BLACK BEARS
Bear State Bruins	3
Charged by a Bear	11

BOTTOMLAND BIRDS
Timberdoodle Time	17
Hunting Snipe: For Real!	24
Gunning for Gooney Birds	31

CROWS
A Calling Card for Crafty Crows	39

DOVES
A Place to Hunt Natural State Doves	47
Whistling Wings and Waterways	53
This Dove Hunting Is the Pits	57

DUCKS
Green-Timber Greenheads	63
Ducks the Color of Autumn	68
Teal, We Meet Again	75
Mud-Puddle Ducks	83
Big-River Duck Hunts	90

ELK
Buffalo River Renaissance	101

FURBEARERS
A Case for Coon Hunting	107
Of Possums and Possum Dogs	111

GEESE
Canadas on the Comeback	119

Snow Storm	124
Specialize for Specklebellies	129

PREDATORS

Bobcat Action	135
The Arkansas Coyote: Nobody's Fool	140

QUAIL

Hunting Arkansas Bobwhites	147
Leapfrog Quail Hunting	153

RABBITS

The Canecutter Challenge	159
Rabbit Tactics: Lewis Peeler Style	165
Rabbits without Rover	169

SQUIRRELS

Crowley's Crackers	177
A Fishy Way to Squirrel Hunt	184
Outfoxing Ol' Foxy	190
Peak Hunting for Bushytails	195

WHITE-TAILED DEER

Wilderness Whitetails	205
Farmland Deer, Arkansas Style	211
Hunting the Rut	218
Big Bucks on "The Refuge"	225

WILD HOGS

Hunting the Legendary Razorback	231

WILD TURKEYS

On Being a Turkey Hunter	239

SPECIAL STORIES ABOUT ARKANSAS HUNTERS

The Rabbit Man	249
Limbgripper Jim	255
Gene Moore	261
Appendix: Arkansas Hunting Information Sources	269
Index	273

Illustrations

All photos by the author.

1.	Arkansas's namesake, the black bear	2
2.	A squalling bear cub up a tree	12
3.	Woodcock hunters	16
4.	The American coot, a member of the rail family	30
5.	Successful crow hunters	38
6.	A good dove hunting area	46
7.	Wing shooting for mourning doves near a waterway	52
8.	Setting dove decoys by a gravel pit pool	58
9.	Mallards pitching into a green-timber reservoir	62
10.	A colorful wood duck drake	70
11.	Hunter with green-winged teal	76
12.	Duck hunting on small out-of-the-way waters	84
13.	A beautiful sunrise on a big-river duck hunt	92
14.	Elk along the Buffalo National River	100
15.	A coon hunter's baying hound	106
16.	White possum	112
17.	Canada goose	118
18.	Flock of snow geese	126
19.	White-fronted geese	130
20.	Bobcat	134
21.	Quail hunter and pointing dog	146
22.	Quail hunter firing on flushing bobwhite	154
23.	Swamp rabbit	158
24.	Lewis Peeler and his dogs, Reb and Bear	166
25.	Rabbit hunting without dogs	170
26.	Calling squirrels	176
27.	A river float squirrel hunt	186
28.	A handsome fox squirrel	192
29.	A gray surprised by team hunters	196
30.	White-tailed deer	204
31.	George Hobson and his record whitetail	210
32.	Rutting-season whitetail	220
33.	A White River National Wildlife Refuge buck	226

34. Razorback tusker	230
35. A successful wild turkey hunt	238
36. The Rabbit Man, Hugh "Ed" Middleton	248
37. Limbgripper Jim and the author's sons	256
38. Gene Moore	262

Acknowledgments

Some of the articles composing this book were originally published in the following magazines:

"Charged by a Bear" (originally published as "There's a Bear in My Face"), *Explore Arkansas,* March 1999;

"Timberdoodle Time" (originally published as "Arkansas Woodcocks"), *Arkansas Sportsman,* December 1993;

"Whistling Wings and Waterways" *Arkansas Fins & Feathers,* September 1984;

"Green-Timber Greenheads" (originally published as "A Marvel of Mallards"), *Sports Afield,* December 2000;

"Teal, We Meet Again" (originally published as "Arkansas Teal Tactics"), *Arkansas Sportsman,* September 1996;

"Mud-Puddle Ducks" (originally published as "Arkansas' Mud-Puddle Ducks"), *Arkansas Sportsman,* December 1996;

"Big-River Duck Hunts" (originally published as "Big-River Ducks"), *Arkansas Sportsman,* December 1988;

"Snow Storm" (originally published as "Stuttgart Snows"), *Arkansas Sportsman,* January 1998;

"Bobcat Action," *North American Hunter,* November 1999;

"The Arkansas Coyote: Nobody's Fool," *Arkansas Sportsman,* February 1988;

"The Canecutter Challenge" (originally published as "Swamp Rabbits: Small game challenge in the southeast bottoms"), *Arkansas Hunting & Fishing Magazine,* January/February 1989;

"Rabbit Tactics, Lewis Peeler Style" (originally published as "Tactics for Arkansas Rabbits—Lewis Peeler Style"), *Arkansas Sportsman,* November 1989;

"Rabbits without Rover," *North American Hunter,* November/December 1996;

"Crowley's Crackers," *Arkansas Sportsman,* September 1995;

"A Fishy Way to Squirrel Hunt" (originally published as "Floating for Squirrels"), *North American Hunter,* September 1998;

"Outfoxing Ol' Foxy" (originally published as "Outfoxing Arkansas Fox Squirrels"), *Arkansas Sportsman,* September 1990;

"Peak Hunting for Bushytails" (originally published as "Peak Hunting for Natural State Bushytails"), *Arkansas Sportsman,* October 1987;

"Wilderness Whitetails," *Field & Stream,* October 1990;

"Farmland Deer, Arkansas Style" (originally published as "Arkansas' Farmland Deer"), *Arkansas Sportsman,* October 1993;

"Hunting the Rut" (originally published as "Hunting the Rut for Arkansas' Big Bucks"), *Arkansas Sportsman,* October 1986;

"Big Bucks on 'The Refuge'" (originally published as "White River National Wildlife Refuge: Arkansas Haven for Trophy Whitetails"), *Arkansas Sports Scene,* November 1990;

"The Rabbit Man," *Southern Outdoors,* May/June 1992;

"Gene Moore" (originally published as "A 'Natural' Philosophy for Big Delta Bucks"), *Arkansas Sportsman,* November 1987.

Introduction

When it comes to hunting, I like variety. I enjoy chasing swamp rabbits with beagles and treeing coons with hounds. I've tried my hand at calling in coyotes and bobcats, and love watching crows flock to a caller playing their fight song. Woodcocks are perhaps my favorite game birds, but I enjoy hunting them no more than hunting mallards and wood ducks in green timber or pass-shooting doves in a sunflower field.

Bow hunting for deer was a favorite pastime in years gone by, and I still hunt them with muzzle-loader and modern gun. I've been an ardent squirrel hunter since age ten and an occasional quail hunter just as long. Now and then I've stalked marshes for snipe and coots and, shooting geese, lain in a spread of decoys. Years ago I hunted possums daily with an unusual treeing dog named Rusty.

I feel fortunate to live in Arkansas because here, all these forms of hunting and more are available. We can't hunt moose or mountain lions or bighorn sheep, but the Natural State has given up some impressive elk to hunters in recent years, and we have plenty of black bears to pursue thanks to a successful restoration effort. The many grouse family members hunted elsewhere aren't available in Arkansas, but if a hunter worked at it, he could bag twenty species of waterfowl in a single season. Maybe our quail hunting doesn't measure up to that found in Texas or Kansas, but you won't find better squirrel and rabbit hunting anywhere.

Changes in antiquated laws have made wild hogs, the razorbacks of legend, legal to hunt for the first time in more than a hundred years, and these fierce destructive beasts have become increasingly plentiful—too plentiful—in many counties. Good hunting opportunities are the result.

Our wild turkey population continues growing as well, with superb hunting available statewide for those who enjoy pursuing this monarch of game birds.

If trophy bucks are your thing, look no further. The number of huge Boone and Crockett whitetails taken here in recent years is astounding.

What I'm trying to say is this: Arkansas offers quality hunting opportunities for a wide variety of game birds and game animals. And if I have done my job well, this book can help you immerse yourself in the incredible diversity found here. In the pages that follow, I'll share with you tips for hunting nearly every game species in the state, insights into the best places to hunt, and a compilation of interesting historical facts that should help you better appreciate the efforts of the Arkansas Game and Fish Commission and other agencies and organizations who restored hunting in this state to quality levels never before seen.

I couldn't do this by myself, of course. I've relied on the help of some of Arkansas's most skilled hunters, people who graciously allowed me to go afield with them to listen and observe. The things they've taught me, the words they've spoken, are written here to provide a lasting guide for others to follow.

Many of our state's biologists and researchers have been kind enough to let me pick their brains and tag along when they were in the field. They, too, have been good teachers, and much of what I've learned from them is in this book.

I've delved into the works of the many excellent hunting scribes who have called this state home, including contemporary writers like Jim Spencer, Gregg Patterson, John Heuston, Mack Ray, Charlie Bridwell, Mike Pledger, Michael Cartwright, and great writers from the past such as Charles Fenton Mercer Noland. The words they've written are a treasure trove of information about hunting techniques, biology, blue-ribbon hunting grounds, history, and the true essence of the hunting experience. They have taught me more than I could learn in several lifetimes of hunting, and I am grateful to those who have allowed me to share their words here.

Much that you will read here is borne from my own experiences hunting in Arkansas. I've pursued game on most of the state's wildlife management areas and national wildlife refuges, on many private clubs, and on lands opened to me by generous individuals willing to share the bounty found on their private holdings. I've hunted the mountains and the river bottoms, flooded woods and agricultural fields, suburban areas and backcountry wilderness, but there is much I've yet to do, much more I've yet to learn. I hope, however, what I've written here will lead you to a greater understanding of Arkansas's game animals and hunting, an understanding that will lead you to new adventures and memorable experiences.

May your hunting always be fruitful.

Bear State Bruins

> "Devil's Fork of the Little Red River (Ark.)
> *Feb. 15th, 1837*
>
> "Dear Mr. Editor,—Being that this is a rainy day, I thought I would write you about the bear hunt."

So begins the story of "Pete Whetstone's Bear Hunt," the first of forty-five Pete Whetstone letters written by Charles Fenton Mercer Noland for the New York *Spirit of the Times*. Noland was one of Arkansas's earliest and most prolific outdoor writers. He moved to Batesville in 1826, and there, under the pen name Pete Whetstone, he wrote many stories about his hunting and fishing adventures in Arkansas.

While Noland hunted deer, turkeys, ducks, prairie chickens, and quail, and fished for everything from "bull minners to ponderous cat," his favorite sport was hunting bears. Some of his Batesville friends kept packs of bear dogs, and Noland frequently went along on hunts to areas around the town of Oil Trough, the Devil's Fork of the Little Red River, and War Eagle Creek. "Pete Whetstone's Bear Hunt" chronicles one of those hunts, during which a "tremendous bear" was wounded by Whetstone and his hunting companions. Whetstone's dogs continued after the bear and finally cornered it.

"When we overtook them," Noland wrote, "they had him at bay; two dead and three crippled dogs told of the bloody fight they had had. Sam Jones fired; the wound was that time mortal. At the crack of the gun, the dogs again clamped him; with a powerful reach of his paw, he grabbed the old General, and the next moment fastened his big jaws on him; this was more than flesh and blood could stand: I sprung at him with a butcher-knife, and the first lick sent it to the handle. He loosened his jaws and Sam Jones caught the old General by his hind legs and pulled him away. I gave him one more stab, and he fell dead."

Tales like this one by Noland, and those of other writers such as Tom Breese, John Gaskins, William Quesenberry, and Thomas Thorpe, made

---

In the nineteenth century, Arkansas was known as the Bear State, a nickname derived from the large number of black bears found and hunted here.

Arkansas nationally famous as an unrivaled bear-hunting territory. In fact, the bears of which they wrote became larger-than-life symbols for frontier society. It was no accident, therefore, that Arkansas was unofficially nicknamed "The Bear State" early in its history.

Arkansas bear hunting was popular long before Noland's time and had its roots with native Americans. Indians used bear skins for robes, the teeth and claws for adornments, and the meat and fat for food. Bear oil rendered from the fat was used for cooking and as a flavoring. The oil often was mixed with red dye, scented with sassafras, and rubbed on the skin and hair. Newborn babies were rubbed with bear oil to protect them from insects.

The Indians preferred hunting bears in winter. They would locate a bear denning in a tree and burn it out. As the bear climbed out to escape, it was easily killed. This practice continued with early European explorers. On April 22, 1721, the journals of French explorer Bernard de La Harpe record, "... we killed a bear and a cub bear which we made come out of a hollow tree with fire."

Bear skins and oil were the foundation of a large hunting industry centered around Arkansas Post during French and Spanish occupation of the state. Bear oil didn't turn rancid as fast as butter or lard and was preferred for cooking. Hollowed-out logs and empty rum pots were filled with bear grease and shipped to Arkansas Post and then to New Orleans. Thousands of bears were killed annually.

In the spring of 1806, nine hundred thirty bear skins and a "considerable quantity" of bear oil and tallow were exported from Arkansas Post by one company alone. Huge quantities of bear skins and oil sewn up in deer skins were shipped downstream to New Orleans where bear skins sold for one dollar and oil for one dollar per gallon.

Bear meat, often made into "bear bacon," was a staple food of early Arkansas settlers, and domestic goods were often paid for with bear skins and oil. The oil was highly valued by early residents of the Ozarks. In *The History of Lawrence, Jackson, Independence and Stone Counties* published in 1904, Dr. Simeon Bateman, an early resident of the area, is quoted: "Bear's grease was as good as butter. We used bear's oil in place of lard and ate it like molasses."

Unfortunately, the presence of so many bears made raising livestock a precarious venture. "Uncle Mel" Robinson who lived in Jackson

County in 1831 later reminisced, "We could raise no hogs. The bears carried them off. One night a bear came and stole a pig and the next day we got the bear and the pig, too. The bear had eaten a little of the pig's shoulder and was asleep."

Dr. Albert Honor who grew up in Phillips County told that virtually all the boys who grew up there in the nineteenth century dreamed of going on a bear hunt down in "The Bottoms." He confessed that he never got to go on a bear hunt himself, but he made these observations as a child:

> They were bound for "The Bottoms," and would hunt in the canebrakes and big timber between Helena, Arkansas City and the White River.
>
> There was no intention of shooting any bear: this was below the dignity of a bear hunter. The hunting was done by dogs who would find, chase and "bay" a bear. Once the bear was bayed he would fight the dogs that ran at him from every point of the bay circle.
>
> When the men reached the bay, one or more of them would go in to kill the bear with a knife. Mr. Opp had a great reputation as a killer of bears. Before going in to kill the bear, Mr. Opp would exact a promise of no shooting unless "you think I am being killed."
>
> With every pack of bear hounds was one or more shepherd dogs. These dogs did not enter the chase nor the fight until their master went in, then they were fresh and kept biting the bear from unexpected quarters while their master was busy cutting the bear's throat.
>
> Once the bear was dead, it was lifted from the ground and hung by its fore feet, using rope or "galluses," or anything handy, to a limb five or more feet from the ground.
>
> Then the bear was dressed and the heart, lungs, liver, and other "innards" given the dogs . . . While all the dogs feasted on bear innards, the bear was skinned, untied, and taken back to camp. The first bear to be killed on the hunt was consumed by the hunters while in camp. There were many stories about bear stew and camp stews. Some of the stories were undoubtedly embellished by the whiskey drunk directly from stoneware gallon jugs which were an integral part of bear hunting equipment.
>
> Other bears killed were brought back to Helena and often one

was displayed in front of Mr. Burton's meat market on Rightor between Cherry and Ohio Streets. There a choice cut could be purchased by a non-hunting game lover.

George Robertson of Paducah, Kentucky, also came to hunt bears in the nineteenth-century wilderness south of Helena. Loading their hunting gear on steamboats, a party of as many as thirty men would land near Modoc and camp nearby. "I remember one occasion, it took ten wagons and forty mules to move our camping equipment into the woods where we pitched camp," he said.

And how many bears would they kill on a single trip? "Well," he replied, "I remember that on one of them we killed thirty two. I packed the meat down in a hollow cypress tree camp near mine."

Unfortunately, this indiscriminate killing of bears by early Arkansans and subsequent habitat reductions signaled the demise of the black bear in Arkansas. Hunting was prohibited by setting a closed season in 1927. By that time, bears had long since been wiped out in the Ozark and Ouachita Mountains and only forty to fifty remained in and around White River National Wildlife Refuge in southeast Arkansas.

The Arkansas Game and Fish Commission reported in 1928 there probably were about twenty-five bears in the state. None had been seen except in the White River country where they ranged on both sides as far north as St. Charles, although "considerable bear sign" had been located by a state trapper in the hill country west of Hot Springs.

Black bears, the commission continued, "are fully protected by law until 1931: however, sentiment favorable to protection has not crystallized as rapidly among our citizens as legislative action indicates.

"As a general rule the average person believes in killing a bear on sight and, if one is not easily sighted, there is strong inclination to get the dogs and chase him down. When brought into court for ending the life of a bear the killer usually proves that the animal was destroying crops, poultry or livestock for him and thus creates a knotty problem for the judge or jury. We are hopeful that as the black bear is reestablished in considerable numbers he will grow in popularity and his protection become assured from the public sentiment standpoint."

In 1949, the Game and Fish Commission decided to try halting the bear population decline and released four bears in the Ozarks—two in the Black Mountain area and two in Stone County.

Ten years later, the Game and Fish Commission began a concerted effort to reestablish the species. It entered into an agreement with the Minnesota Department of Natural Resources and the Canadian province of Manitoba under which Arkansas would trade bass and wild turkeys for the privilege of trapping black bears for transfer to the state. From 1959 until the program ended in 1968, a total of two hundred fifty-four black bears were trapped and released in remote areas, primarily in the Ozark and Ouachita National Forests where habitat was considered excellent. This was then, and still is, the most massive bear restoration program ever conducted in the United States.

Since the original releases, the bear population has expanded rapidly. The state's population was estimated at six hundred to seven hundred bears in 1973, and, today, the population is approaching four thousand bears statewide.

The Arkansas bear hunting season reopened in 1980 after a fifty-three-year hiatus. The first hunt was restricted to four wildlife management areas—Piney Creeks between Russellville and Jasper; White Rock, which covers a large part of four northwest-Arkansas counties; Buffalo River near Jasper; and Gulf Mountain near Clinton. Permits for the first two areas were limited to two thousand while only one hundred fifty were issued for Buffalo River and Gulf Mountain.

The hunt was set for December 1–6 to protect females, which usually den earlier than males. Hunters were allowed to take only adult bears, those weighing more than seventy-five pounds, but could not take sows with cubs at their sides.

Preseason harvest predictions never exceeded twenty. The 1,334 hunters who actually participated bagged five bears. The hunters also learned that bear hunting is hard work, and skills that have been dormant for fifty-three years must be honed for success.

The objective of the first bear hunt was to provide quality recreation for Arkansas sportsmen and, at the same time, to collect some badly needed biological data on our bears. The use of dogs and baiting was not allowed on this and subsequent hunts to insure the population would only be lightly harvested. As a result of these restrictions, harvests over the years have been relatively modest, ranging from 5 to 207 bears.

Bear hunting in the Natural State remains relatively popular, and it appears hunters can look forward to a short bear season or seasons each year. In fact, it's likely hunting opportunities will expand in the near future, and hunters may able to pursue bears in the Delta region of the state, in addition to zones in the Ozark and Ouachita Mountains where they've been hunted for more than two decades. Early estimates from an on-going population-dynamics study indicate there are six hundred to eight hundred bears in the Delta population, which is spread out north to south from Cache River National Wildlife Refuge to just below Arkansas City, and east to west from Helena to Stuttgart. The greatest bear densities occur on White River National Wildlife Refuge, with an estimated four hundred to five hundred bears. Biologists have proposed a hunt in this region to evaluate the impact of harvest on the population, to collect valuable biological data, to reduce the number of conflicts between humans and bears and to provide increased recreational opportunities for Arkansas hunters.

Although bear-hunt success rates are relatively low in Arkansas, you can improve your chances of bagging a bruin by following some basic guidelines. If you're new at this game, you should first study several good books on bear hunting, research the sport on the Internet, and/or pick the brain of a veteran hunter. The more tricks you have up your sleeve, the better your chances for success. Space limitations allow only a cursory explanation of basic bear-hunting techniques here.

You'll also need to do some research to pinpoint good hunting areas. Harvest statistics available from the Game and Fish Commission can help you find a wildlife management area or county with a healthy bear population. Then it's a matter of homing in on good bear habitat and looking for sign.

In the mountains, bears like to move around near bluffs. Wooded stream bottoms also are attractive, as are clearcuts. Studies of bear stomach contents show their most important autumn food is acorns, hence the large number of sightings in oak/hickory woodlands and mixed stands of hardwoods and pines. The next most significant foods were pokeberries and leaves, which grow in forest openings. Other significant bear foods include hickory nuts, persimmons, insects, and carrion.

Spend as much time as possible scouting for signs of bear activity in the area you intend to hunt. Look for some of the food sources mentioned above, take note of their location, and check them daily to see if they've been visited. Watch for bear tracks around watering holes. Large, soft black droppings full of seeds and acorn shells also are indicative of bears' presence. Droppings often are found on logs, along with hair left when bears sun themselves. A bear meandering along a stony outcrop often leaves a trail of overturned rocks where it searched for insects. Bears sometimes scar tree trunks with their teeth and claws, another sign that can help bear hunters locate a promising area.

When hunting, remember that bears have keen senses of hearing and smell, and are highly attuned to anything out of place in their environment. To prevent a bear from winding you, try one of the products deer hunters use to mask or eliminate human odor. Some hunters actually use the bear's sense of hearing to their advantage by using predator calls that imitate injured rabbits. Bears sometimes are attracted to these.

Some hunters sit on a stand, waiting for a bear to come to them, but because a bear may roam over many square miles, some successful Arkansas hunters say it is best to cover lots of ground, moving slowly and quietly as you might do if you were still-hunting for squirrels.

Selecting the right weapon for bear hunting is important, and knowing how to skillfully use it is even more important. Most experts recommend rifles .30 caliber or larger. Black-powder hunters have excellent success with 370-grain maxi-balls propelled by eighty to one hundred grains of FFG powder. Bowhunters shouldn't use anything lighter than a fifty-pound bow, and even presharpened broadheads should be honed to a perfect razor edge to penetrate bears' thick hide, fat, and muscle.

Knowing where to shoot a bear also is important. Broadside and head-on shots are the preferred choices for gun hunters. A bruin hit in the shoulder blade area won't travel far. For head-on shots, aim for the center of the chest.

The best shot for archers is not a broadside shot, but one where the animal is angling slightly away. Try to place the arrow just behind the nearest shoulder, midway between back and belly. This gives a clear shot at the vital area without interference from the front leg or shoulder. Broadside shots behind the shoulder blade will also kill.

A bear's heavy fat layer prevents free external bleeding, making it difficult to track. For this reason, many bowhunters use a string tracking device. Available from archery suppliers, each consists of a spool of thread with the end attached to the arrow and the spool attached to the bow. The line plays out as the game flees, leaving a clear trail to follow.

When you find a downed bear, approach it cautiously. If possible, approach the animal's rear from uphill. If the bear isn't dead and is aroused, it's most likely to lunge forward and head downhill. If the bear shows any sign of life, finish it with a well-placed shot.

Bagging an Arkansas bear is challenging, but most ardent bear hunters prefer it that way. To them, that obvious degree of difficulty is the reason for hunting. The hunt is a success whether they kill a bear or not, because they've faced the challenge and tried.

Still, that fractional chance of success is always there. And every bear hunter hopes that maybe, just maybe, this will be their year to bag a Bear State bruin, one of North America's most magnificent and storied game animals.

Charged by a Bear

It is a humbling thing to be charged by a bear. I speak from experience.

Several friends and I had been fishing on the lower White River, at the southern end of White River National Wildlife Refuge. We had seen fourteen bears over the course of our two-day trip and were thrilled each time we saw one. On this particular day, we were motoring back upriver after running trotlines. Four of us were in the boat—me, Cliff, Alex, and Bill. Cliff commented he'd like to photograph a bear if an opportunity arose.

"There's one now," said Bill, who was at the helm. He swung the johnboat toward shore where we saw a sow and cub on a sand embankment. At our approach, the bears ran over the embankment and disappeared.

We were disappointed Cliff didn't get his photograph, but I suggested all was not lost. Perhaps we could photograph the bears' tracks in the sand.

Bill motored us to the bank. Alex, Cliff, and I disembarked. I was walking, looking for tracks in the sand when the bear charged from her hiding place in a band of trees and brush. She came out of nowhere, ran lickety-split up an embankment, stopped at my feet, and stood there for what seemed an eternity, snapping and snarling in my face. I felt her hot smelly breath on my flushed cheeks. At the time, I guessed her weight near half a ton. In retrospect, I suppose she ran about two hundred fifty pounds.

I was completely startled by the bear's appearance, but she made her charge and quickly retreated, doing me no visible harm.

Cliff and Alex witnessed the bear's charge from a distance. They were headed my direction when the sow came at me again. This time I had my camera at the ready, or so I thought. I snapped several pictures, but when they were later processed, I found nothing but blurs on the film. I was running while snapping the photos. Cliff and Alex later confirmed this.

Following the bear's second charge, Alex noted he had seen two cubs, not one. One was now squalling from a treetop. The other was

silent but also up a tree. We now knew we were between two cubs, with a mad mama bear somewhere out of sight in the brush.

To say we beat a hasty retreat is somewhat misleading. Bill had already backed the boat many yards away from the bank, claiming the current was pulling him out. Yet somehow Cliff, Alex, and I managed to cover those few yards without getting wet. You never know you can run on water until you have to.

Having read this, you might be inclined to believe I had a bad encounter with a bear. That evening, as I recounted the story of the bear's charge over and over again to my friends, I thought I had, too. It wasn't a bad encounter, however. It was actually a good one. The bear never touched me, though she easily could have. I'm fat and slow—no match for black bears, which tend to be fat and fast.

What happened that day occurred because I used bad judgment. I inadvertently placed myself and my friends between a sow bear and her cubs—not a good place to be in anyone's book. The sow reacted as nature programmed her to, and the encounter ended as it should. We left the bear's cubs alone, which is all she wanted. And the three bears, as far as I know, lived happily ever after.

How fortunate we are to have a healthy bear population here in Arkansas, especially these native bears inhabiting White River National Wildlife Refuge. Yes, occasionally people have bad encounters. In one incident, an Arkansas man was terribly mauled when he and his dog startled a bear. Sometimes bears destroy beehives or scatter trash about someone's yard or even break into a house looking for food. These are not good things, but they are inevitable in a world where man and wildlife are learning to coexist.

My experience was memorable, exciting, frightening, and a thousand other things. But it was not bad.

If you're a hunter like me, perhaps it is good now and then to stand in the presence of a superior predator, knowing that you are, for once, a potential prey species. A little hair-raising humility can make you a better sportsman.

A squalling bear cub up a tree means trouble for humans on the ground below.

BOTTOMLAND BIRDS

Timberdoodle Time

In autumn, when the weatherman announces the first cold front blowing down from the north, our minds turn to woodcocks. It usually happens the first week or two of November.

Last year it happened in mid-November. The phone rang at 6:30 P.M.

"Did you hear the weather report?" Jim asked, a twinge of excitement edging his voice. "There's a blue norther coming down. The timberdoodles are probably flocking into Lost Pond already. I'll pick you up at five tomorrow morning. You bring sandwiches, and I'll bring coffee. Patterson's going with us."

We drove over from Little Rock, and at seven, we were making our first push through bottomland timber adjacent east Arkansas's L'Anguille River. Like most woodcock hunters, I prefer you don't know the exact location of my hunting spots, so I'll call this one Hugh's Hollow.

This particular covert is a classic woodcock hospice of dense sweet gum saplings and honeysuckle thickets. A beaver slough slashes the edge, feeding water into the spongy ground beneath the canopy of oaks and tupelos. The territory is thick and uncivil; it's hard to find space between the tangles of vegetation to set down your feet.

As we waded into the thicket, I saw the first signs that our timing was right: white splatters on the leaves and little holes in the mud, like someone had been poking around with a stick. Then ten yards out front, from the depths of the sweet gums, came a sharp, ascendant twittering. A brown, fist-sized bird spiraled skyward through the branches.

I lost sight of the bird almost immediately in the crisscross of leafy limbs, but by some fluke of luck, it presented Jim an uncommonly clear shot, and he killed it. The shot rumbled. The woodcock fell at his feet.

"In case you didn't know, boys, this is what we're looking for," he said, holding the timberdoodle up for us to see.

The second bird came out low and fast. I shot, missed, and it flew into the nether reaches of the covert. After it we went, and when it flushed again in characteristic fashion, Gregg mounted, swung, and fired

---

Woodcock hunters must brave dense thickets to find their quarry.

in one quick fluid motion. A detonation of feathers showed he had found his mark.

Gregg found the woodcock in a patch of honeysuckle. Jim came over, and we admired the singular beauty of this unusual woodland ghost. Its bill was like a knitting needle, its legs weak and squatty, the tail just a little tuft of stubby feathers. The soft plumage was warm earthy brown flecked with black and cinnamon. Broad black bars crossed the crown between big ebony eyes.

As we stood, another woodcock put up in the cover beside us, whistling away through the bottoms.

You could probably tally the number of hard-core woodcock hunters in Arkansas on your fingers and toes. Woodcocks are pretty much an unexploited resource here. Hunting for these brassy little devils hasn't caught on in the Natural State like it has in New England and other areas.

The reason woodcocks are neglected in Arkansas is no real mystery. Because the birds are small and cryptically colored and hide in dense cover, many Natural State hunters aren't even aware of their presence. Those who do know the woodcock spend the bulk of their time hunting more favored game animals when woodcocks are in season.

To top it off, woodcock hunting is anything but easy. Gunners must brave the gnarly thickets and boggy bottoms woodcocks frequent. And while buried to the ears in a latticework of vegetation, they must try to snap-shoot a crooked-flying, brown-feathered blur that has the nerve-jangling habit of flushing directly underfoot. Tough hunting like that discourages many people.

The lack of hunting pressure does not reflect the number of woodcocks found here. Evidence suggests 80 percent of North America's woodcocks winter in Louisiana, and nearly all those birds pass through Arkansas during their annual migrations to and from the North Country. Our population of wintering and migrant woodcocks is substantial, especially in eastern and southern lowlands.

Recognizing good woodcock habitat is one key to successful hunting, for these coverts concentrate the birds and provide consistent shooting. In Arkansas, woodcocks frequent moist bottomlands near waters surrounded by heavy brush eight to fifteen feet tall. Look for damp, loamy soil along creeks, springs, sloughs, and beaver ponds where woodcocks can probe the soft ground for earthworms, their favorite food.

Young woods with a good understory of swamp privet, sweetgum, honeysuckle, dogwood, ash, small maples, willows, and/or switch cane seem especially attractive. In the best areas, the understory is thick, but in more open woods, isolated patches of cover often harbor woodcocks as well.

The most common sign of woodcocks is the chalky whitewash of droppings they deposit on the forest floor. Normal weather quickly obliterates this, so finding it indicates birds are, or recently were, nearby. Watch, too, for probe holes in soft earth around ponds, creeks, and other waters. These are made by the woodcock's long bill when it probes the ground for worms.

Some woodcocks live year-round in Arkansas and nest here. Before cold weather sends flights down out of the north, hunters must be content with the sporadic action offered by these few residents. The best hunting, however, is provided by large influxes of migratory birds. Hunters intercept these woodcocks as they head to Louisiana, typically from early November through early December.

Weather reports offer clues on when to expect the migrants. Major influxes of woodcocks usually precede strong autumn cold fronts pushing down from Canada and the northern United States. Most move out well in advance of snow or ice that locks out their food supply.

On several public hunting areas in east Arkansas, I've found woodcock coverts thick with birds in November and December. Usually, there had been a series of days with winds from the south that stalled their migration. These small birds don't move well against a wind, and such weather causes large groups of timberdoodles to stack up in holding areas. The first change in wind will send them southward again in an enormous group, and it is the fortunate longbill hunter who is in good cover immediately after such a group arrives.

To avoid frustration, it's important to remember that most Arkansas woodcocks are just passing migrants. If you time your hunt properly, coverts may be bristling with birds. But miss them by a day, and the only trace of timberdoodles will be their white "splashes" on new-fallen leaves. Pinpoint several likely coverts to increase your chance for finding timberdoodles on any given hunt, and visit these coverts several times during the season before giving up on them.

Fortunately, woodcocks usually return to the same coverts year after year. If this year's scouting proves fruitful, you'll have several known coverts to hunt again next season.

For most of us, woodcock hunting is a jump-shooting sport. The trick is to locate a good area, then work the cover meticulously. A woodcock prefers not to fly. He'd rather sit on the ground and let you walk right past. To foil this instinctive gambit, adopt a walk-then-stop pattern of hunting, pausing a minute or so every twenty feet as you walk through cover. Woodcocks are a nervous lot, and won't sit long if a hunter stops nearby and looks around.

Dogs are another element in many successful hunts, the favored breeds being close-working dogs such as Brittany spaniels and German short-hair pointers. Woodcocks hold quite well for pointing dogs, and since woodcocks have excellent camouflage, dogs can help find many downed birds that otherwise would be lost. Because woodcock habitat is usually thick, it's wise to attach a bell to your dog's collar so you can better track it and tell when it goes on point.

Assuming you're lucky enough to find and flush a woodcock, with dogs or without, you're still a ways yet from putting meat on the table. Woodcocks fly slowly, but erratically, like a filled balloon turned loose to sputter through the air. On top of that, it can be extremely difficult to follow through with a shotgun in the thick cover where they usually hide. The woodcock is an elusive target.

Woodcocks do have one endearing flight trait that works in the hunter's favor. When flushed, they seldom fly far. Typically, they rise on whistling wings then flutter back to earth within fifty or sixty yards—sometimes still within shotgun range. If you blow your first opportunity, mark the bird down and try again.

As far as equipment is concerned, hunting woodcocks is essentially the same as quail hunting. Most hunters prefer short-barreled, improved cylinder shotguns for quick snap shooting and easy maneuverability in tight, brushy quarters. Low-brass shotshells with number 7-1/2, 8, or 9 shot work great; the birds are easy to bring down if you can hit them. Other recommended items of equipment include a hunter-orange cap and shooting vest for visibility to other hunters; shatterproof shooting glasses for eye protection in brush; and shooting gloves and tough, canvas-fronted brush pants to fend off briars and thorns.

Most prime habitat once used by woodcocks has been destroyed by stream channelization, wetland drainage, and clearing of bottomland hardwoods. But the hunter who does his homework still can find woodcock coverts full of birds.

Some of the best woodcock territory is in southeast Arkansas, along the White River from Augusta to the Mississippi River. Four public hunting areas along this stretch have good woodcock populations.

Henry Gray/Hurricane Lake Wildlife Management Area covers 17,524 acres of prime timberdoodle habitat just southeast of Bald Knob along the White and Little Red Rivers and Glaise Creek. Eleven thousand acres are flooded each fall and winter, and in most years, woodcocks can be found in thickets at the edge of shallow backwaters. Wattensaw WMA, a 19,184-acre area near Hazen, is bounded by the White River and Wattensaw Bayou, both of which provide wet bottomlands and plenty of young hardwood thickets attractive to woodcocks. White River National Wildlife Refuge encompasses 160,000 acres of superb woodcock habitat along nearly one hundred miles of the White River. Trusten Holder WMA near the confluence of the White and Mississippi rivers is a bonanza for woodcock aficionados willing to scout the area's 8,173 acres of Delta bottoms.

Other southeast river bottoms also support thriving public-lands woodcock populations. On the Cache River south of Augusta, hunters find good woodcock hunting on 6,284-acre Rex Hancock/Black Swamp WMA. Dagmar WMA covers 9,720 acres of timberdoodle territory on Bayou de View west of Brinkley. Bayou Meto WMA, a blue-ribbon woodcock hot spot, provides 32,250 acres of public woodcock hunting land southwest of Stuttgart.

Other good bottomland woodcock areas open to the public in this region include sixty-five-thousand-acre Felsenthal National Wildlife Refuge in the Saline-Ouachita river bottoms near Crossett, 6,100-acre Overflow National Wildlife Refuge west of Wilmot, and 8,904-acre Cut-Off Creek WMA southwest of Dermott.

Stream floodplains in northeast Arkansas also provide excellent gunning for savvy woodcock hunters. This region is especially good early in the season as the first migrants pass through on their southward migration.

Some of the best northeast hot spots are along the St. Francis River. This big bottomland stream snakes its way from Missouri's boot heel south to the Mississippi River at Helena and is accessible via numerous state roads off U.S. Highways 63, 64, and 79, and Interstate 40 near Jonesboro, Marked Tree, Parkin, and Marianna.

St. Francis Sunken Lands WMA near Marked Tree offers some of the best public hunting on the river. Almost all access on this 27,858-acre area is from the river, and the Game and Fish Commission provides three boat ramps to accommodate its use. A fair number of woodcocks also frequent the St. Francis National Forest near Marianna. Most of this 21,202-acre area lies atop Crowley's Ridge, but several thousand acres of bottomlands lie adjacent the river on the eastern edge of the national forest.

The bottoms along the L'Anguille River, a tributary of the St. Francis, are more famous for their duck hunting than for woodcocks, but hunters still can find pockets of good woodcock hunting in the 40,000 acres of remaining bottomland hardwood habitat between the Cross-Poinsett county line and the St. Francis National Forest near Marianna. Access is via State Highways 42, 284, 306 and 1, near Cherry Valley, Wynne, Pine Tree, and Haynes. Almost all these lands are privately owned, but woodcocks aren't considered glamour species like ducks and deer. Landowners frequently grant hunting permission for timberdoodles when they might refuse a request to hunt premium game.

In southwest Arkansas, woodcocks can be found on 16,900-acre Sulphur River WMA, fifteen miles south of Texarkana. Dams and levees on Mercer Bayou aid in flooding to provide some of the best woodcock habitat in this part of the state. Access by road is limited (most travel is by boat or on foot), but woodcock hunting can be excellent at times.

My friends and I wound up our morning of woodcock hunting with a grand total of eight timberdoodles, an average of almost three apiece. That doesn't sound like many, and it's not. But like most woodcock fans, we don't measure the success of our hunt by how many birds we shoot.

Back at the truck, we admired our harvest. "You know," Gregg said, leaning against the pickup, "I've done a lot of hunting in my time, but none more fun than I had today. It doesn't get any better than this."

Jim and I agreed. It's a demanding sport, this woodcock hunting. You wear yourself out fighting through brush, hoping to find some little brown birds that may be there or may not. And if they are, if you're lucky this time, then they'll flush right under your feet, and you'll twist yourself into a knot trying to shoot them before they spiral away through the timber. You'll kill a few, and miss a lot more. But next year, when the weatherman talks about that first blue norther heading your way, you'll get woodcocks on your mind, and the next morning, you'll be out there trying again.

Hunting Snipe: For Real!

Ask an Arkansas hunter to join you for a snipe hunt, and you must be careful how you phrase the invitation. Even then, you may get a knowing grin and a polite decline. The image of an age-old practical joke lingers.

You see, there is a snipe hunt, and there is snipe hunting.

1. Snipe hunt: A prank played on an unsuspecting person taken to a remote location to "hunt snipe" with a group. The victim is left stranded, alone, after his companions promise to spread out and drive snipe into the special gunnysack he has been given.

2. Snipe hunting: A legitimate hunting sport in which sportsmen seek small, fast-flying, hard-to-hit, unpredictable, tasty, long-billed birds that frequent open wetlands.

Snipe hunts—the practical joke kind—prompted the phrase "left holding the bag," meaning "to be duped." But don't be duped into thinking snipe are just imaginary birds. They're as real as mallards, quail, and other Arkansas game birds. Hunting them is equally, if not more, exciting.

THE BIRD

The common snipe, also called jacksnipe or Wilson's snipe, is often confused with its close cousin, the American woodcock. But while woodcocks prefer forested wetlands, snipe reside in treeless wetlands—marshes, rice fields, ponds, drainage ditches, and bogs. Other prime snipe grounds include seeps in cattle pastures, damp mud flats exposed when reservoirs are drawn down, and areas where low-growth vegetation borders lakes and slow-moving streams.

On the ground, the unusual snipe looks like a feathered egg on toothpicks. It's a chunky bird, slightly larger than a quail, with an extremely long bill, a distinctive striped head, and a rust-colored tail. The head and dark, mottled upper parts are marked by prominent buff-colored stripes. The buff breast and flanks are heavily spotted and barred; the belly is clear white.

In flight, the snipe resembles a winged golf ball carrying its own tee. Its takeoff has been described as "explosive." The flight is rapid (up to sixty-two miles per hour) and zigzagging, accompanied by a distinctive, harsh "*scaaape*" call. To identify it, watch for the very long, heavy, straight bill; the long, dark, pointed wings; the white belly; and rust in the tail.

A flock of snipe, called a "wisp," may include several hundred birds. When disturbed, the birds freeze or run quickly to cover, winging away if approached too closely.

HISTORICAL NOTES

Snipe were once among the most popular North American game birds. In fact, some researchers believe more snipe have been killed in North America than any other game bird.

Single-day bags of one hundred to three hundred snipe were common in the nineteenth century, and many early American hunters strived to set a record with numbers of snipe shot, a practice common in Europe. Among the most famous of these was the champion shotgunner Capt. Adam H. Bogardus. He often killed 150 snipe a day. His best day was 340.

Another famous snipe hunter was John Julius Pringle from Pointe Coupee Parish in southeast Louisiana. In 1899 his book, *Twenty Years' Snipe Shooting,* was published. In it are accounts of Pringle's best days taken from an 1867–1887 game log.

"Every day on coming in from shooting," Pringle wrote in the preface, "the birds were taken from the game-box of the wagon and laid out in rows of twenty, and the numbers reported to me . . ." During those two decades of hunting, Pringle killed 78,602 snipe that he recorded, including a one-day bag of 366 on December 11, 1877.

During his last years of shooting, Pringle noted a decline in snipe numbers. He blamed the loss of habitat, but while this is often the chief reason for a species' decline, especially today, in Pringle's era the snipe was a noted loser due to overshooting.

Market hunting was part of the problem, as indicated by Capt. George Combs Sr. in *Marsh Tales* by William N. Smith. Combs's grandfather hunted snipe in the mid-1800s. "You see, snipe brought a pretty good price back then," Combs said. "They'd give you twenty-five cents a bird which was damn good money. And Christ, there were so many of them that when they jumped off the bars, they would cover the sun ... They used muzzle guns, mostly ten, eleven, and twelve gauge. Shoot right into the flocks of them, then whistle 'em right back in and shoot 'em again."

There are still dusty snipe decoys in attics and barns, relics of these old shorebird days. Some are crude; others are masterpieces of carving. All bring high prices with collectors, but decoy hunting for snipe is rare today.

At the turn of the century, snipe were among dozens of shorebirds being hunted. Then, in 1913, all but five shorebirds—the snipe, woodcock, black-bellied plover, greater yellowlegs, and lesser yellowlegs—were placed on the list of protected species in hopes of rebuilding seriously depleted populations. In 1926, plover season was closed, and in 1927, greater and lesser yellowlegs joined the protected list, where all remain today. This left only the snipe and woodcock out of a group of hunted shorebirds that once numbered forty-eight.

In 1939, a long, hard freeze on the snipes' Gulf Coast wintering grounds killed tens of thousands of birds. Two years later, snipe season was closed. In his book *The Complete Wildfowler*, famed Louisiana outdoorsman Grits Gresham described what happened.

"Although the complete closure of the snipe season was based on fragmentary reports of the extent of the loss," he wrote, "with virtually no data on snipe populations continent-wide, such total protection could be justified as a precautionary measure. Better to be safe than sorry.

"The error was not reopening a season on snipe until a dozen years had passed—much longer than necessary for the populations to recover completely from one bad winter. During that closed period most of the old-time snipe hunters passed from the scene, and no new ones were developed. Not very many have adopted the sport since the season was reopened ... in the fall of 1953."

And so it remains. Although snipe populations are now healthy, and snipe hunting was allowed in forty-nine states (all except Hawaii) during recent seasons, the U.S. Fish and Wildlife Service estimates only twenty-seven thousand to thirty thousand waterfowlers pursue these curious birds each year.

Should that dampen your interest in hunting snipe? Certainly not.

Bag limits are generous, and snipe are common migrants or seasonal residents in Arkansas. Hunting them is a unique and very challenging enterprise that must be experienced to be appreciated.

THE HUNT

Finding a snipe-hunting ground isn't difficult, but be prepared to walk and wade. Look for areas with shallow water and sparse vegetation, then wade in. If snipe are present, you'll soon flush them. If not, find a new location and try again. With persistence, you'll soon learn to recognize preferred areas.

Jump shooting is the most common snipe-hunting technique. Hunters spread out in proper habitat, gun at the ready, and walk the birds up. Some hunters work in pairs, wading opposite sides of a swale or taking turns driving and shooting. Others stalk snipe from shallow-draft boats, poling through tidal marshes and other snipe habitat to flush their quarry. Snipe often fly over duck blinds, and duck hunters probably bag more of them than most other hunters.

Snipe usually hold tight in cover, allowing one to approach within good shotgun range. They are ghosts on the ground, however; it's a rare hunter who can spot one in vegetation before it flushes. Just when you decide you've made a mistake in marking him, the snipe jumps from a spot where you just looked. It flies as though it doesn't have any idea where it's going, but nevertheless is in a terrible hurry to get there.

Another disconcerting habit of the snipe is the "up-up-and-away" flush. Startled birds often rise straight up, flying upward until they're mere specks in the sky. Anyone with good eyes should watch such snipe, for if the shooter remains motionless, the bird will eventually pitch and land, usually within thirty yards of where it first flushed. The hunter then can flush it again—and miss it again.

Fast, accurate gun handling is a must for the successful snipe hunter. The bird's erratic flight pattern and small size make it an extremely difficult target. A straight-away shot is rare. Instead, the snipe moves much like a balloon that's been inflated and suddenly turned loose. Any hunter who bags two birds for every five shots fired can demand (and deserves) all the respect he can muster.

Although some authors recommend a properly trained bird dog for retrieving downed snipe, in *Twenty Years of Snipe Hunting*, J. J. Pringle noted dogs interfered with his shooting. "As a rule, when the birds were abundant, I kept the dog (setter or pointer) at heel, and only used him to 'find dead,' not to retrieve, for a dog sent out to retrieve would have put up many birds which would have gone off, some of them unshot at..."

If you use a dog, you'll want one that stays close, almost by your side. If a dog is not used, carefully mark the position of downed birds. The snipe's camouflage coloring blends perfectly with mud and grass, making it very hard to find.

It's also wise to focus your attention on the area immediately ahead of you when flushing snipe. Carry your gun at the ready, and ignore derisive snipe cheeps to the right or left—unless birds are scarce enough that each individual is an event.

HERE TODAY, GONE TOMORROW

The best-looking snipe habitat may be devoid of birds, even though they were abundant yesterday. Like woodcocks, snipe travel south a jump or two ahead of freezing weather. They feed primarily on insects, worms, and other small invertebrates captured by plunging the long bill straight down into soft earth or mud. Frozen ground sounds a death knell, so snipe move south ahead of freezing weather.

Knowing when to expect the migration helps. In Arkansas, it usually comes around mid-November, though some flights might not wing in before December. Serious snipe hunters, few though they may be, listen to weather reports from the north to time incoming flights.

Hunting pressure doesn't often cause snipe to abandon good areas, but it does make them increasingly wild. If you visit the same area several days in a row, they may get so wild that you're wasting your time. It's possible to walk for hours, putting up scores of snipe, without a single one in range. Alternating hunting days on several good areas is best.

Hunters should learn to positively identify snipe. These birds are easily confused with yellowlegs, dowitchers, and other shorebirds that may be present and illegal to hunt. The snipe's short orange tail and raspy "*scaape, scaape*" call are good, but not infallible, identification characteristics. Before hunting, compare snipe with their look-alikes in a good bird-identification guide, or have a veteran snipe hunter teach you how to properly identify your target.

It's difficult for some to understand why anyone would aspire to be a snipe hunter, if indeed, they are so hard to hunt, so hard to hit, and so small. The snipe hunter comes home with aching legs that have dragged hip boots through miles of sticky gumbo, red eyes that have stared for hours at grass and weeds the same color as snipe, and aching arms that have held a shotgun until the fingers will hardly open. And what does he have to show for all this effort? If he's lucky, enough meat for a couple of small servings.

So why bother? All I can tell you is the real allure of hunting snipe must be experienced to be understood.

Next time someone asks if you want to go snipe hunting, don't be too quick to call his bluff.

Gunning for Gooney Birds

"Why is it you like hunting rails?" a friend asked. "You wear yourself out wading through ankle-deep mud and tangles of cattails and buckbrush, hoping to find some little funny-looking birds that may be there and may not. And if they are there, if you somehow miraculously timed it right, then every bird you find will flush right under your feet and scare the wits out of you. You'll twist yourself into a knot trying to shoot them before they sputter away, and if you're really, really lucky that day, you'll actually kill one or two.

"When you come crawling out of the marsh with those two little gooney birds," he continued, "you'll have so many briar scratches, it'll look like you fell in a nest of bobcats. And what do you have to show for all this effort? Enough meat to feed a shrew.

"I just don't understand it," he said.

"It's fun," said I.

"Then maybe it's not just the birds who are gooney," he replied.

I felt it best to withhold the fact that I also hunt coots.

There's no question about it—rails are curious birds. So are coots, gallinules, and moorhens, three other webless migrants that can be hunted in Arkansas.

What is even more curious to many Arkansas sportsmen is the fact there are actually folks who hunt these birds. A few will admit they see one or the other now and then during seasons for other game. And one or two more will confess to taking an occasional shot, mostly out of curiosity. But hunt them? On purpose?

It's difficult to explain why anyone would want to hunt these comical birds, even for a gooney bird fan like me. It's a self-punishing sport where hours are spent busting brush and tackling ankle-deep muck. Tangles of saw-like leaves and vines eat at your clothes and skin. It's

Although common in Arkansas, the American coot, a member of the rail family, is ignored by most hunters.

nothing but hard work, pushing past snags and struggling to put one foot in front of the other.

It's certainly not the birds' culinary potential that attracts sportsmen. All these webless migrants are good eating, but a plump bobwhite or rice-field mallard is tastier by far. And you might more profitably try to put meat on the table by hunting squirrels with a slingshot.

Nor is there much glory in shooting them. I don't know a single taxidermist who could make a living from the number of gooney birds he mounts in a year.

No, hunting these birds is more a matter of infatuation, a love of the loony. It's a special hobby, an acquired taste. Many hunters consider it folly—a waste of time, energy, and ammunition. These hunters have arrived at a single and definite conclusion: they won't act the fool and chase gooney birds.

For the died-in-the-wool wetland bird hunter, however, desperation and determination go hand in hand. The more he misses and the more he fails, the harder he works at it. When he experienced his first hunt for wetland migrants, he was hooked for life because of his continuing resolution to find the successful combination.

Or else he's just plain crazy.

Today, only a handful of dedicated Arkansas gunners pursue coots, rails, gallinules, and/or moorhens. Prime hunting is available in many areas, but few hunters have the knowledge to hunt webless migrants successfully.

How 'bout you? Looking for challenging alternatives yourself? If so, here's how and where to hunt coots, rails, moorhens, and gallinules.

COOTS

Of all our common game birds, none is less hunted than the American coot. This black bird with the white beak frequents flooded crop fields, lakes, ponds, marshes, and other watery habitats throughout Arkansas. Some know it as mud hen, marsh hen, or whitebill. Folks in southern Louisiana call it *poule d'eau*. Although often seen swimming with ducks, it is a member of the rail tribe, and like rails, it is quite tasty when properly cared for and prepared.

I have seen on some Arkansas oxbow lakes and large reservoirs, flocks of coots numbering in the hundreds, sometimes thousands. Rarely is one seen alone, preferring, it seems, to swim and forage in groups of a few to many birds. They're usually found in shallow water where they feed on aquatic vegetation and small invertebrates.

The word "coot" is a synonym for fool or simpleton, and with good reason: these birds are dumb as dirt. They sometimes sit on shore basking and preening, and on several occasions when I was younger, I managed to catch one by simply running it down. Coots have weak wings and require a long watery runway to accomplish their sputtering, walk-across-the-water takeoff.

Most coots harvested in Arkansas probably fall to hunters bored by the lack of action for other waterfowl species. They can be hunted by design rather than accident, however, simply by scouting for flocks and boating into a position where you can hide and ambush them. They love the security of flooded button willow thickets, and I've taken many by wading into such an area and stalking them with a shotgun.

As table fare, a coot won't equal a plump acorn-fed mallard or corn-fed dove. But as the old adage goes, "Don't knock 'em till you've tried 'em." The heart-dark meat of these overlooked game birds embodies a hearty flavor well suited to a variety of unique, and very tasty, recipes.

Skin, don't pluck, the coots you harvest, and place the meat on ice as soon as possible. Most hunters save only the breast meat, as the legs, wings and other parts are too puny to make them worth saving. Slice the skin over the coot's breast, roll it back and lay off the two fillets with a sharp knife. Most cooks place these in a favorite marinade, then refrigerate for twenty-four to forty-eight hours before cooking.

RAILS

Rails aren't hunted much in Arkansas, not for lack of huntable numbers, but because most Natural State hunters know little about them. Rails are secretive and spend most of their time hiding in dense wetland vegetation, flying only when hard pressed. Few sportsmen see rails because few look for them.

Two species—the sora and Virginia rail—can be hunted in Arkansas. Yellow, clapper, black, and king rails, which also visit the state, are protected. Soras and Virginia rails are especially numerous from September through December in the rice fields and cattail marshes of east-central and southern Arkansas.

The sora offers the best hunting opportunities, being much more plentiful and generally easier to find than the Virginia rail. It's a plump little grayish-blue and brown bird about the size of a quail, with a short yellow bill, barred flanks, and black face.

Virginia rails also are quail-sized. Good identification marks include the long bill, rust-colored breast, gray cheeks, and strongly barred black-and-white flanks. A good bird identification guide can help you learn to distinguish soras and Virginia rails from protected species.

How do you hunt them? On the Gulf and Atlantic coasts where rail hunting is most popular, they're hunted by poling flat-bottomed boats through marsh grasses, using the boat as, say, a fourteen-foot flushing dog. You could try the same in cattail marshes and rice-field flumes here in Arkansas.

If you're a real eager beaver, you can slip into your waders and try walking rails up. In the gumbo-bottomed environs where they're usually found, this is no more arduous than climbing Mount Magazine with a cannonball strapped to each leg.

Florida rail hunters have a unique hunting method well suited for Arkansas jump-shooters. The hunters line up about one hundred feet apart. Connecting each hunter in the line is a nylon cord, and fastened to the cord are a number of cans with pebbles or marbles sealed inside. The hunters walk slowly along, the cord follows, dragging across the vegetation, and the pebbles clank loudly in the cans. One guy follows about fifty yards behind the line of hunters. Rails let hunters walk right past them without flushing, but when that cord and cans come over them, they fly.

Rails are great confidence builders. They can make it *seem* as if you're a good wing shot. You see, "marsh hens" fly less than fast. If they were airplanes, they'd be C-130s with two engines out. Their flight is slow, low, and lumbering. Straight away, too. Miss more than one or two, and you should be considered too dangerous to handle a gun.

MOORHENS AND GALLINULES

Purple gallinules and common moorhens, two closely related water birds, are the rarest, and least hunted, of Arkansas game birds. Of the two, only the moorhen occurs in any appreciable numbers during hunting season, and this species is extremely difficult to find and hunt. Still, for hunters who enjoy a challenging change of pace, trying to bag an Arkansas moorhen could make for a fun fall outing.

The moorhen is closely related to coots and rails. It's a duck-like swimming bird, slate-gray in color with a prominent red bill tipped in yellow and a red shield extending up its forehead. It has a white band of feathers on its flanks, another sure mark.

Look for these handsome birds in or near dense vegetation around quiet, shallow ponds, marshes, and lake edges. They're often seen walking on lily pads or feeding along edges of open water; when disturbed, they seek cover in heavy vegetation. They constantly pump their head and tail when walking, and like rails, their flight is slow and weak.

In most waters, the best hunting is from boats, as walking a marshy, mucky lake or pond shore is difficult. Lightweight johnboats and canoes are most serviceable, since they are easily maneuvered over and through weeds and grass. A good technique is to spot the birds from long distances with binoculars and motor to a position about one hundred yards away. Then pole or paddle close, slowly and quietly, for a shot. By law, the boat can't be under power (even drifting from a shut-down engine) when a hunter shoots.

WHERE TO GO

Scouting is important for successfully hunting gooney birds. Coots are abundant in Arkansas, and usually easy to find, but Virginia rails, sora rails, and common moorhens are uncommon migrants found only in small localized areas. Their secretive behavior puts the hunter at a distinct disadvantage. Purple gallinules are unlikely to be encountered during hunting season. They're rare summer residents seen in only a few locations in Arkansas. Before hunting season begins, those that visit the state have moved on to warmer climes.

When searching for public-lands hunting opportunities, focus on wildlife management areas where the appropriate wetlands are found—brushy lake edges for coots, densely vegetated marshes and small ponds for rails and moorhens. Wildlife management areas where these habitats are found include Harris Brake, Petit Jean, Bayou Meto, Dagmar, Wattensaw, St. Francis Sunken Lands, Trusten Holder, Henry

Gray/Hurricane Lake, Rex Hancock/Black Swamp, Sulphur River, Big Lake, Dave Donaldson/Black River, Holland Bottoms, Ed Gordon/Point Remove, St. Francis National Forest, Bois d'Arc, and Shirey Bay-Rainey Brake.

Many Arkansas wing shooters consider it crazy to hunt rails, gallinules, moorhens, and coots. "They're just a bunch of gooney birds," some say. "Why should I waste my time on them?"

Discover the truth for yourself. The real allure of hunting webless migrants must be experienced to be understood. Don't knock it till you've tried it.

A Calling Card for Crafty Crows

I flipped the switch on the electronic caller and began playing a cassette tape labeled "Fighting Crows." From the speaker came the loud cawing sounds of dozens of crows stirred into a frenzy by some unidentifiable enemy.

A flock of crows, like a street gang, is always ready to rumble. These birds love a group fight with an enemy, whether it be an owl, hawk, fox, or cat. When an enemy is spotted, the crows gather round and begin cawing loudly, inviting other crows to come and join in the fray. These fighting sounds can draw in scores of crows and keep them so fired up they will ignore all dangers around them, even hunters. I was counting on this behavior when I turned on the caller.

I had joined two friends—Joe Mosby and David Settlemoir—for a crow hunt on a farm near Little Rock. Before turning on the caller, the three of us, dressed in camouflage clothing, had concealed ourselves in dense undergrowth on a woodland edge. We were positioned twenty yards apart, with a good view of the surrounding countryside that would allow us to see crows flying in as they were attracted to the caller. We scattered a few full-body crow decoys in the corn field around us; a great horned owl decoy was strategically placed in a tree above our heads. Crows hate owls. If they saw this lifelike replica when they approached, they'd move in close and focus their attention on it instead of us.

What surprised me most was the quickness of the crows' reaction. We heard a few distant crows as we set up to hunt, but none were visible. But when the sounds of fighting began, there was an immediate response. Nearly half a mile away, I saw a crow leave the woods and begin flying our way, then another and another and another. The trees around us were swarming with cawing crows within minutes.

We waited until several crows were within shotgun range; then, as we had previously agreed, I fired the first shot, the signal to "Take them!"

I dropped one crow then another, as did David and Joe. The crows were so intent on harassing the owl, the first shot didn't frighten them

---

Crows respond readily to electronic or hand-blown callers.

away, as one might have expected. Several continued their noisemaking, and those met their maker as well. Before the crows wised up, we had killed perhaps a dozen, and I found myself hooked on crow hunting, a sport that until that day had been as unfamiliar to me as hunting tigers in India.

Most humans don't care much for crows. These large black birds are beneficial consumers of harmful insects and important scavengers, helping clean up roadkills, dead fish, and other carrion. Unfortunately, crows also destroy crops like pecans and corn. They hunt constantly for eggs and nestlings, and in areas where crows are numerous, they may seriously impact populations of game birds, songbirds, and herons, making it necessary to control their numbers. Hunting them offers a means of control and a first-rate challenge for sportsmen.

Two species of crows—the American crow and fish crow—inhabit Arkansas year-round. Both are legal game for hunters during open seasons, which typically run from early September through the end of February, Wednesdays through Sundays only. Mondays and Tuesdays are closed to extend the season and allow as many open weekends as possible. This is necessary because crows are federally protected migratory game birds, and federal guidelines stipulate that crow season may be no longer than 124 days.

American crows live in a variety of habitats, including farmlands, woodlands, and even urban areas but seem especially fond of large open farm-country fields. They usually stay in small groups in spring and summer but form flocks of twenty-five to fifty or more birds in autumn and winter. In some states, roosts containing up to half a million American crows have been reported. One large concentration seen in Arkansas was a roost on Lake Millwood occupied by twenty-five thousand birds.

Fish crows favor marshes, swamps, rivers, lakes, and other wetland habitats. In Arkansas, they frequent the countryside surrounding big slow-moving rivers such as the Arkansas. Though common in some localized areas, sometimes forming flocks of fifty or more birds, they are, overall, much less common here than American crows.

Farmers have no love for crows, and if you conduct yourself in a courteous and respectful way, you should have little trouble gaining permission to hunt crows on private lands. Almost all our wildlife management areas also harbor healthy crow populations that can be hunted.

When you find a huntable concentration, you then must decide where to set up a stand. Some hunters learn the daily flight patterns of crows as they travel between roosts and feeding areas, then set up beneath these flight paths to take their quarry. Others prefer to drive through the countryside searching for small bands of feeding or calling crows. A quick blind then is constructed, or the hunter conceals himself in some other manner. The calling then begins.

Electronic and hand callers both are used. Each has a place in crow calling, and very often their use overlaps.

Hand callers are inexpensive, easy to carry, and easily mastered. Picking from the many models available is a matter of personal preference, but some features should be considered. Avoid callers that are too "windy" (callers that require a lot of air to blow). Crow hunting, unlike most types of game calling, requires extended calling with a lot of volume. A windy caller will wear you out in a hurry. Also, look for callers that have a movable reed rather than a fixed reed. This allows tuning the caller to produce sounds ranging from a young bird's high falsetto to the guttural rasp of an old-timer.

Electronic callers, which play compact discs or cassettes, offer several advantages over hand callers alone. They can produce the sounds of multiple crows simultaneously, something difficult to do with a single hand caller. Your hands aren't busy when shooting time comes, because the caller can be turned on and left alone. The sounds played are the ultimate in realism; the sounds of real crows often are used to create the compact disc or cassette. Novice crow hunters can experience fun results with these units right off the shelf.

Some veteran crow hunters combine the use of hand and electronic callers for an even more effective calling effort.

If you intend to use a hand caller, practice diligently to learn the variety of calls used in various situations. There are many variations of the two basic call types—friendly and fighting—that usually are employed. Each has subtle variations that make it effective for a particular setup or situation. Having a veteran caller teach you is the best way to learn, but instructional videotapes and audio cassettes also are available to assist you.

Using an electronic caller is easy. Insert the tape of the call type you want to use, then turn the caller on. An electronic caller can produce combinations of sounds, such as multiple fighting crows, that can't be duplicated by a single hand caller. And with an electronic caller, there's no worry about fatigue. Carry a spare set of fresh batteries and you can call crows continuously for hours. On the down side, an electronic call doesn't "talk" *to* the crows, it talks *at* them. This failure to actually converse with crows can limit a hunter's success.

Decoys aren't absolutely necessary for crow hunting, but they help focus a crow's attention away from the hunter. Two types—silhouette and full-body—frequently are used, often together. Silhouette decoys can be made from cardboard for just pennies, are easy to carry and can be quickly set up. They're not as durable, however, as full-body decoys, which usually are made of hard plastic. They're also difficult to use in trees. Full-body decoys are more realistic and durable and set up very quickly. They cost more and are bulky, however. If you use this type, purchase those with a small eye on top of the decoy, which allows it to be pulled into a tree.

If you intend to set up a "crow versus owl" scene, you'll also need an owl decoy. Most commercial models resemble the great horned owl. Some are made full-body style in hard plastic, others cardboard silhouettes imprinted with photo-realistic owls. Owl decoys often can be purchased in garden stores.

Two types of decoy setups—friendly and fighting—are used. The friendly setup mimics a group of foraging crows going about their business. This display type should be placed where crows normally feed, usually in a field, orchard, or dump. If trees are nearby, place a few as high as possible in the branches to give your setup long-range visual appeal, as well as to simulate the crows' natural habit of posting sentries. "Feeding" decoys on the ground should be randomly spaced at the edge of gunning range, about thirty to thirty-five yards. Do not place decoys too close to your stand or blind, giving the birds a reason to stare in your direction.

With the friendly setup, most hunters put out as many decoys as possible to simulate a group that has found a feast. Don't despair, however, if you only have a few decoys. You can add a few dead crows to your decoy spread when the shooting begins.

The fighting setup, which is most popular, simulates a situation where crows are in conflict with an owl. In the past, hunters used live owls as decoys, but that practice is now illegal. Instead, the hunter uses an artificial owl positioned on a fence post, the top of a small tree or even a long pole, so every crow in the vicinity can spot it. Unlike the friendly setup, position most of your decoys above the ground in surrounding trees and brush. In a real fight between crows and an owl, the crows that aren't flying usually sit in surrounding trees to scold the owl.

Pump or semiautomatic shotguns loaded with number 6 or 7-1/2 shotshells are perhaps the most popular firearms for crow hunting, but a .22-caliber rimfire rifle or small caliber muzzleloader also can be used. All guns should be customized to cover high-gloss finishes and/or reflective surfaces, which crows may see.

When you begin hunting, try to avoid these common mistakes:

Overhunting an area. Crows are smart; they remember. It may be tempting to constantly revisit an area where you had a great shoot, but if done too often, the birds get call-shy. It's best to scout for several good areas then "leapfrog" from one to another to avoid problems.

Not being properly camouflaged. Crows easily detect colors, shapes, and silhouettes that are out-of-place. Wear complete camouflage on body, head, and hands that matches your surroundings. Crow hunters have a saying: "You can never be too well camouflaged."

Premature cessation of calling. Some hunters cease calling when shots are fired, thinking crows will leave when shooting begins. Though this sometimes happens, crows often get so worked up, they'll return to the decoys again and again if you keep up a steady stream of calls, even during gunfire.

Calling with too much volume. Some electronic callers can be cranked up to produce a tremendous call volume when needed. This can be helpful for getting the attention of distant crows, but too much volume can be detrimental when birds are near. Reduce the volume to a "normal" level as crows approach.

Leading birds too far. Crows typically move slower than other game birds, especially as they pass the decoys. Many first-time shooters lead them too far when shooting. It's impossible to give hard and fast rules relating to shot lead, but you'll normally find your target with a beak-length lead after crows enter the decoy zone.

Not carrying a spare caller or batteries. Calling with a hand caller requires lots of blowing and usually a lot of spit. This causes reeds to stick or freeze up, especially during extreme cold. Have a spare caller hanging around your neck in case of a failure. Carry spare batteries and a spare calling tape for electronic callers.

All this may seem like a lot to learn and remember, but don't let that intimidate you. The more you learn about the various nuances of crow hunting, the better hunter you'll become. But even beginners can be successful at pursuing these abundant black rascals. Only a few basic items of equipment are necessary, and none are hard to use. The sport is challenging and simple at the same time, and will help hone your calling and shooting skills.

Best of all, you can hunt crows near home no matter where you live in Arkansas. Crows are abundant in all counties. And with a season that spans half the year, you should find ample opportunity for many trips afield. Once you've tried crow hunting, you'll be glad of that. Because once you're hooked, like me, you'll want to go crow hunting as often as you can.

A Place to Hunt
Natural State Doves

The opening of dove season is one of Arkansas's great social events. In grain fields from Blytheville to Texarkana, hunters numbering in the tens of thousands gather in September to celebrate the break of the long hunting drought.

Thousands of other hunters sit on the sidelines during the kickoff, wishing they could play but not certain where to go. "It's tough finding a good place to hunt doves these days," I often hear. "I'd like to be out there on opening day, but so much land is posted nowadays, and the public hunting areas aren't really managed much for doves."

Landowners worried about liability and tired of cleaning up after slob hunters often post "No Trespassing" or "No Hunting" signs on their property. More than two million acres of public land are open for hunting, but crops attractive to doves are planted on only a small percentage of that acreage. Management practices usually are aimed at deer, ducks, turkeys, and other "glamour" game animals instead of creatures such as mourning doves that prefer open crop fields.

That's the bad news. The good news is, doves remain extremely plentiful in the Natural State, and despite the prevalence of posted ground and the lack of dove management on public lands, you still can find excellent shooting opportunities throughout the state if you make an extra effort. The following vignettes will give you some options to consider.

PAID SHOOTS

From their hiding place in a sunflower field, a hunter and his son watch the sky for incoming birds. It's the boy's first dove hunt, and he's eager for action. He fidgets on his seat, a five-gallon bucket, gripping tightly the twenty-gauge he has practiced shooting for weeks.

"There, son," the father whispers. "See them coming across the field? Get ready."

Finding a good dove-hunting area requires some prehunt preparation from the hunter.

Four doves cross the expanse at breakneck speed, coming straight toward the two hunters. The doves wheel away as they near, and it looks like they will pass out of range. But something turns them once again. They cross from left to right less than thirty yards from the man and boy. And when it is time, the father calls the shot. "Now, son. Get 'em!"

The youngster stands, picks a bird, swings with it as it passes, and pulls the trigger when he establishes the proper lead. The dove falls. The father's follow-through is not so good. He misses. Three birds continue flying along the field's edge. Other hunters are positioned to intercept them farther down, and they do.

"Great shot, son! Great shot. Let's go retrieve your bird."

It is the first bird of several the youngster will kill that morning. By noon, his shoulder will be black and blue after shooting three boxes of shells. But he will not notice until much later. For a twelve-year-old just experiencing the joys of wing shooting, the excitement is overwhelming.

"I'm glad I looked at those advertisements in the newspaper," the man tells his wife that night. "It was well worth the hundred dollars I spent for John and I to enjoy a really great hunt."

I've heard some hunters say they'd never pay for the privilege to hunt. But if you enjoy fast-paced wing shooting, you'd do well to consider a paid hunt on private land. In recent years, I've seen hunts advertised for as little as twenty-five dollars for a half-day shoot, and as much as one hundred fifty dollars for an all-day hunt in a fancy blind, with lunch served on the premises. You'll have little trouble locating hunting areas of this type if you scan the classified ads of major newspapers and state-oriented magazines in the weeks just prior to the season opener.

If you don't have time to scout out a good dove hunting area, or want to treat friends or clients to a good hunt, this definitely is the way to go. You're almost guaranteed lots of shooting because these areas are intensively managed specifically for mourning doves. Most pay-to-hunt lands now feature sunflower fields, which attract doves like kids to an ice-cream truck. Save five dollars here and ten dollars there, and you'll soon have enough for a great opening day hunt.

HUNTING BY PERMISSION

In August, he stopped by and knocked on the farmer's door. "Hello, Mr. Johnson," he said when the man answered. "My friends and I still want to hunt doves on your place when the season opens, and I wondered if you'd mind me doing some scouting today. I'd like to see if I can figure out how they're coming and going from the field so I can pick some good stands."

"Well, it would be pretty hard to refuse a guy who spent a whole weekend helping me fence the back forty," the farmer replied. "Tell you what. Let me grab my hat and some binoculars and we'll drive out in my truck together. I've been watching those doves myself, and I might have some pointers that will help you out."

The farmer's advice was invaluable. On opening day, the hunter and three friends managed a dozen birds apiece in the fifty-acre grainfield. The action was fast and furious.

When the hunt was over, they picked up their spent shotshells and carried them out. The doves were dressed, and the leavings put in trash bags. They stopped at the farmhouse on their way out to thank the landowner.

"We cleaned up when we left, and made sure your gate was shut," one of the hunters told him. "And we brought you a mess of doves already dressed and ready to cook. We appreciate your hospitality."

"Come back any time," he said. "You boys are always welcome here." The farmer smiled the next week when a thank-you note arrived in the mail.

Because most prime dove-hunting lands are privately owned, most sportsmen must turn toward private lands to meet their hunting needs. Knocking on the landowner's door and asking permission to hunt each time you visit is common courtesy. But this isn't a guaranteed way to gain access. Sometimes the landowner reserves hunting privileges for family and friends. Some simply won't let anyone hunt, fearful of liability or wary of bad seeds who cause problems. It's been my experience, though, that many landowners will grant hunting permission, even on posted land, if you take time to get acquainted before hunting season and show that you're different from the scores of other folks who come to his door each year asking the same favor.

The true sportsman is a real friend to the landowner. Your contribution might be nothing more than a willingness to spend a little time visiting. In other instances, it may be something more concrete, like helping build a new fence or even offering to pay for the privilege to hunt.

Hunters should always pick up spent shells and litter—that left by other hunters, too. Hunt only where the landowner wants you to, keeping safely away from his house, barns, and livestock, and respecting his crops. Don't stretch or break fences you cross, and latch gates securely when you pass through. Leave everything as you found it, or better, and let the landowner know you appreciate the opportunity to hunt on his land. That means sharing your game with him, sending him a thank-you note, and always letting your good manners show.

If you want private landowners to be your friends, try being a friend to them.

PUBLIC LANDS HUNTING

It was near dusk when the birds started coming in. The strips of grain in the food plots didn't look like much, but they were enough to draw a few hungry doves each morning. When they came, the man and a friend were waiting to take them.

The man had scouted the wildlife management area three times prior to opening day before finding this hidden treasure. Most hunters would have overlooked it, so small was the place. But the man was patient and thorough, and soon had figured where many birds were feeding. They bagged four doves apiece at the food plot that morning, then moved to a small pond to hunt in the afternoon. The doves liked the open mudflats around the half-dry pond, and could be counted on to drop in at 4:00 P.M. each evening to water. A few decoys by the water's edge helped draw them the last few critical yards into shooting range. The shooting wasn't fast but it was steady, and each man shot a half-dozen more birds to add to the morning's bag.

Despite what many hunters think, you can find good dove hunting on wildlife management areas and other public lands. In fact, on a few areas, managers plant food plots and fields that draw doves in numbers that rival Delta farmlands. Personnel in the Wildlife Management

Division of the Game and Fish Commission can provide information on public lands open to dove hunters and details about specific tracts planted with grain crops attractive to doves.

On areas where dove fields aren't planted, you still can find doves. Scouting is the key to success. You still look for open areas where doves are feeding, but you also look for other things that attract doves. For instance, many wildlife management areas provide good roosting cover for doves, although there may not be good dove food in the area. Doves may feed in adjacent fields on private land, then come into the brushy areas on the wildlife management area to roost. By scouting in late afternoon, you often can find a flight lane leading into or across a portion of the wildlife management area where you can intercept birds. The doves may not be roosting in it but may be flying over part of it—over open areas, along power lines or gas line rights-of-way, etc. Small ponds and streams with open banks may provide shooting for doves coming to water, and weed fields or food plots may draw small numbers of feeding birds. Scouting prior to hunting season can lead you to many good hunting areas others overlook.

Worried about a place to dove hunt this season? You shouldn't be. As you can see, hunters willing to spend some time scouting always can find a place to hunt in the Natural State. Hitting the doves at which we shoot . . . that's the tough part.

Whistling Wings and Waterways

"Heads up!" The muffled shout came from my right. I looked around just in time to see a high-flying mourning dove speed across the river, then suddenly drop low near the cottonwood tree I hid by. Before I could raise my twelve-gauge, Jimmy Peeler fired, dropping the bird with a clean shot.

"Nice shot!" I called out. Then Jimmy's brother Lewis was yelling and pointing behind us.

"Birds coming in over the trees."

Three doves were nearly on top of me, dodging and dipping like bantam kamikazes out of control. When they were directly in front of me, I shouldered my shotgun and fired at the trailing bird. It faltered a little but kept racing along like demons were nipping at its heels. I followed it and fired again. It wasn't a perfect shot, but the bird fell in a patch of weeds forty yards out. I ran to retrieve it.

Before I was back in position, someone called "Bird," and I dropped to a squat as a tight group of five or six doves winged by out of range. Lewis was ready and downed two as the cluster broke up. Gray streaks skedaddled for safer air space in all directions.

Two streaks veered my way. I shot twice and missed. Jimmy lowered the boom on one, and the other hugged the ground as it rocketed across the river. I pulled three shotshells from my second box and pushed them into the belly of my Browning.

If you want to enjoy fast-paced wing shooting like this, head for the nearest Delta river on opening day. That's right, I said "river." Not milo field or corn field or sunflower field. River.

Like most dove enthusiasts, I've spent hundreds of hours pursuing doves in harvested croplands where they feed. And I've enjoyed extraordinary dove hunts in this type of habitat. As often as not, however, I head straight for one of east Arkansas's major waterways when looking for an action-packed dove shoot. Unbeknownst to most hunters, doves concentrate in phenomenal numbers along rivers like the St. Francis, the

---

Waterway hunts near dawn and dusk often produce good wing shooting for mourning dove enthusiasts.

lower White, the lower Arkansas, and the Mississippi. And because most land bordering the main river channels is in public ownership, there's little problem finding a place to hunt.

Hunting waterways comes naturally for me. My first dozen dove hunts took place along the St. Francis River Floodway in Cross County when I was a teenager. On my first such outing, Jimmy Peeler positioned me under a tree above the almost-dry stream bed.

This muddy ditch and the terrain in general weren't too exciting to a fourteen-year-old kid. I doubted dove hunting was as sporting as Jimmy and Lewis had described it, and my surroundings seemed to prove me right. I was nodding off when the first shots rang out from down the levee.

"Get ready," Jimmy shouted. "Birds comin' in."

Suddenly, there they were, wings whistling. Some streaked in from downstream. Others blazed in behind us from across the river. As I swung on one, several more appeared, flaring as our guns boomed. For ten minutes, the action was nonstop, then there was a short lull. I found, to my amazement, I'd gone through more than half a box of shells. My shotgun barrel was hot, my knees were weak, and in the midst of all that bedlam, I had downed only two birds.

From then on, I was hooked on dove hunting. And today, after many feeding-field hunts, I still find that nothing quite touches the waterway shoot for fast action and consistent success.

Doves usually water twice daily—once in the morning after feeding and again in late afternoon before going to roost. One might think such striking game birds would prefer sparkling clear water, but doves usually drink at muddy ponds, seeps, mudholes, and streambanks. A farm pond or stretch of riverside with a wide swath of open dirt or mud is ideal, especially if it's located near roosts or feeding areas. Doves will circle swiftly, eye the water hole for signs of danger, then, if all looks safe, swing in to alight a few feet from the water's edge. From there they walk to the water to drink.

These sporty game birds are attracted to Delta waterways for other reasons, too. Mourning doves visit "graveling" sites daily to pick up tiny pieces of grit their gizzards need to grind seeds. Sand and gravel bars along rivers provide a readily available source of this important dietary component.

Rivers also serve as reference points for flying doves. When moving between feeding, watering, graveling, and roosting sites, doves follow easily recognizable travel lanes like streams and adjacent tree lines. Positioning yourself along or at the ends of these flyways is the key to dove-hunting success.

Some waterway hunting sites, like river levees, can be accessed by roadway. Others, such as river sandbars, can only be reached by boat or by walking in. Regardless of where you hunt, though, you'll need to spend time scouting for areas used by huntable concentrations of birds.

When you've located an area harboring good dove numbers, use binoculars to determine activity patterns throughout the day. If you plan to hunt a sand or gravel bar, the best hunting may be at midday when birds usually gravel. If birds are using your portion of the waterway primarily as a travel lane, shooting action probably will peak near dawn when birds are flying to feeding areas. If doves come to drink at your chosen hunting site, you'll probably need to be there in late morning or near dusk. Dove hunting is a sport of ambush, and knowing where and when doves roost, feed, water, gravel, and fly determines where and when you should hunt.

Of course, the best dove hunting areas provide all the amenities of life close at hand. Pinpoint a locale with feeding, roosting, graveling, and watering areas all in close proximity, and you can enjoy exciting wing shooting throughout the day.

Without doubt, the best dove hunting in Arkansas is found in the eastern Delta. Within this vast agricultural region are dozens of waterways where Arkansas sportsmen can enjoy incomparable wing shooting.

The largest of these waterways, the Mississippi River, offers excellent dove shooting in selected locales along Arkansas's eastern border. When water levels aren't too high, big river sandbars attract concentrations of doves traveling between feeding and watering sites.

On the St. Francis River and St. Francis River Floodway, which run from Phillips County north to the Missouri boot heel, hunters may find doves at selected sites along the floodway levee in Cross and Poinsett Counties, and when water levels are low, around exposed mudflats where doves come to water. Numerous cottonwood trees along regularly traveled dove flyways provide excellent cover for waiting hunters.

The White River is another dove hunting mecca. Much of the

lower river, from Newport downstream to the river's mouth, is bordered by crop fields that attract tremendous concentrations of mourning doves. To coax these birds into shooting range, position dove decoys at the water's edge on mudflats and sandbars, or in small, dead, leaf-bare trees along scouted flyways. A camouflaged hunter can squat at the edge of nearby vegetation and pick his shots as doves pass close to investigate.

The Arkansas River provides superb waterway dove hunting from Fort Smith across the state to the Mississippi River. Here, as elsewhere, pre-hunt scouting is important in determining when and where the sportsmen should hunt. Most hunters select an ambush site along flyways between adjacent agricultural lands and evening roost sites, but the savvy hunter also may pinpoint huntable concentrations around gravel and sand bars.

Regardless of which waterway you hunt, take care to avoid trespassing on private land, especially when hunting along levees where a lot of land is leased and posted. It's also imperative to follow the rules of safe boating and hunting. All the rivers mentioned, except the St. Francis, have heavy barge traffic that can cause problems for the unwary boater. Always wear a life jacket when boating and know what's beyond your target in the direction you're shooting.

Hunting rivers for doves may sound a bit offbeat, but like the old adage says, "Don't knock it till you've tried it." For doves, Arkansas's Delta waterways provide all the amenities. And for dove hunters, few places can provide a bigger dose of action, fun and excitement.

This Dove Hunting Is the Pits

When scouting for mourning doves, most Arkansas hunters head straight for farm country where harvested fields of sunflowers, millet, wheat, or other seed crops attract hungry birds.

"Most dove hunters hunt grain fields, and that's about it," says Lewis Peeler, a veteran dove hunting enthusiast from Wynne, Arkansas. "But that doesn't mean grain fields are the only place you can hunt. Gravel pits also attract lots of doves, especially around midday when doves leave feeding areas to get water and grit. Many hunters don't know this, and if they live in an area where gravel is mined, they're missing some excellent shooting opportunities."

Gravel, a loose mixture of small rocks and sand, is a key ingredient in concrete and is often used for surfacing rural roads. In many areas, it's obtained by removing surface soils and stripping away the underlying gravel with heavy equipment. The open pits left behind are common throughout much of the Natural State, and many attract large concentrations of doves.

"Doves are drawn to gravel pits for several reasons," says Peeler. "The main attraction is water. Many pits aren't well drained, and water fills the holes left by digging. The water is usually muddy from runoff, and for whatever reason, doves like to drink muddy water. Few plants grow around the water holes, so the banks are open. Doves like that, too, because it lets them watch for danger while drinking and fly away quickly if there are any threats."

Another gravel pit attraction, says Peeler, is a readily available source of grit.

"Mourning doves pick up little bits of grit every day so their gizzards can grind the seeds they eat," he notes. "That's why you see doves sitting on gravel roads and on the shoulders of highways. That's also why they flock to gravel pits. There's plenty of sand and other grit, and there's no traffic to disturb them while they're getting it."

Open perches are an added enticement.

"Anyone who hunts doves very much knows how they're attracted to dead trees," Peeler says. "If there's an old snag on the edge of a field or watering hole, they'll light in it and sit a few minutes to rest or watch for danger before they fly down. That's another reason doves like gravel pits.

When workers are digging gravel, they push dirt up around trees, and the trees later die. So there usually are several dead snags for birds to use.

"When you have all three elements—water holes, graveling sites and dead trees for perching—together in one small place, then you've got a topnotch dove hunting area. If you can add to those a nearby feeding area—a field of milo or other grain close to the pit—then the shooting can be almost unbelievable."

Peeler, like most hunters, usually hunts doves in harvested crop fields. Gravel pits, he says, serve primarily as back-up sites when field hunting gets slow.

"I usually hunt fields in early morning or late afternoon, because that's when doves generally feed," he says. "Around midday, though, doves usually leave the fields to water and gravel, and the action tapers off. That's when I head for the pits."

Peeler scouts the pits ahead of time to determine the birds' activity patterns. "I watch where they're flying over, where they're coming into the pit. Then I position myself accordingly, hiding in the edge of timber or some high weeds. Camouflage clothing is important to help you remain undetected, and in the last few years, I've become a real believer in dove decoys. A few decoys set on bare branches or at the edge of the water help attract passing doves and draw them in close so I have a better shot."

Peeler, who usually hunts gravel pits on his property, stresses the importance of visiting with the landowner before you hunt.

"Nearly all gravel pits are privately owned," he says. "Most folks, like me, don't mind you hunting inactive pits, because there's not any equipment or cattle to worry about, no houses nearby. Still, you should always take time to ask permission first. And then drop back in to say thanks and offer the owner some of the birds you shot. It's just common courtesy, and it'll pay off when you want to come back and hunt again.

"You'll want to come back, too," he continues. "Sometimes when you're hunting a gravel pit, the shooting seems like it'll never end. Then there's a lull in the action, and you realize that in fifteen minutes you've gone through an entire box of shells. Your barrel's hot, your knees are weak, and you know, without a doubt, you gotta come back for more."

A few decoys set by a gravel pit pool can draw doves into shooting range.

Green-Timber Greenheads

As the shower drew near, a hush swept through the flooded timber—the calm before the storm. We watched the tempest take shape as one might watch a rain squall on the horizon, and knew, in seconds, we'd be caught in the deluge.

"My God!" one of the hunters whispered.

Then the birds began to fall.

They plummeted into the flooded trees from a single point of the compass, wings cupped, feet splayed, the emerald heads of the drakes glistening in sharp contrast to the vivid crimson and orange of the autumn-colored oaks. One landed with a splash, then another and another. In seconds, the air was full of them. The soft whistling of their wings filled our ears.

I tried guessing their numbers, but it was useless. One might easier count snowflakes in a blizzard. One hundred? Five hundred? I could not determine, but in less time than it takes to tell it, they covered the shallow water before us like a warm feathered blanket. The sky, dark with their forms just seconds before, shone bluebird-blue again.

All was silent now. My hunting companions and I were afraid to move, afraid even to breathe, for fear of destroying that magic moment. But despite our best intentions, the inevitable happened. Somewhere within the flock, a wary susie flushed. Something in her tiny brain told her something wasn't quite right, and she shot from the water like a stone from a catapult. The entire flock followed in an explosion of swamp water and feathers.

We watched them leave, a backward-played video on nature's TV screen. As quickly as they had come, they were gone.

I have witnessed many wonderful things during forty years of hunting, but none more memorable than that shower of mallards, which fell last fall. Under different circumstances, some ducks never would have left that hole. In this instance, however, not a shot was fired. My friends and I had our limits. We were simply observers.

Mallards pitch into a green-timber reservoir on the Poor Boy Hunting Club near Stuttgart.

Three hours earlier, before first light, we had boated to brush-covered blinds in the flooded timber. Sammy Faulk, a friend from Louisiana, had joined me for a hunt on the Poor Boy Duck Club just outside Stuttgart, Arkansas, the Rice and Duck Capitol of the World. Here, mallards and flooded green timber are the basic ingredients in a decades-old duck-hunting recipe.

Our hunting spot, the "South Hole," was a small clearing amidst hundreds of acres of pin oaks flooded with shallow water. When we reached it, after navigating a maze of narrow woodland boat trails with a small spotlight, Sammy and I climbed into a blind. Our hosts, Vernon Baker, Bob Bendigo, and George Peters, remained outside. Wearing waders and standing close beside trees in the almost-knee-deep water, the three men, almost invisible in their tree-bark garb, made the sounds of mallards feeding, gabbing, cajoling their friends in the sky to come down. Occasionally, one man swirled his foot in the water, sending ripples through a small block of decoys. Ripples in the water convince flying ducks that their kind are feeding below.

Weather conditions were ideal for a timber hunt. The sky was robin's-egg blue with wisps of white clouds. No ice was on the water, so the birds were flying. A cold front had passed the night before, and with it came a new wave of ducks. The sky at first light was alive with mallards.

The callers called. The ducks responded. The whole thing seemed choreographed.

A pod of greenheads and susies rocketed by at treetop height and banked sharply in response to Vern's hail call. Vern turned this way then that, trying to keep an eye on the mallards speeding through the maze of trees. A staccato burst of feeding notes was the final persuader. The birds circled once, cupped their wings, and came in through the canopy. We each dropped a drake.

Hundreds of mallards traded through the timber. George called. A flock whirled and came our way. They circled twice, then gave to the pull of gravity, falling through the trees. Two. Four. Ten. A dozen. Two dozen. When all was right, George signaled: "Get 'em!" And some got got.

By ten, we were celebrating our good fortune over a welcome cup of coffee back at the clubhouse. Other hunters were coming in, too, and we swapped "How'd you dos" on the front porch. All agreed it was a fine morning for hunting green-timber greenheads.

This was just one of many successful green-timber duck hunts I've enjoyed in Arkansas. Not all were as exciting as this one, but I can say with certainty Arkansas serves up the finest timber hunting in the world. Most years, the Natural State ranks number one in mallards killed, and the focal point of this harvest is the Grand Prairie region around Stuttgart.

Field shooting and reservoir hunts figure heavily in the Arkansas duck hunting equation, but these are not the essence of Stuttgart duck hunting. What exemplifies Stuttgart is shooting in flooded green timber. Hardwoods cover the bottomlands in this region. On private clubs and many public hunting grounds, water is pumped into the woods before duck season and held there by levees and stop-log structures. Mallards, wood ducks, teal, gadwalls, and other puddle ducks flock to these shallow green-tree reservoirs to feed on acorns and other favored foods. When the ducks leave in spring, the water is released. Thus it does not kill the trees.

Artificial impoundments of this sort aren't the only draw for wintering ducks. Thousands of acres of naturally flooded woodlands still stretch along the region's big rivers, despite the prevalence of rice, soybean, and wheat farming. These, too, draw ducks like squirrels to a bird feeder. The largest such areas are Bayou Meto Wildlife Management Area, a world-renowned green-timber waterfowling hotspot covering 32,250 acres just southwest of Stuttgart, and 160,000-acre White River National Wildlife Refuge, part of the largest contiguous tract of bottomland hardwoods remaining in the United States. The allure of green-timber mallard hunting attracts thousands of visitors to these areas and to scores of commercial hunting lodges around Stuttgart.

Timber hunting is the purest form of duck hunting, and in many ways the hardest. You don't need a boat, a dog or even decoys, though these figure into most men's hunting. Timber shooting can be distilled down to three essentials—a man, a call, and ducks.

The call is the key. Flying birds must be right over a decoy spread before they can see it. Consequently, the oversized blocks of decoys used in open water or field hunting don't work here. Sound in the form of duck talk attracts birds in green timber.

Hunters try to "read" the ducks and call when appropriate, using a combination of hail calls, feeding calls, and quacks to bring birds in. Mallards respond differently to calling each day. The best hunters recognize this and change their approach to be successful.

The average Stuttgart duck hunter's pacifier was replaced with a duck call at a very early age, so many hunters here are experts at the craft. Those less confident in their calling skills, and those wanting an added advantage, place a dozen or so decoys in a small opening to keep the birds coming those last critical yards. Blending into the shadow of nearby trees, some hunters call while others slosh the water with enthusiastic kicking to get the decoys moving around and create the impression of mallards feeding on acorns.

Shooting can be fast and furious. Hard-to-see ducks in tall timber can be on top of you before you realize they are near. You must decide in a split second if they're within range, if they're going to drop in, or if they should be taken on the pass.

You probably would take more birds if you stuck to pass shooting exclusively, even though it's tricky to track, lead, and shoot a bird in the scant seconds before it's swallowed in the maze of branches. Too often mallards that appear to be coming in will circle and circle, then disappear when they spot something out of place. But resisting pass shots holds a special reward. Few sights in the sport of hunting are as magnificent as a flock of ducks skimming the winter-bare treetops, wings cupped in classic fashion, as they drop from the sky into a flooded forest.

In November 1999, my son Matt and I accompanied Jim Spencer of Little Rock for a timber hunt on Bayou Meto WMA. Jim has been hunting Bayou Meto for decades, and through Jim's generosity, Matt and I experienced a moment the two of us will always remember.

Wading into flooded timber at first light, we took a stand in a small opening and watched thousands of mallards trading back and forth overhead. Most were too high for shooting, but Jim's expert calling convinced several to drop in. At noon, when shooting hours ended, we had six mallards for our efforts.

What happened next was almost too astounding to believe. All shooting ended. We unloaded our guns and sat back to watch. Mallards that flew high all morning started dropping into the timber. It began as a trickle of ducks, but the trickle soon grew to a flood, and mallards were splashing down all around us. As the water became crowded with birds, those trying to land were forced to circle and look for open water. Thousands and thousands of them flew round about us, circling through the woods like a huge feathered whirlwind. The three of us were mesmerized.

Moments like that, after a successful hunt, embody the true green-timber experience.

Ducks the Color of Autumn

Shooting a wood duck in flooded timber is like trying to gun down a stone released from a slingshot, only harder.

I came to this conclusion while hunting early-season ducks in a green-tree reservoir near Stuttgart. Mallards had not yet made their way into Arkansas's Grand Prairie in appreciable numbers, but wood ducks, year-round residents in the Natural State, were buzzing through the pin oaks like bumblebees round a flower garden. My "purist" waterfowling companions, who hunt only mallards, agreed that the lack of greenhead action made woodies fair game—for me. They wouldn't join in my follies, but I was told I would be "allowed" to try pass shooting some of the birds streaking past our blind.

The wood ducks usually appeared in pairs, squealing loudly as they flew past. *Oo-eek! Oo-eek*. Their distinctive flight calls left no doubt how they earned the nickname "squealers." Those that weren't calling still were audible on their approach. The noise made as air rushed through their pinions closely resembled the sound of a bottle rocket fired on the Fourth of July.

It seemed that shooting one would be an impossible task. And in several instances, my assumption was correct. Many birds passed at such breakneck speed, there wasn't time to shoulder my shotgun and shoot. No problem, I thought. I'll just keep my gun at the ready and take the next one that comes by. But after fifteen minutes waiting, I no longer could maintain a shooting stance. And, as one might expect, the instant I brought my shotgun down, two woodies flashed across the opening in the timber right in front of me.

My hunting companions found all this rather humorous. "You might as well give it up, Sutton," one of them said, chuckling. "You'd have better luck hunting quail with a pea shooter."

Undaunted, I continued my quest. And at ten o'clock, almost four hours into the hunt, everything came together—sort of. I shouldered my shotgun, and almost immediately a pair of woodies came into view, flying fast from right to left, my favorite cross-shot swing. I aimed ahead of the lead bird and fired. The rear bird fell.

"That bird out front was just moving too fast for me to draw a bead on it," I told my hunting buddies. "So I had to take the one behind it."

"Well, lucky for you," Bob said as he waded back with the duck in hand. "The one you got was a drake. It sure is a beauty."

Bob held in his hand a bird more beautiful than any I had ever seen, a bird of such gorgeous coloring, it hardly seemed real. Its glistening green head was crowned with a short rakish crest; its back was a blend of magnificent blues and purples that shimmered and glinted like metal in the sun; its breast was rich chestnut, and its sides the color of marigolds. The bird's glossy bill was painted with broad brush strokes of red, black, and white, and the large crimson eyes bore likeness to the glowing coals of a campfire. So brilliant were these colors, and so sharply contrasted, that the bird appeared to be painted. It was as if some skillful artist had spread upon its plumage the richest and most vivid pigments at his command; and yet there was nothing artificial in the effect produced, but, on the contrary, a perfection of beauty as natural as the beauty of a flower.

When I was a youngster hunting ducks along the L'Anguille River, we rarely saw wood ducks, and never shot them. They were scarce then, victims of market hunting and destruction of their bottomland hardwood habitat. Populations were protected by law. Fortunately, in the thirty-five years since I started hunting ducks, the wood duck has rebounded remarkably, and now ranks among our most plentiful game birds. We can hunt them without fear of harming the population, and for that, I am glad. I did not mind passing them by when they needed protection, and when mallards are plentiful in the woods I hunt, I probably won't give a second thought to taking wood ducks. But on days like that day last fall when mallards are scarce, the abundance of wood ducks gives me opportunity to take home game for the table. And for me, that, as much as anything, is the reason I hunt. I see beauty in wood ducks, but when I am hunting, my eyes follow them through the timber like a cat watches a bird. I hunt wood ducks because I know they provide the makings for memorable dinners.

And so, after admiring the wood duck I shot that morning, I returned to my hunting. And by noon, when our hunt ended, I had one more wood duck for the dinner table.

"You should be glad, Sutton," one of my companions said, "that you don't have to rely on your shooting skills for *everything* you eat."

That I was. But I was already looking forward to the day when I could try again for these autumn-colored birds. Wood ducks are

challenging targets to be sure, but that's one things that sets them apart from other, more commonly hunted species of waterfowl.

If my story has convinced you to give them a try this season, read on and learn more about their incredible history and some tactics that may help you bring more home for the dinner table.

YEAR-ROUND RESIDENTS

Of the fifteen species of ducks most likely to be killed by Arkansas hunters, only the wood duck lives here in appreciable numbers year-round. The number of wood ducks in Arkansas swells during spring and fall migrations, from mid-February through April, then again from August through November. But woodies always are common in larger forested stream bottoms and forested swamps. They're among the most abundant of all our ducks when hunting season opens in November. Most years, they rank second in harvest totals in Arkansas (behind mallards), composing around 10 percent of the take.

HISTORICAL NOTES

Wood ducks are common now, but they haven't always been plentiful. Near the turn of the century, populations reached all-time lows as a result of disappearing bottomland forests and market hunting. Wood ducks numbers fell so low the hunting season was closed for twenty years. It reopened in 1941 with a modest one-bird limit in fourteen states.

Unfortunately, the decline in Arkansas had not ended. Files at Big Lake National Wildlife Refuge showed one thousand to five thousand young and adults present during summer in the 1940s, but only five hundred in the 1950s, and fewer yet in the 1960s.

Many folks believed wood ducks could never recover, but they were wrong.

Thanks to its amazing resiliency and sound wildlife management, the woodie staged a remarkable comeback. Artificial nest boxes built by government officials and conservation-minded citizens, the construction of thousands of wooded ponds, and the comeback of the

---

The colorful wood duck drake is among the world's most beautiful waterfowl.

beaver (which creates prime nesting and rearing habitat for wood ducks) have all helped increase and stabilize wood duck populations. At Big Lake National Wildlife Refuge, for example, a nesting box program produced three thousand young in 1971. At White River National Wildlife Refuge, the decades-old nesting box program was discontinued because the extensive forested bottomlands there are now believed to have enough natural nesting cavities to accommodate the estimated summer population of three thousand birds. Dam construction on our big rivers also may have boosted woodie numbers. At Fort Smith, wood ducks were considered rare prior to the damming of the Arkansas River in the late 1960s. Today, wood ducks are common there.

LIFE HISTORY NOTES

The most secretive of our waterfowl, wood ducks rarely are found on large expanses of open water. They are creatures of deeply forested wetlands, seeking the seclusion of cypress swamps, timbered river bottoms, and willow-lined creeks. So strong is the bird's attachment to woodlands that even during migration it is seldom found away from trees.

Trees supply wood ducks with nesting sites and much of their food. Young are raised in tree cavities twenty to fifty feet above ground within a few yards of quiet, undisturbed bodies of water, from March through July. The wood duck's diet in Arkansas consists largely of acorns, pecans, and other woodland and wetland seeds.

Although seen statewide during warm months, these beautiful ducks become increasingly rare in upland areas as autumn approaches. Few are seen after October in the western Ozarks, and wood ducks are rare or very uncommon in all northern areas of the state during winter. During hunting season, large numbers are seen with regularity only in the forested lowlands of eastern, southern, and central Arkansas. Hunters should take this into account when planning a hunt.

HUNTING WOOD DUCKS

To successfully hunt wood ducks early in the season, first you must find them. If you fish on creeks, rivers or ponds, or squirrel hunt near water, you may already know of spots where wood ducks hang out.

Beaver ponds, sloughs, creeks, rivers, farm ponds in woods, floodplain potholes, and forested swamps all can hold substantial numbers of woodies. There's excellent hunting for wood ducks on nearly all bottomland wildlife management areas and national wildlife refuges within the winter range described above, but only footwork and advance scouting will actually tell you if the ducks are there. Among the many public hunting areas worth investigating are White River, Felsenthal, Overflow and Cache River National Wildlife Refuges, and Wattensaw, Henry Gray/Hurricane Lake, Dagmar, Rex Hancock/Black Swamp, Dave Donaldson/Black River, Earl Buss/Bayou de View, St. Francis Sunken Lands, and Bayou Meto Wildlife Management Areas. Check a current hunting regulations guide for rules and seasons on each area before hunting.

On certain rivers and bayous, float hunting can be extremely effective. Canoes or johnboats can be used, but canoes often are better because of their easy maneuverability and narrow profile. Regardless of the craft, camouflage it before each hunt with camo netting or splotches of flat brown and green paint. Dead branches or brush draped over the bow add to the effect.

Two hunters work better than one for float hunting. One paddles from the rear while the other handles the gun in the bow. Both should keep a low profile, sitting, if necessary, on the boat's floor. Keep the boat headed straight downstream, and remain immobile and silent. When approaching stream bends, hug the inside edge. This allows a closer approach to birds that may be around the bend.

Thousands of acres of flooded timber are along the L'Anguille, Cache, St. Francis, Black, White, Red, Ouachita, and Mississippi Rivers, with healthy wood duck populations available for hunting. But float hunting smaller streams often is best, streams like Bayou de View, Big Creek, Big and Little Bayou Meto, Bayou Bartholomew, Moro Bayou, Dorcheat Bayou, Bodcaw Bayou, Sulphur River, and Bayou Des Arc.

Hunting "mud-puddle" habitats—small, out-of-the-way waters such as beaver ponds, brush-entangled swamps, little overflow lakes, and backwoods farm ponds—is another way to zero in on wood ducks. Foods in these secluded stillwaters attract the birds in great numbers.

Jump-shooting is one technique for hunting these waters. The hunter studies the contour of the land surrounding the water then figures the best way to sneak within gunning range without being detected. It may mean walking a quarter-mile then belly-crawling fifty yards to the water's edge. Or it may be as simple as slipping into some brush on the outside of a pond levee.

You also can sneak into the area before daylight or a couple hours before dark and wait in hiding until the ducks come. Use a portable blind for this hunting, or wear camouflage and hunker down in brush near the water's edge. Some hunters use three or four mallard decoys to help draw the birds in, but this isn't always necessary, especially if wood ducks are using the spot regularly.

Of course, timber hunts made Arkansas waterfowling famous, and to enjoy wood duck hunting to its fullest, one should don waders and camouflage clothing and be waiting, waist-deep in the water of a flooded pin-oak flat, when wood ducks come roaring in at dawn or dusk. Decoys are unnecessary, although a half-dozen mallard sets may serve to put the birds at ease and coax them to circle overhead before pitching in. There's no need for fancy calling either, so even novice waterfowlers can go it alone.

Quick instinctive shooting is best, especially during the first few minutes after legal shooting time. Woodies are on top of you in flooded timber almost before you can spot them, especially on foggy mornings. The ducks appear out of the mist and vanish quickly if you react too slowly. If you miss your first few shots, however, don't despair. Odds are you'll be able to adjust your shooting in time to bag some woodies.

Arkansas winters more wood ducks than any state in the Mississippi Flyway except Louisiana. Our bottomland rivers and wooded pools provide winter homes not only for wood ducks that nest and are hatched here, but for thousands of birds from breeding grounds in the Great Lakes region.

Like me, many Arkansas waterfowlers remember days when wood ducks were illegal game. But thanks to intensive management and protection, hunting opportunities for these home-grown ducks are plentiful again. The mallard is monarch among Natural State duck hunters, but the wood duck is the handsome prince of our woods. Hunting this autumn-colored bird is a magical experience not to be missed.

Teal, We Meet Again

In the half-light of a September morning, we set the decoys.

"This one goes here," my friend says, a thoughtful decision born of careful observation and past experience. Line, anchor, and hand-hewn block of cork sing through the chill air, landing with a hollow-sounding splash. The teal decoy bobs upright, then swings into place as it is snubbed short by the tightened anchor line. It dances in the pre-dawn breeze, suddenly alive.

"Now another over there, and one here in front of me."

Slowly the picture takes shape, creating an illusion of nature and life. The placid brown water gains dimension and depth as decoy after decoy is placed, each carefully gauged to complement the whole.

Black willows and buckbrush cuff the river backwater we've chosen to hunt. Muted reds and golds tint the eastern horizon. We move ashore and watch as the last ripple from the last decoy drifts outward and dies.

"Not quite right," comes my friend's critical judgment. He wades out to a decoy just beyond good gun range and pulls it a bit closer. Another has lost its balance weight and is riding awry. He plucks it from the water and retires it for the day.

We move into our driftwood-and-willow blind and admire our creation over a cup of coffee. The sun rises, and the Arkansas River is postcard perfect. The water is a misty mirror reflecting the fluid orange sky. Canada geese call from a sandbar downstream as we enjoy those last few introspective moments before the gun.

"See them?" he asks, nodding upstream.

Heading our way, a ragged flock of fast-moving ducks twists and turns in the vastness above the big river.

"Blue-wings, you think?"

"I'm not sure," he replies. "But we'll know in a second."

They come like little rockets, each with the same loose wire in their guidance system. They wheel high over our blind, disappearing from sight as we sit breathlessly listening to their whistling wings.

With astounding speed, they turn downwind, following our decoy line. Then suddenly they bank, moving in precise unison, cupping their

wings, splaying their feet and dropping toward our teal blocks with the sound of the wind vibrating through their wing feathers.

"Now!"

We rise to fire. The teal see us and flare straight over our heads in a starburst pattern, daring us to hit them if we can.

I can't. And neither can my partner. The perverse little birds fly away to torment some other poor teal hunters.

That small flight of birds signals the start of the morning's shooting; though, and it isn't long before small bunches of teal are buzzing around here and there. My next opportunity comes when two blue-wings zip in from my blind side and splash down in the middle of the decoys fifty feet from the blind. When it happens, I'm blowing sand out of the receiver of my shotgun, which is laid across my lap. While I'm juggling my gun, trying to get in a position to make a shot, my hunting companion pulls off a snappy double as the pair of birds tries to hightail it out of there.

The sight of two teal floating belly up in the decoys makes the morning heat a little more bearable, and the sight of their brethren flying erratically up and down the river is encouraging. Another small flock comes winging past the blind. I lead the front bird by ten feet and touch off a load of number 6s. I kill the fourth teal back, surprising him as much as me.

At 9:00 A.M., we drop the last two teal of our limits. We make our way through the shallow water to get them, and as I stoop to pick one up, I hear the distinctive burning, rushing sound of another pod of teal passing low overhead. Without standing, I turn to my friend. A broad grin dimples his cheeks.

It's been one heck of a great morning.

The September teal season in Arkansas reappeared a few years ago after being closed for several seasons. When breeding ground counts show teal numbers are high enough, the U.S. Fish and Wildlife Service allows Arkansas and several other states the option of setting a brief, early season to take advantage of the hordes of blue-winged teal, and a few green-winged teal, that pass through in September and are sitting in the

---

Blue-winged and green-winged teal provide an early season challenge for Arkansas hunters.

marshes of Mexico long before the traditional waterfowl season opens in November. That was the case the year I hunted with my friend, and with luck, teal will be plentiful enough to support a September season again this year. If not, there will be plenty of green-wings during the November-to-January season for hunters to target.

Although mallards are king among Arkansas waterfowlers, our state also has a small core of dedicated teal enthusiasts. If you haven't tried teal hunting yet, I suggest you do. Teal are among the most delicious of our game birds, and targeting teal specifically is a great way to add spice to your hunting season.

BLUE-WINGED TEAL: IDENTIFICATION

During years when there's an early teal season, ducks other than teal are strictly off-limits. It's unlikely you'll see other species during September hunts, but it is possible. Therefore it's imperative to know how to properly identify your quarry.

Blue-winged teal arrive in Arkansas before other migrant waterfowl, sometimes as early as mid-July. By early September, they are common in shallow ponds, flooded fields, and along rivers. By early December, all but a few stragglers have moved to their wintering grounds farther south. Green-winged teal are the only other Arkansas ducks smaller in size.

Blue-wings are pint-sized ducks with chalky-blue shoulder patches on the front of the wing. The bill is relatively large. Males are grayish above, tan spotted with dark brown below. A white facial crescent is present by early winter in adults but is usually absent during summer and fall. The female is grayish-brown above, pale gray marked with dark below.

The blue wing patch, the most distinguishing flight mark, may appear white in poor light. Cinnamon teal and shovelers have similar shoulder patches, but cinnamons are rare in Arkansas, and the shoveler's huge spoon-shaped bill distinguishes it. The blue-wing's flight is erratic, and their small size and twisting turns give the illusion of great speed. The small, compact flocks usually fly low and often take hunters by surprise.

GREEN-WINGED TEAL: IDENTIFICATION

The smallest of ducks, green-winged teal are common migrants and winter residents in Arkansas. They may arrive from their breeding grounds by late August, but large numbers are seldom encountered until mid-October. They are found statewide but are most common in lowland areas. Green-wings often feed on mud flats, but where mud flats are lacking, they're usually found in shallow marshes or flooded croplands.

Male green-wings have a brown head, spotted tan breast, and gray sides. The head turns chestnut-colored and has a green ear patch by early winter, when a white vertical crescent behind the breast also becomes evident. Females are grayish-brown, speckled below. The speculum is green on both sexes. Green-wings have shorter necks, bills, and bodies than blue-wings and lack blue on the wing.

If a small duck without conspicuous wing colors flies by, it is probably this species. From below, in flight, the male green-wing shows a light belly; male blue-wings show dark. The flight is fast, buzzy, and erratic, usually low, with compact flights wheeling in unison like pigeons. The wings whistle in flight.

SCOUTING

The secret to finding Arkansas teal is determining where they are likely to be concentrated. Doing that requires knowledge of their habits.

Blue-winged teal are fond of still waters and slow currents. They frequent small ponds and pools where they dabble near vegetation, and often frequent the marshy borders of slow-moving streams such as those of eastern and southern Arkansas. During wet periods, they often alight in pools of rainwater.

Green-winged teal procure most of their food in very shallow water or on land. They are fond of wading and "puddling" in a few inches of water in muddy places or on bare mud flats, often in the company of sandpipers or killdeer. They are particularly active on their feet, walking and running well and often traveling on foot for some distance on land when searching for food or passing from pool to pool.

When alarmed by the hunter, both species spring directly from the water into the air and soon are out of danger; but if some members of the flock are shot down, the rest are likely to circle about and return. Green-wings and blue-wings are naturally tame and unsuspicious.

Because teal and doves often frequent the same water holes, some fans of both sports combine early morning teal hunts with dove shooting when season dates permit. After bagging their allotment of ducks, the hunters hang around the same body of water for the daily visitation of thirsty doves.

Many sportsmen also combine the pleasures of hunting and fishing on a single trip, hunting teal early and fishing the remainder of the day. You can scout for tomorrow's teal hot spot while you fish.

GUNS AND LOADS

Teal cannot be killed efficiently with low-velocity dove loads, but because teal are small, many hunters try shooting them with such shells. High-velocity steel shot loads are necessary. Number 6 or 4 shot are the preferred sizes.

Teal are easy to decoy. Most shots are close—twenty to thirty yards—so an open-choke shotgun works better than a tight choke, especially with steel shot. Steel shot has a pattern tighter than lead. Improved cylinder is a good choke choice for decoying teal, but when pass shooting, many waterfowlers prefer a modified choke.

To improve your odds for success, it's a good idea to try a few practice rounds at a local skeet field, or better yet, shoot a few rounds of sporting clays, the clay-bird game that simulates most hunting situations. Practice your shooting with the gun unmounted (away from your shoulder) as you call for the target. Failure to mount the gun quickly and properly is one of the worst habits into which the average teal hunter falls. Teal are among the fastest game birds and often pop into shotgun range when the hunter least expects it. Pour a cup of coffee, break out a sandwich, or step from the blind on a nature call, and it's the teal's cue to come rocketing out of nowhere, sizzle across your decoys, and disappear before you can lay hands on a gun.

DECOYS

Being trusting, unsuspicious ducks, teal decoy well without calling. That's good news for hunters like me who are less than proficient at blowing a call.

When hunting small waters such as ponds, six to twelve decoys usually are enough. When hunting larger waters—big rivers or lakes, for example—it's best to carry at least two to three dozen decoys to gain the birds' attention. Mallard decoys work OK, but small-bodied teal decoys are even better. These are available from many manufacturers, and the extra cost of owning a few is well worth it when you plan to hunt teal specifically.

The pattern of your decoy set is vital in attracting teal and luring them where you want them to land. Most patterns have an opening or pocket facing downwind where the decoying birds should land. These patterns often are described as C, V, and J patterns, after their shape as seen from above. The opening or pocket should be well within shotgun range and encourage the most ideal angle of approach. Decoyed teal land into the wind, which should be coming from the back of the blind, encouraging the normally difficult-to-hit teal to come in straight toward the gunners. It's also important to place decoys where flying ducks have a good view of them. If decoys are hidden by a high bank, trees, or other obstructions, they are useless.

ARKANSAS TEAL-HUNTING HOT SPOTS

Almost all good teal habitat in the state will harbor a few to many birds sometime during the season. But some areas stand head and shoulders above the rest for consistently good hunting.

The biggest chunk of good teal habitat in the state is the Arkansas River Valley, from Fort Smith on the west to the Mississippi River on the east. The river is bordered by thousands of shallow backwater areas where teal congregate in huge numbers. The river from Pine Bluff downstream usually provides the best hunting, but hunters who scout prior to hunting should have no trouble pinpointing huntable concentrations of teal throughout the river's length.

Wildlife management areas owned or managed by the Arkansas

Game and Fish Commission also provide fair to good teal hunting. Some of the best include Bayou Meto, Nimrod, Sulphur River, Bois d'Arc, Shirey Bay-Rainey Brake, Henry Gray/Hurricane Lake, Dave Donaldson/Black River, and Rex Hancock/Black Swamp, but be sure to consult a regulations guide prior to hunting to be sure these areas are open.

Some of Arkansas's big lakes also provide a temporary home for migrating teal. Bull Shoals and Norfork in north Arkansas are good bets, and Millwood Lake in southwest Arkansas is extremely good most years.

Many more large and small hot spots are scattered around the state. I've killed teal in mid-field mud puddles the farmer plowed around and while floating rivers like the L'Anguille and upper Ouachita. Pre-season scouting will help you zero in on areas with good hunting.

No matter where you hunt, you'll probably burn a few shells before you can consistently connect with teal. Even the most skilled Arkansas hunters know to take along plenty of shotgun shells and patience.

That's part of the fun of hunting these fast little game birds. No matter how you hunt them or where or when, teal always offer plenty of challenges.

Mud-Puddle Ducks

It was nothing more than a big mud puddle, but it provided the perfect setup for luring passing ducks off the large river nearby. It wasn't even a mud puddle, except during wet weather. Even a moderate dry spell transformed the pothole into just a low spot in a large soybean field adjacent the St. Francis River in Cross County.

A friend and I hunted the pothole during our teenage years. Our tactics were simple but effective. We placed all four of our old plastic duck decoys in the water hole, which was about twenty-five yards wide and fifty yards long. They were anchored with discarded spark plugs and set close to a patch of smartweed on the upper end. We hid in a makeshift blind in a little thicket of black willows bordering the pool and waited for the ducks to drop in for a visit.

Most hunts were after school or on weekend mornings. We'd slip into the willow blind, then train our eyes just above the treetops along the river. When visibility was good, we'd see the ducks when they broke away from the river flyway and headed for our hole. When conditions were otherwise, we often were surprised by an unobserved flight coming in behind us and landing among the decoys.

We didn't own camouflage clothing in those days, and often as not, the ducks would spot us and flare away before entering our limited shooting range. About half the time, though, our blue jeans and khaki shirts went unnoticed, and the birds swept in, dipping and tilting in the breeze, wings cupped, circling the hole before making a final splashdown in the shallow water before us. When they drew near enough, we blazed away with .410 and twenty-gauge.

There never were many birds—usually two or three at a time, never more than three or four flights during a hunt. Sometimes they were mallards. Other times, green-winged teal, shovelers, pintails, or the occasional prized gadwall. We never used a call, never more than the four decoys. But they came anyway. And during the two seasons we hunted them, we kept our families well fed on plump waterfowl.

Over the years, we hunted big water and small, but the simplest hunts are most memorable. With our four decoys in a gunny sack slung

over the handlebars of my Honda 50, we'd head for a local farm pond or bean-field pothole. I enjoyed the quiet and the color of that kind of hunting.

After college, I started hunting ducks seriously again, usually in public hunting areas. Unfortunately, many early hunts on public land were marred by unsociable exchanges. Gunfire, skybusters, and numerous other annoyances detracted from the number one reason for duck hunting—being there. So I gradually withdrew from the crowds and started once again looking for solitary little pockets of water that might lure a few passing birds. Surprisingly, I found that I saw, decoyed, and shot far more ducks on small, seldom-hunted waters than I did on huge, well-managed public hunting grounds. And I began to enjoy the hunts again, which was all that mattered.

Arkansas has thousands of small potholes, ponds, sloughs, marshes, and out-of-the-way oxbow lakes. Most draw modest numbers of ducks each season, but in the aggregate, they total thousands of birds. Except for a piddling few potted by farmers, these flocks hardly hear a shot fired. Hunting these "mud puddle" duck haunts can be a provocative endeavor, especially for average hunters who must make quick forays and can't afford fancy equipment.

The gear needed to hunt mud-puddle ducks shrinks back to a level approaching sanity. A shotgun, warm clothes, waders, and a few decoys comfortably carried over the shoulder in a burlap bag are the only necessities. A good retriever is a big help, and maybe you'll want to bring along a duck call if you're inclined to learn how to use it well.

Equipment that isn't needed includes large boats, outboard motors, trailers, and the dozens of decoys it takes to deploy a big-water spread. Both my budget and my self-opinion thanked me when I eliminated these things from my hunting list.

The mud-puddle waterfowler usually can find waters within a short drive or walk that draw a few sizable flocks of ducks. Sometimes, on very small ponds or potholes, he gets only one or two shots, or one or two ducks, during a quickie hunt. By planning, however, he can repeat these brief hunts, or line up a series of small water holes for longer "make-the-rounds" hunts. The mud-puddle duck hunter who learns

---

Small out-of-the-way waters often attract enough ducks for a good morning hunt.

the "how" of it may wind up the season with as many birds as those spending hundreds of dollars traveling to prime waterfowl wintering grounds.

The newcomer to small-water duck shooting should begin by combing his vicinity for possibilities. Not all small waters offer good shooting, and the astute waterfowler quickly discovers that of scores of possible locations, only a few appeal to the birds. Invariably, such spots are the ones where favored duck forage is abundant, so it's important to check the grub list when scouting for small water bodies likely to attract ducks. When a pond or pothole with an abundance of the most desirable items turns up, it's almost sure to provide excellent shooting.

Because numerous ducks species visit Arkansas in winter, all of them eating scores of different plants and seeds, complications in the grub-list scouting game might seem insurmountable. Fortunately, most Arkansas hunters prefer gunning for the seven species of puddle ducks that frequent the state in winter. Of the scores of foods these ducks eat, only a couple of dozen favorites make up some 90 percent of the diet. And of these, no more than half are prime choices in Arkansas. Using a plant identification guide from the library, you can learn to recognize a few of those mentioned below, and you're in business.

Wood ducks are partial to white oak and pin oak acorns in flooded, timbered bottoms, and sometimes feed on seeds of button willows and bald cypress. Mallards prefer acorns or crop grains—rice, soybeans, wheat, and corn—and often eat seeds of smartweed, wild millet, bulrush, pondweed, and button willows. Pintails are grain lovers, too, but often frequent shallow water where seeds of smartweed, pondweed, bulrush, wild millet, and bur reed are abundant.

Wigeons and gadwalls prefer leaves and stems to seeds. Most are found on small bodies of water with dense beds of pondweed, coontail, and/or spike rush. Green-winged teal like to feed on mud flats where they glean the seeds of smartweed, wild millet, bulrush, pondweed, milfoil, sedge, bur reed, and some grain. Shovelers prefer shallow waters where aquatic invertebrates—small crayfish, mollusks, and insect nymphs—are available. Vegetative forage includes seeds of bulrush, pondweed, smartweed, will millet, button willows, water willow, and bald cypress.

You can figure out the potential productivity of some small waters without learning plant taxonomy. For example, puddle ducks are birds that tip up to feed but seldom if ever dive and feed deep. If a pond is steep-banked and deep at the edges, it may not produce enough food to attract or hold these ducks. Many farm ponds are kept "clean," with as few weeds as possible. Likewise, these are seldom selected by ducks.

Small-water hunters should try pinpointing several likely locations, each with different favored forage. This enhances the success potential and the variety of birds. One year I discovered a large farm pond with a heavy growth of coontail that drew several small flocks of gadwalls. A second location was a small isolated beaver pond where a heavy crop of acorns fell into the water, attracting mallards and wood ducks. A third spot was a mostly drained catfish pond the landowner let me hunt. Small invertebrates here attracted sizable flocks of shovelers. By staggering my shooting at the three locations, resting each in between, I put ducks on the table all season.

When you have noted the waters most likely to appeal to ducks as foraging areas, consider also which may have appeal as roosting sites. For example, wood ducks commonly fly to very small holes rimmed densely with button willows to spend the night. Teal often roost in potholes edged with cattails. Mallards feed in many ponds but like to get into flooded timber or sloughs for the night. Arkansas has many of these. If you know where feeding and roosting waters are, you can time your hunts to find the birds at home.

Just about any beaver pond has the potential for attracting puddle ducks. Fortunately for ducks and for duck hunters, beavers run rampant in Arkansas these days. Trapped nearly to extinction by the mid-nineteenth century, the Natural State's largest rodent has rebounded with astonishing verve, establishing itself in just about every location offering its two basic needs: water and trees. You can poke any spot on your favorite topo map and bet there are beaver ponds within five miles.

Some beaver ponds are more productive than others. One of the best situations is a small creek with beaver ponds strung one after another for a considerable distance. Wood ducks, teal, and mallards will work back and forth over several ponds that are bunched up, with the greatest activity occurring during early morning and late afternoon.

When ducks do come, they usually are close and fast. There's little time to think, just seconds to decide which bird to swing on, no time to calculate proper lead. Everything either comes together in an instant, or it doesn't.

Farm ponds also offer exciting shooting possibilities. Those covering an acre or less usually offer only a single shooting flurry per visit. On these, it's important to figure out how to approach without alerting ducks. If you know birds on a certain pond usually feed at the shallow end, then it's necessary to approach so you're in range. If a cold wind is howling, ducks will usually be on the protected side, if there is one. In a gentler breeze, they may be on the wind-blown side because stirring water brings them food.

Some ponds never hold more than two or three birds, transients dropping in for a short visit. A friend of mine told of hunting one such pond on his property. He hunted thirty minutes each morning before going to work, then thirty minutes late in the afternoon. "Some visits I wouldn't see a bird," he says. "But during the first month, my score was twenty-six ducks. It was great. I was hunting within a hundred yards of my house."

Another prime "mud-puddle" duck location is flooded timber along waters off the beaten path. One of my favorite hunting spots is a long forgotten slough in the middle of a forty-acre woodlot. As far as I know, no one but me has ever hunted ducks there because when seen from the nearest road, a quarter mile away, it appears to be the most unlikely spot in the world for bagging a duck. Wood ducks come here, though, feeding on abundant acorns fallen from surrounding oaks, and on occasion, I've bagged a fat mallard that came to roost near dusk.

When hunting small-water duck haunts, remember two things: such restricted locations call for a minimal number of decoys, if any, and too little calling is preferable to too much. Ducks get suspicious if you get carried away, and when water is calm, three dozen decoys may look exactly like so many plastic ducks. Make your spread match the waters—small. Use a call if you must, but sparingly. The guy who cranks out a rousing highball at birds hovering over a beaver pond or backcountry slough is going to bag few, if any, birds. On potholes near big water, it's OK to get loud to catch the attention of distant birds, but slack off when they show interest.

If you find that a few decoys are needed, place them so the wind gives them a bit of life. If they sit too quietly, you may want to run a piece of monofilament fishing line to a couple. A jerk may be all that's needed to bring in birds that haven't quite made up their minds. Take along a casting rod and surface plug, a great way to retrieve birds on still days.

Blinds seldom are necessary. Small waters are too easy for ducks to study in detail with a single overflight, and any built blind arouses suspicion. It's better to become part of the scene. Wear camouflage clothing that blends with the surroundings, and move as little as possible. Flop down atop a beaver house, hunker among cattails, stand against a tree in the shadows, squat among cypress knees in a slough.

When ducks are directly overhead, cease all calling and stay absolutely still. Don't look up and give them a chance to spy a shiny face. If you're weak-willed, try a face mask like those used by turkey hunters or some judiciously applied camo face paint. Hide well, and more ducks will come your way.

There's no doubt that Arkansas serves up some of North America's finest duck hunting. Huge waterfowl concentrations gather each winter on huge public-hunting areas managed by the state or federal government. Unfortunately, public-hunting grounds also attract the most duck hunters. Under these conditions the hunt hangs in a precarious balance between traditional waterfowling and orchestrated shooting.

That's why I like to prowl the creeks and little oxbows, or sit by an isolated farm pond or in a switch-cane blind on a backwoods slough. There have been days when the sound of wings was noticeably absent. Those days were not in the majority, though, and they still outranked the days on Bayou Meto or Dagmar or White River that were ruined by the skybusting gunnery and inept calling of hunters a short distance away.

I hope the day never comes when I no longer am awed by wood ducks streaking through the bone-white sycamores or surprised by a dozen mallards exploding from a puddle where they just shouldn't be. On mud-puddle hunts, I dictate the quality of the hunt. The pressure is off, the crowding is gone, and the excuses are mine and mine only.

That's the way duck hunting was meant to be.

Big-River Duck Hunts

It's 4:00 A.M., 5:00 A.M., I'm not sure. No one in his right mind is up this time of day or night, whatever it is. I'm trailing my hunting partner through a cocklebur field to a sandbar on the Arkansas River. It's pitch-black outside. Mean little cockleburs are stabbing my ankles. Mouth's as dry as a Canadian pothole.

Suddenly, I'm clotheslined at the waist. "Watch the fence," my buddy notes.

Sure. Thanks.

"I'll carry the decoys, you carry my bag, OK?" Whatcha got in here, pal, a case of shells? Must be at least a case. And a six-pack of sodas. Gun in one hand, bag in the other, cockleburs swarming in my socks. I must be crazy.

Finally, we reach the sandbar. I know it is a sandbar because my face is buried in it. Darned rock. "Don't trip on that rock," he calls from up ahead. Yeah, right.

The sun rises, despite my apprehension, and the Arkansas River is pretty as a picture. Knucklehead wades out in the shallows and sets the decoys.

Canada geese are calling from a sandbar downstream, but the ducks aren't flying. I twist the top off a soda. Sand grates the glass like fingers scratching a chalkboard.

Better load my shotgun. Ooooooh! Another chill down my spine. Sandy receiver sounds like a coffee grinder.

A pair of scaups buzz through the chute. The great white hunter tries dumping one on the pass. Fast little buggers. They fly on. I'm caught dumping sand out of my boots. Couldn't reach my gun.

Three hours later, we call it quits. Several flights of ducks pass by out of range, but besides the scaups, none are close enough for a shot. My friend, undaunted, shrugs his shoulders and says, "Well, that's river hunting."

They're a different breed, these river hunters. Two McNuggets short of a Happy Meal, one of my friends would say. It's tough hunting, perhaps the toughest there is, both in ducks bagged and effort expended.

Still, big-river duck hunting draws a devoted cadre of fans. Why?

Listen to Jim Spencer of Little Rock who's been hunting big-river ducks for decades.

"I like the grab-bag aspect of it," he says. "There are more than just mallards to shoot. There are gadwalls, scaup, pintails and all the divers. You never know what you'll shoot at next, and that adds to the fun. And when shallow waters freeze, moving rivers don't. That concentrates ducks in a smaller area, and hunting can be spectacular."

Big-river hunting requires specialized skills, starting with the ability to locate hunting areas with concentrations of ducks.

"Where you hunt depends a great deal on weather conditions," Spencer says. "If a blue norther passes through with a calm, cold high pressure system behind it, look for hunting areas close to current because that's where open water will be. If it's rainy and windy, look for sheltered places where ducks find protection from the elements. Hunt the lee side of islands or behind dikes or levees. If the weather's too frigid, and it's raining and windy, too, then just stay home."

Spencer believes in the efficacy of large decoy spreads. "In timber, you hardly need decoys," he says, "because when you see ducks, they're in working or shooting range. Big water is different; you may see a flock of ducks two miles away, and they must be able to spot your spread. You need a visual attractor, and the more decoys you've got, the better your visual attraction is. Take at least three or four dozen."

Most hunters using large decoy spreads leave a pocket of open water in the spread to encourage the ducks to land there. "You want an open spot in your decoys within gun range," Spencer says. "Set the decoys around the open spot close together when the wind is blowing. Set them more loosely in calm weather."

Good, loud calling is best.

"Forget the feeding call," says Spencer, "because river ducks are resting, not feeding. The highball is all that's needed, and make it loud."

Spencer usually hunts from a camouflaged boat. "Most of my hunting is boat stuff," he says, "because it's difficult to find a place on shore to set up a blind. I usually hunt from a boat that's hidden in some bushes or other cover. A fourteen- to sixteen-foot wide-bottomed boat with a twenty-five to thirty-five horsepower motor is ideal."

Safety is the most important consideration when hunting big-river ducks.

"You have several factors working against you," Spencer says. "One is the sheer big-water aspect. You often encounter big wave action or other problems absent in ricefields or timber. And the wind really cuts into you out there, so it's always better to be overdressed than underdressed. You can always pull something off."

Each passenger should wear a personal flotation device; the boat operator should wear a kill switch. When boating at night, run slowly, always watching for other boats and obstacles such as wing dikes and sandbars. The motor and batteries should be in tip-top shape, but carry paddles for each hunter. Carry a waterproof fire-starting kit and some high-energy emergency foods like chocolate bars. And always file a trip plan with a friend or relative. Let them know where you're going and when you'll return.

Some of Arkansas's big rivers are consistently more productive due to location, density of flights, nearby food supplies, current speed, and lack of human intrusion. These are the prime hotspots for late-season waterfowlers.

The White River below Highway 64 at Augusta, one of the state's most fantastic river-hunting areas, is accessible via several public-owned hunting areas. Just below Augusta, the White forms the border of Henry/Gray Hurricane Lake Wildlife Management Area, a popular green-timber duck hunting hot spot for hunters from the Searcy/Bald Knob area. Continuing southward through the rich agricultural lands and hardwood forests of the southern Delta, the river bypasses the community of Des Arc, then runs along the east side of Wattensaw WMA, another favored duck hunting area covering over nineteen thousand acres of bottomlands north of Hazen and De Valls Bluff. The southern reaches of the river bypass Clarendon and Crockett's Bluff, then run ninety miles through White River National Wildlife Refuge before joining the Mississippi River in Desha County.

The White is accessible via numerous state and county roads off Interstate 40 and U.S. Highways 64, 79, and 165. A good set of topographic maps, available from the Arkansas Geological Commission, will allow you to pinpoint a good stretch for hunting.

A beautiful sunrise is reason enough for a big-river duck hunt in the minds of many Natural State hunters.

The White is a superb duck-hunting stream, and hunters encounter everything from hooded mergansers to Canada geese resting on its muddy currents. Mallards and wood ducks are especially common, handsome prizes for the river hunter. A few teal may be around if the winter is mild, and always there are wigeons, gadwalls, ringnecks, shovelers, and pintails to round out the hunter's bag.

Because the lower White is so broad and expansive, most hunters stay off the river proper and hunt flooded green timber at streamside. Look for a place off the main river where there's an opening in the timber. Then, set out a dozen or two decoys, hide your boat and back up beside a big tree. If you're in a fairly remote location, the ducks almost always work well, and you can call them into the decoys.

Most hunters prefer rainy, drizzly days for river hunting. Those are days when there's more shooting in the rice fields and on the dead-timber reservoirs. And that means more ducks flying to the river and more shooting for river hunters.

Even on the best days, river hunting is hard work, and you'll have to scout to find the best areas. Look for something unusual that will give you an advantage. For instance, George Peters, a river hunter from Little Rock, once described for me three holes he's checked on the White River at Hurricane Lake WMA. All look basically alike, he said, but one is far more productive than the other two. That's because the trees over that hole are slightly lower, ducks are funneled in closer to the decoys, and they're more readily called. A slight variance like that can spell the difference between shooting a limit or going home empty-handed.

During late portions of duck season, the Mississippi River is another prime place for ducks. "Ol' Muddy" is the major artery of the Mississippi Flyway, a 742,000-square-mile area covering fourteen states and Canada. When conditions are right, fast action and swarming ducks help the avid waterfowler heat up, despite the chilly weather.

With literally hundreds of miles of river to hunt along Arkansas's eastern border, it's again important to scout before hunting. The key to success is knowing the river stage before you head out, so you can effectively plan where to hunt. At six feet and below, sandbars are productive. From six feet to twelve feet, the slackwaters behind the dikes are the best places, especially for divers such as scaups and ringnecks. A river stage of twelve to twenty feet puts ducks in flooded timber. And when the river is really high, twenty-five to twenty-six feet, it's time to find a flooded rice or bean field. River stages are printed in the newspapers of nearby towns.

Safety considerations are especially important when hunting the Mississippi. Hunters should have an in-depth knowledge of the river's whirlpools, sandbars, dikes, buoys, snags, and fog to navigate safely, because the Mississippi simply won't tolerate disrespect or an indifferent attitude. Make a mistake, and you could pay with your life.

Check your fuel supply before you leave shore to be sure it's ample for your boating needs, and always carry a compass. Fog is one of the biggest hazards when river hunting, and without a compass, you have no business being out there.

Big-river hunters should also beware of barge traffic. The enormous wakes thrown by these massive machines can easily swamp even a large boat, especially if the operator is foolish enough to try to cross a wake while under power. Passing barges also can swamp shallow-draft boats secured near shore, or send one that hasn't been tied properly floating free, leaving you stranded. Consider that when settling in to hunt.

The Arkansas River is another big stream where Natural State ducks find dependable wintering habitat. Because the river runs from Fort Smith to the Mississippi River, it's easily accessible to a large part of the state's duck hunting populace, a fact that makes it one of Arkansas's most popular areas for river waterfowling.

The Arkansas River always has been an excellent place to hunt ducks, but until recent years, it was overshadowed by the superb hunting in the rice fields and flooded river bottoms in the east Arkansas Delta. There's still superb hunting in the Delta, of course, but due to a combination of less wintering habitat, more posted land, and smaller fall flights of mallards, the quality and quantity of that hunting have suffered somewhat.

Meanwhile, the Arkansas River has seen few detrimental changes. In fact, if anything, this river may be even more attractive to ducks. There's more soybean and corn agriculture along the Arkansas now, and the McClellan-Kerr Navigation Project has helped stabilize the river and its backwaters, providing a dependable wintering area for waterfowl.

One often-used hunting tactic here is locating sandbars beneath major flyways by using binoculars to survey the areas. First, locate sandbars with ducks passing overhead, then pinpoint those with other attractive characteristics. The best have a southern exposure with a tall growth of shoreline willows to break the north wind. They also have a decent area of water that isn't over two or three feet deep, because puddle ducks rarely dive to get grit. Good sandbars also are out of the current, so ducks don't have to swim hard to stay on the bar.

Most big-river hunters shoot from a boat hidden in some bushes or other cover as a matter of necessity, simply because it's difficult to find a place on shore where you can set up a blind. When hunting sandbars, however, it's often possible to build a make-shift blind using materials indigenous to the river. Use materials such as old sticks or driftwood that don't look out of place, and keep a low profile. A big high-profile blind on a sandbar is obvious to ducks.

Although the White, Mississippi, and Arkansas Rivers offer some of the best waterfowling in the Natural State, there are many other big rivers worth trying as well.

In southwest Arkansas, hunters can ply the waters of Sulphur River and Mercer Bayou on Sulphur River WMA south of Texarkana. Waterfowling enthusiasts also can scout for sometimes heavy duck concentrations on the Red River near the Arkansas-Texas border.

East Arkansas offers public hunting on several top-notch waterfowling rivers. Two wildlife management areas—Dave Donaldson/Black River and Shirey Bay-Rainey Brake—provide excellent gunning along the Black River. Flooded green timber along Bayou de View is open to hunters on Earl Buss/Bayou de View WMA near Hogue and Dagmar WMA near Brinkley. The Cache River, world renowned for its quality waterfowling, flows through two public hunting areas—Cache River National Wildlife Refuge and Rex Hancock/Black Swamp WMA near Augusta. And the St. Francis River, one of east Arkansas's largest streams, is accessible to duck hunters via St. Francis Sunken Lands WMA near Marked Tree.

Sportsmen in south-central Arkansas can experience first-rate duck hunting on two big rivers—the lower Ouachita and Saline. The portion of the Ouachita downstream from Camden offers the best possibilities. Saline River hunting gets progressively better as one travels downstream from Warren. Felsenthal National Wildlife Refuge offers public hunting along portions of both rivers.

If you measure success by the number of ducks killed, big-river duck hunting probably isn't for you. There are, however, many positive aspects to this arduous sport. Wind, spray, and open space are heady wine for duck hunters. You're out there alone, without competition. You see wild places and wild things—eagles, geese, the occasional deer, and, if you're lucky, ducks. Lots of ducks. But that plays second fiddle to just being there.

"A big river has a way of making a man in an open boat feel very small and vulnerable," Jim Spencer says. "That's a good thing to be reminded of every once in a while."

Amen to that.

Buffalo River Renaissance

The elk seems the most unlikely of animals to be pursued by Arkansas hunters. This huge stately member of the deer family just doesn't seem to belong here. "You have elk hunting in Arkansas?" I often hear from incredulous hunters elsewhere when I mention the big bulls taken in recent years. "You gotta be kidding me."

In the minds of many, elk are associated the mountainous West. Few know that before European settlers came to this continent, elk inhabited most parts of the United States. They thrived from California to the Atlantic and from Canada to Mexico, but during the early years of settlement, overhunting and habitat changes began taking a toll. Elk soon were gone from the East, then from the prairies as people moved westward. The mountains remained their last stronghold. Had elk not been remarkably adaptable, they might now be extinct.

The eastern elk, the subspecies native to Arkansas, *is* now extinct. Historical records indicate it persisted no later than the 1840s.

The earliest record of eastern elk in Arkansas comes from Jean Bernard Bossu, captain in the French Colonial Marine who visited Arkansas Post in 1751. He recorded elk in his list of Arkansas mammals. Because the Delta was the only part of Arkansas with which he was acquainted, presumably he was referring to elk in this region.

Another record was left by John Billingsley who lived in the west Arkansas community of Big Mulberry in 1816. Billingsley recalled that he and his family lived there two years "enjoying all the luxuries of life that a new country could afford, such as buffalo, bear, deer, elk and fish and honey."

If we read the journals of Henry Schoolcraft, one of the first skilled observers to write about the natural history of the Ozarks, we may infer that elk still thrived in the Arkansas Ozarks at least as late as 1818. He saw them in November that year, just across the border in Missouri, while on a tributary of the North Fork of the White River.

"We now entered on a very elevated tract of land," he wrote, "barren

---

Thanks to a Game and Fish Commission restoration effort, elk once again are common along the Buffalo National River.

in appearance, but still covered with oaks ... This ridge appears to be a favorite haunt for elk and bear, which have been frequently seen in our path. The enormous size of the horns of the elk give that animal an appearance of singular disproportion, but it has a stately carriage, and in running, by throwing up its head, brings the horns upon its back, which would otherwise incommode, if not entirely stop, its passage through a thicket."

While visiting a home in southeast Missouri in 1834, not far from the upper end of the big St. Francis River swamp, G. W. Featherstonhaugh, a geologist, learned "there were still a great many elk" in the bottoms. This swamp reached far down into eastern Arkansas, and that portion south of the Missouri-Arkansas line probably provided equally favorable conditions for elk.

Published accounts by later explorers who visited Arkansas—Thomas Nuttall, Jean Filhiol, Frederick Gerstaecker, William Dunbar—did not mention elk in what is now this state, but historical records indicate that Elkhorn Tavern, the scene of a Civil War battle in Benton County, was named for a pair of antlers taken from an elk killed in the area by a settler sometime in the 1830s. Those horns perhaps came from one of the last native Arkansas elk. By the time Arkansas achieved statehood in 1836, elk had been exterminated in most, if not all, of the state.

We don't know the exact day when the last Arkansas elk perished, but the species' disappearance was complete and long-lasting. For nearly a century, the haunting bugles of elk were absent from Arkansas's wild lands.

Then, in 1933, the U.S. Forest Service introduced the Rocky Mountain subspecies of elk in Franklin County's Black Mountain Refuge. Three bulls and eight cows from Wichita National Wildlife Refuge in Oklahoma were released. The population grew to one hundred twenty-five by 1948, increased to an estimated two hundred by the mid-1950s, then vanished. No one knows what caused these elk to disappear, but illegal hunting probably was the culprit.

Twenty-five years later, the Arkansas Game and Fish Commission began another attempt at reintroduction. In 1981, volunteers hauled the first load of elk from Colorado and Nebraska to their new home in the Arkansas Ozarks. Between 1981 and 1985, 112 elk were released at five sites near Pruitt in Newton County. All release sites were on or adjacent Buffalo National River lands.

The elk herd took root, then took off. In the ensuing years, elk have been reported in at least eleven counties—Washington, Carroll, Boone, Marion, Newton, Searcy, Stone, Conway, Pope, Van Buren, and Faulkner. But most of the 450 or so elk now thought to be in our state occur along sixty-seven miles of the upper and middle Buffalo National River corridor in Newton and Searcy Counties, primarily on public land administered by the National Park Service. Their range in Arkansas covers approximately 315,000 acres. Gene Rush/Buffalo River Wildlife Management Area, which borders Park Service property along the river, is included in this area, and elk also are found seasonally on surrounding private lands.

In summer 1997, an Elk Committee formed by the Arkansas Game and Fish Commission drew up a proposal for a carefully controlled, ten-bull, ten-cow permit hunting season for 1998. The proposal went through the regulations process, and the hunt was scheduled: a split season, September 21–25 and December 7–11, 1998. Seven bull tags were to be issued for the September hunt, and three bull and seven cow tags were allocated for December. The remaining three cow tags were good for both segments.

One bull permit was donated to the Rocky Mountain Elk Foundation and brought $42,500 at its 1998 benefit auction. Another bull permit, along with a custom-made rifle and a guided-hunt package, was given away in a donation raffle sponsored by the Arkansas Chapter of the Elk Foundation. This brought another $40,000. The Game and Fish Commission received 85 percent of the proceeds from these two permits, with the money earmarked for the elk program. The other eight bull tags and ten cow tags were awarded at a public drawing August 1 at the first annual Newton County Elk Festival at Jasper.

On September 21, 1998, Melvin Farris of Drasco, Arkansas, killed the first legal modern-day elk in Arkansas—a 5x5 bull taken on Gene Rush/Buffalo River WMA at 8:25 A.M. Then Michigan resident Leon Searles took a magnificent 8x7 bull at 10 A.M. near Erbie. Late Monday afternoon, seventeen-year-old Austin Branscum of Searcy tagged a 5x5 bull, also near Erbie. Richard Bearden, a Pine Bluff resident, killed a 5x5 near Carver, and Jimmy Minton of Story killed a 3x4 the same afternoon.

The rest is history. Elk hunts have been held in the state each year since that model beginning, and with the elk herd healthier than ever, the hunts are likely to continue on an annual basis. Hunters lucky enough to draw the right permit have a chance to take a bull of extraordinary size.

During the September 2000 hunt, Hunter Short of Magnolia got a good look at a huge bull. Short, who had a permit for that hunt, stalked the animal, then passed up an unsure shot though it was close to him. That bull was a 9x12. That's nine points on one side of the antlers, twelve on the other. Short, an experienced elk hunter, said, "I have a mount in my den that has a forty-eight-inch spread. The one I saw on Buffalo River was bigger than that."

Short and his companions said the bull likely weighed about one thousand pounds. "It was the biggest I've ever seen," Short said, "and I've hunted a lot all over the West—Colorado, New Mexico and other places. It had a massive set of horns."

An elk like that would be the trophy of a lifetime for any elk hunter. And if that elk ever is taken, and chances are it will, it will bring newfound attention to Natural State elk hunting. I can hear it now:

"You have elk hunting in Arkansas? You gotta be kidding me."

FURBEARERS

A Case for Coon Hunting

"Let's sit and listen," Leon said.

I did as my hunting companion suggested, moving closer to the campfire to warm my backside. It was cold outside, but the frigid temperature seemed to clarify the January air. The stars were never brighter. I stared up at them and focused my attention on the sounds of Leon's dogs far off in the St. Francis River bottoms.

I wish I could describe for you the sound made by two redbone hounds chasing a coon at two o'clock in the morning on a clear, cold winter night. But I can no more describe it than I can describe the aroma of a cake baking in the oven or the feel of an autumn breeze touching my skin. It can't be done.

Suffice it to say that two coon dogs out there in the darkness on the trail of an Arkansas raccoon have a sound all their own. I've listened to the doleful sound of a wolf howling in the far reaches of the wilderness, but a lone wolf's howl is no more mournful than a redbone's cold-trail bawl. The eerie noise of a screech owl calling from the darkness raises chill bumps on my skin, but not as quickly as the cry of a coon hound picking up a hot trail. No one who has heard a pack of coyotes yipping hysterically as they chase some unseen prey can deny they sound as wild and ancient as the back-country ridges along which they run. But when a redbone or bluetick or Catahoula hound, or any other coon dog, is running those same ridges, his chorus sounds even more wild and ancient. If you sit by a campfire on a cold winter night and listen to him, your mind is bound to wander back to a time when nearly every Arkansas hunter owned a coon dog or two and followed them nightly through the woods with a carbide light on his head and a .22 rifle in his hand.

I thought about these things as I huddled by the fire that night not far from the St. Francis River. I listened as the dogs made those indescribable sounds, and during those hours spent listening, I was as happy as a man can be.

"They're turning back this way now," Leon said. "Sounds like ol' King is hot on his trail, and Rusty's not far behind."

To a coon hunter, no music plucks at the heartstrings more than the baying of a hound.

The chase moved quickly through the bottoms from east to west, carrying the dogs and the coon away from the river. For this we were happy. When a coon takes to water with dogs hot on his heels, he may swim quickly until the hounds are in the water with him, then turn and climb on the head of one of the canines. If the coon is big enough, he may drown the dog during the fight that ensues.

Fortunately, our happy state of affairs continued. The dogs kept pushing the coon our way, and when they were less than a quarter mile away, the sound of their barking changed in tone.

"They've treed," Leon said. "Let's go."

My companion rushed off into the black woods, leaving me to follow as best as I could. He reached the big oak where the dogs had treed, well ahead of me, and was playing the beam of his flashlight on the branches above when I arrived.

The scene under the tree was pure bedlam. The hounds were bawling, leaping, and clawing furiously at the trunk. Above the excited dogs, Leon's beam of light was playing back and forth in the treetop as he tried to locate the ruby eyes of our quarry. The animal was so well hidden, we thought at first it had taken to a hole. Then Leon spotted it.

"Near the top," he said. "On the left." He focused his light there, and the chase ended when I shot the coon with my rifle.

Indians in Arkansas were hunting raccoons before Hernando de Soto visited the state in 1540. Not only was the long, warm fur prized, but the savory flesh, not unlike the dark meat of chicken in texture and flavor, was highly relished. (Many Arkansans still enjoy the delicious taste of coon meat, particularly barbecued coon, which is the featured entrée each January at the Gillett Coon Supper, a political rally that attracts many well-known personalities to this Arkansas County community.)

Henry Schoolcraft, in his journal of travels in the region in 1818 and 1819, mentioned that raccoon hides were among the exports from the upper White River country. In "A Survey of Arkansas Game" (1951), Trusten Holder reports, "In 1885 a pelt brought 25 cents, which was a good price in those days. As late as 1919, raccoons were much more plentiful than they are now, old-timers say. Some farmers declared that about the time of World War I raccoons were so numerous that it was hard to grow corn. Raccoons were poisoned to protect the crop. About 1935 a low ebb seems to have been reached in most parts of the state. After the beginning of World War II both prices and numbers of pelts have rapidly increased.

"It is evident," he wrote, "that raccoons have been increasing in nearly every part of the State during the last few years."

Arkansas Democrat columnist Bill Apple, in a column on December 16, 1956, stated that the raccoon "has made a comeback unparalleled by any other game animal in the state, with the possible exception of the deer herd."

The 1930s and 1940s apparently were tough years for raccoons. Coons were hunted and trapped extensively for food and pelts during the Depression, and den trees often were cut to get at coons inside. The Game and Fish Commission started a restocking and education program to help stem the downward population trend. Sportsman's groups got together and agreed they would not cut den trees. "With this aid," said Apple, "Mister Raccoon made his comeback."

During the 1970s and 1980s, the price of raccoon pelts soared to its highest level ever as the demand for fur increased in Europe and Asia. The prime pelt from a large animal sometimes brought twenty-five dollars or more during that period, and this high price drew more participants into the sport of coon hunting. On a good night, hunters with a well-trained hound might bag ten or more coons and obtain two hundred dollars or more for the pelts. I knew individuals during this period who quit their day jobs and hunted raccoons full-time for a living.

Heavy hunting and trapping pressure kept raccoon numbers in check, but raccoons are prolific, and the population remained healthy statewide. Then, in the late 1980s and early 1990s, sustained campaigns by animal rights groups against people wearing furs led to a decline in the demand for pelts, particularly in Europe. The fur market crashed. Raccoon pelts worth thirty dollars in 1970 brought only a tenth of that in 1992. Raccoon hunting and trapping no longer were lucrative businesses; the number of participants declined dramatically. As a result, raccoon numbers skyrocketed.

The Game and Fish Commission's veteran animal nuisance control officer, Rocky Lynch, said in 1992 that raccoons were the animals about which he received the most calls in populous central Arkansas. By 1994, raccoons were so plentiful, the Game and Fish Commission extended the hunting season on them for more than a month into the spring. The

2001–2002 Arkansas Hunting Regulations guide listed raccoons as legal game for hunters during all but three months—April, May, and June. No other game animals could be hunted for such an extended period.

Today, despite the long season, despite the overabundance of raccoons in nearly every county of the state, few hunters pursue these ringtailed bandits. The Game and Fish Commission wishes more would. Raccoons are very efficient predators on the nests of both ground-nesting and tree-nesting birds. They eat eggs and young birds. They have been implicated in study after study—some of them here in Arkansas—of preying on the nests of many bird species, from Neotropical songbirds to ducks and geese to wild turkeys. No wildlife manager worth his salt wants to eradicate raccoons, but they do need some form of control, not only for their own good, but for the good of their wildlife neighbors. Right now, raccoons are too numerous.

If you're already a coon hunter, great. If not, I encourage you to give coon hunting a try. The pelts aren't worth much any more, but I can say from experience, a dinner of roast or barbecued coon is one of the finest you'll ever sit down to. And besides, I've always believed that a hunter who hunts simply for monetary gain isn't much of a hunter at all. Coon hunting offers much more than a monetary return.

I can still remember the last week I hunted coons with Leon. There were many more long chases across the bottoms and ridges, through cane thickets and briar patches, across sloughs and through soggy swamps. Even with good lights to shine on our path, it wasn't exactly like pounding the smooth pavements, and after that long night of coon hunting, I had plenty of scratches and bruises, and sore muscles to boot. It was all worth it, though, for those glorious hours spent listening to the hounds.

When the dogs would tear off on a chase, we'd build a fire and wait. "Let's sit and listen," Leon would say. And so we would. We would sit and stare at the stars or the flames of the fire for hours, saying nothing. Talk was an interruption. We were there with one purpose in mind: to tune our ears to the baying of the hounds as they trailed a raccoon across the river bottoms. And if we killed a coon now and then . . . well, that was just a bonus.

During those times, sitting by the fire and listening to the chase, I was as happy as a man can be.

Of Possums and Possum Dogs

Does anyone know if you can buy a good possum dog nowadays?

When I was a kid I had a dandy, an old black-and-white setter named Rusty. He belonged to my uncle, actually, but when Rusty failed to show an interest in pointing quail, and began exhibiting a knack for tracking and treeing possums, my uncle loaned him to me permanently.

To a twelve-year-old boy, a dog that'll tree possums is just about the finest animal one can have. At least that's the way I saw it. I'd turn Rusty out every afternoon, and we'd make our way off to the woods near home. He'd track and tree; I'd shoot. Most times we'd have a one-possum day, occasionally a two-possum day, and very rarely a three-possum day. I sold the pelts to Red Hendricks, a local fur buyer, for one to three dollars each. On a good three-possum day, I earned as much as I did driving tractor ten hours on the farm, so those days always were cause for celebration. Rusty's reward for each possum we got was a nickel can of Vienna sausages.

One day an old man came by and offered me fifty bucks for ol' Rusty. I told him Rusty wasn't really my dog to sell, hoping he'd go away, but my uncle had told him about Rusty's exploits as a possum dog and had told the man if he wanted to buy the dog, and I was willing to sell, that was just fine with him. I told the man I'd just as soon not.

"Can't say I blame you," he replied. "A good possum dog is getting hard to come by."

Rusty ran off chasing a possum the next fall, and never came back. I never found out what happened to him, and never saw another dog that took after possums the way he did. I don't reckon I ever will. The possum pelts that brought three dollars back in the 1960s and 1970s won't bring a quarter now. And though there were plenty of folks who liked a good meal of roast possum and sweet potatoes back when I was kid, I imagine nowadays most people would eat a box of nails before they'd lay their grinders into a piece of possum meat. Because folks aren't after possums to eat, or for their furs, I don't imagine there's much of a market for possum dogs.

It's funny how times change. For hundreds of years, possums were considered something of a delicacy in Arkansas and throughout the

South. One early reference is found in *The True Relations of the Gentleman of Elvas,* a narrative account of Hernando de Soto's expedition through the South, written by an anonymous Portuguese soldier and published in 1557. Elvas notes that when de Soto's men had exhausted the provisions they brought from Cuba, they had "such a craving for meat that when the six hundred men who followed Soto arrived at a town, and found there twenty or thirty dogs, he who could get sight of one and kill him, thought he had done no little . . . The dogs were as much esteemed by the Christians as though they had been fat sheep." Another narrative of the expedition, taken from the diary of Rodrigo Ranjel, de Soto's private secretary, talks about the "little dogs" being "good eating" and goes on to say, "These are dogs of a small size that do not bark; and they (the Indians) breed them in their homes for food." Some scholars believe these "little dogs" actually were possums.

Almost three centuries later, John James Audubon, the famous naturalist and painter, provided more insight into the human craving for possum in his *Quadrupeds of America, 1846–1854:*

> On a bright autumnal day, when the abundant rice crop has been yielded to the sickle, and the maize has just been gathered in, when one or two slight white frosts have tinged the fields and woods with a yellowish hue, ripened the persimmon, and caused the acorns, chestnuts and chinquepins to rattle down from the trees and strewed them over the ground, we hear arrangements entered into for the hunt. The Opossums have been living on the delicacies of the season, and are now in fine order, and some are found excessively fat; a double enjoyment is anticipated, the fun of catching and the pleasure of eating this excellent substitute for roast pig.

Another interesting nineteenth-century account is provided in the October 28, 1886, edition of the *Arkansas Gazette,* in which "A Gazette Man Describes a Hempstead County Possum Supper":

> Last evening at 8:30 o'clock a goodly company sat down at the hospitable board of the Lazarus House to partake of a sumptuous "'possum supper," at the invitation of Messrs. R. P. Williams,

---

Possums aren't hunted much any more, but decades ago, when possum hunting was popular, a white possum like this would have been a special prize.

Louis Sarazin and Wash Hawthorne, three mighty 'possum Nimrods, who a night or two since slew four of the "pesky" but toothsome critters. The critters were cooked and the feast prepared under the able direction of Mrs. Molly Blackmore, the proprietress of that favorite hostelry, the Lazarus House, and her cooking won well deserved encomiums from one and all. It was indeed a treat and one scarcely knows to whom to accord the most praise—the Nimrods who captured them, the cook who cooked them or the Great Father who made them.

That possums were considered good table fare is borne out again by Benton, Arkansas, native Patrick Dunnahoo in his self-published book, *Putting the Big Pot in the Little One* (1988). Dunnahoo interviewed a Mrs. Marshall Little who "recalls an unusual Thanksgiving dinner which she attended in the 1920's . . . One family which lived near the school, invited the entire student body—all fourteen of them—and the teacher to come to Thanksgiving dinner during the school's noon hour . . . Mrs. Little remembers the dinner as a lavish feast of baked possum and sweet potatoes, Irish potatoes, turnips and other vegetables, sweet potato and pumpkin pie . . ."

Over in Mena, folks were eating possums, too, and making a big deal about it. We have Ernie Deane to thank for this remembrance, published in his *Ozarks Country* in 1975.

> The only organization I ever heard of whose members were dedicated to the catching, cooking and eating of 'possum wasn't in the Ozarks, but in the Ouachitas farther south. This was the Polk County 'Possum Club, founded in pre-World War I days at Mena near the Arkansas-Oklahoma border.
>
> Annual feasts held by this club attracted national attention and were attended by captains and kings of industry and politics, as well as ordinary hill folks. For weeks before the banquet, hunters caught 'possums in the wooded hills. But rather than killing them right off they put the critters in cages and fed 'em well on sweet potatoes and persimmons. The banquet itself was noted not only for its main dish, but also for its great spirit of fun and carrying on. To my regret, opportunity never came for me to be there for one of the feasts.

Deane wrapped up the account by posing a question to his readers. "Are 'possums still caught and eaten in the Ozarks, or can 'possum meat be bought . . . ? I honestly don't know, but I'd like to find out."

Twenty-six years later, I'd like to pose the question again, and ask another: Does anyone know if you can buy a good possum dog nowadays?

It's a shame, but I'm betting you can't.

Canadas on the Comeback

We waited in the middle of a plowed corn field, scanning the early morning skies above a small spread of decoys. All was quiet for many minutes, then in distance, we heard the first melodic strains of flying geese.

It was hard to pinpoint them at first, but after a minute or two, I could make out the birds floating in the tangerine sunrise. Adrenaline stirred my senses. They were coming our way.

Minutes passed like hours. The calls of the Canada geese grew in volume. Their forms grew in size. We could tell now there were twenty or more coming toward us in a V-shaped wedge. The flock broke up. Some began swinging north, away from our spread. But some held a steady course that soon would take them over our heads.

Two hunters began calling. Would it be enough to attract their attention? I gripped my shotgun tightly and wondered.

The last five minutes seemed like a hour. More of the flock broke off, turning back toward another field. Fewer than a dozen remained, but these were convinced our spread was real. At one hundred yards out, they cupped their wings and began swinging back and forth in the air as they flexed their rudders and dropped their landing gear.

Too late the birds realized our ruse. As one hunter shot, then another, they tried to turn and gain altitude. I swung on one giant bird and fired. It hit the ground with a hard thump as I tried unsuccessfully to get another bird in my sights.

When it was over I realized I was shaking. Excitement does that to me. And this type of hunting, my friends, is exciting.

Canada goose hunting means shooting geese, of course, but it is infinitely more. It is pleasure in perfecting an elusive skill with a fowling piece; it is a glorious sunrise or a vivid sunset; it is listening to nature's most beautiful music; it is a special kind of companionship with men you enjoy and admire.

More, it is the thrilling aerial antics of a flock of wild Canada geese,

---

Canada goose populations have rebounded in Arkansas, and hunting these magnificent waterfowl is popular once again.

their haunting calls on a misty morning, the wonder they create as they wing in toward your spread of decoys. Most of all, it is being outdoors in winter, when all of nature unfolds before you. Until you have sat in a decoy spread and watched a winter day begin, develop, and then decline, you have missed one of life's greatest pleasures.

Canada geese are a special prize for Arkansas hunters. Overhunting and changing agricultural practices in states north of Arkansas caused the number of Canada geese to plummet below the threshold of good hunting in earlier decades. The Arkansas season closed from 1980 till 1989, allowing the flock to recover. Numbers increased from two thousand to three thousand birds in the early 1980s to tens of thousands today. The Game and Fish Commission reopened Canada goose hunting on a limited basis in 1989, and it has remained open in selected zones since.

Arkansas's Canada goose restoration program was carried out in two distinct phases involving two subspecies of Canadas—the interior Canada goose, a migratory bird that spends only the winter in Arkansas, and giant Canadas that live in the state year-round.

The first phase of restoration involved interior Canadas. Juvenile birds captured in northern states were brought to Arkansas and kept in pens approximately three years, until becoming sexually mature. Then they were released, allowing them to migrate north. The object was to imprint these juvenile birds on their adopted southern home, so they would return to Arkansas, bringing their immature offspring with them and thus increasing Arkansas's wintering population of Canadas. The program worked.

The other phase of the restoration program involved giant Canadas, which have wingspans up to six feet, making them the largest of waterfowl except the swans. Historically, this unique subspecies lived in the prairies of the United States and Canada. Rather than making long migrations twice each year like other subspecies, giants stayed in the same area year-round and made only short migrations. Unfortunately, giants vanished from much of their former range by the mid-1900s due to uncontrolled shooting and wetlands destruction in the late 1800s and early 1900s. In fact, the giant subspecies was believed extinct until 1962, when Harold Hanson of the Illinois Natural History Survey determined that Canada geese wintering at Rochester, Minnesota, belonged to this subspecies. Subsequently, several remnant populations were found. After the rediscovery of giant Canada geese, many states, including Arkansas, initiated or intensified efforts to reestablish resident flocks.

Arkansas's effort to establish a flock of giant Canadas started in earnest in 1981 with the importation of eggs, juvenile geese, and adult birds from Ontario, Tennessee, Illinois, Ohio, and Mississippi. Imported geese and those raised from eggs were released primarily in the Lake Dardanelle area.

In 1983, the Game and Fish Commission established a captive breeding flock of giants at "The Goose Pens" near Clarksville. After 1985, most of the geese released in Arkansas were offspring of this captive flock. From 1986 through 1990, over forty-three hundred geese were released in the Arkansas River Valley.

These released geese, their young and geese that adopted Arkansas from other areas are thriving. During a survey of the Arkansas River between Plumerville and Ozark in 1983, biologists found 25 goose nests. In 1992, they found 326 nests on a much smaller segment of the Arkansas River. Today, there are so many giant Canadas nesting in the river valley, it would be impossible to count them all.

When Game and Fish biologists began the Canada goose restoration effort more than two decades ago, none could have envisioned this amazing success story. Overall, Canada geese in Arkansas are doing very well. That translates into increased opportunities for sportsmen interested in goose hunting.

Canada goose hunting rarely is conducted on Arkansas's public hunting areas. There aren't enough grain fields to attract geese on a regular basis to wildlife management areas, and the national wildlife refuges with decent Canada goose populations—Wapanocca, White River, Holla Bend, and Big Lake—typically have closed seasons. There is, however, excellent hunting on public lands within and adjacent to the Natural State's big rivers, particularly the Arkansas River where giant Canadas are most abundant.

Sandbars and islands provide good spots for hunting big-river Canadas. Scout for those beneath major flyways, using binoculars to watch for birds using or passing through the area. The best have 1) a southern exposure with a fairly tall growth of shoreline willows to break the north wind; 2) an expanse of shallow (two to three feet deep) water where geese can feed and eat grit; and 3) are out of the current so geese don't have to struggle to stay put. Most big-river goose hunters shoot from a boat hidden in bushes or other cover, or hidden in natural cover on the sandbars or along the river.

Place a few full-body decoys and/or silhouettes on the water and on the sandbars, keeping them a good distance away from vegetation and other cover where Canadas may perceive a predator, or hunter, to be hiding. Set the decoys to take advantage of the goose's tendency to alight with the wind in their faces. Walking and swimming geese also prefer to be facing and/or moving into the wind, so decoys should be positioned in this manner.

Another characteristic of Canada geese is their setting down at the head of the resident flock. They prefer to glide over the top of the birds on the water or in fields, setting down in front of them as opposed to behind birds that already are there. I suppose they may instinctively feel that feeding opportunities are better on ground that has not yet been picked over by other geese.

On big rivers, you can see and hear geese coming for quite some distance. They also can see and hear you from way out there. Use high-pitched hail calls to get a flock's attention from a distance, and as the birds draw near, limit your calling to a few honks and clucks to avoid spooking the birds.

Most ardent goose hunters turn to private lands for their bounty because that's where most geese are concentrated. Good areas to scout include harvested fields of winter wheat, oats, barley, and corn silage, all prime feeding sites. Standing crops usually are ignored because geese prefer to feed where they have a clear field of vision around them. Try to locate several fields to hunt in, because Canada geese tend to feed in family units, and once a group has been shot at, survivors aren't likely to return to the same field again. This also is a good reason to take a few birds and leave a field as quickly as possible. Late-arriving birds that aren't molested might be counted on for future hunts.

One good way to pinpoint private lands hunting areas is to contact the Cooperative Extension office in the county you plan to hunt. Agricultural agents work closely with local landowners and often will share information about farms where crops attractive to geese have been planted. A couple of friendly phone calls using the farm agent as a reference may confirm the presence of geese and secure hunting permission.

When a goose field is located and hunting permission secured, head to the field to analyze what parts the birds are using. Normally geese stay well away from fencerows, ditches, and other cover. Therefore, set your decoy spread so there will be as much open space as possible around you. A spread with four or five family groups of five to seven birds apiece works very well.

Hunters should be in the field with decoys set long before the feeding birds arrive. Sometimes geese arrive right after sunrise, but other times they trickle in throughout the morning.

Elaborate blinds are nice but not necessary, because the typical goose field probably will produce only one or two good shoots before the birds wise up. Most hunters simply lay on their backs in the decoys and wear camouflage clothing that blends well with the ground.

Most important, the hunters must remain absolutely motionless until birds are well within shooting range. Avoid the temptation to shoot when the first birds start dropping into your set-up. Veteran waterfowlers hold off until the lead geese are touching down and geese in the rear of the flock are well within gun range before making their move. If approaching birds seem reluctant to land, flare off at the last minute, or land consistently outside the decoy placement, chances are the birds are spotting the blind, hunter movement, or something else that makes them nervous. Don't hesitate to move a blind or decoys if necessary to lure birds well within shotgun range.

All these things require lots of time and hard work. You need to scout, set up realistic decoy spreads in key locations, be well camouflaged, know how to call, and be creative. It's worth the effort, though. The end result is a face-to-face encounter with huge wild geese that will leave your heart pounding and provide memories long treasured.

Snow Storm

The snow geese look like a wall of thick white smoke in the distance—rising, swirling, falling again on a winter wheat field near Stuttgart. The already large flock continues swelling as other geese fly in from all points of the compass.

"It'll be difficult competing with a flock that big," proclaims our hunting guide, Mark Ragland. "But some will pass over us on their way to join them, and maybe we can coax them into our little flock of decoys instead."

"Little" is not an appropriate word to describe the group of decoys in which we lay. There are a thousand at least, including full-body models and hundreds of white trash bags draped over soybean stalks to imitate a flock of snows. Still, Ragland is right. Even though this is my first time to hunt snow geese, I know it will be hard to draw birds our way when ten thousand live, calling snow geese are feeding in fresh-sprouted wheat just a half mile away.

For the first hour after dawn, I lay on a sheet of plywood in the harvested soybean field and watch as geese skirt our spread to land with the distant flock. The scene in our field seems surreal, with eight hunters dressed in long white smocks and white toboggans laying amidst a thousand trash bags. It looks like some bizarre KKK ritual or a late-season Halloween with everyone dressed as ghosts.

Finally, off in the distance, I see a flock of snows making a bee-line our way.

Ragland sees them, too. "Wave your flag!" he calls to his partner. At his command, the man raises a white flag tied onto a long pole. He begins waving it over his head, back and forth in wide arcs, the plastic square rippling and popping in the early morning breeze.

The progress of the geese against the wind is slow, but they come steadily and straight on. Soon, individual birds can be distinguished, and their high-pitched calls ring out above the flagging sounds. Some birds begin a rocking, side-to-side, tipping motion. They've spotted our spread and are looking us over.

Ragland and his partner lower the flags and begin calling with tube calls. A dozen geese swing low, their feet outstretched as they drop toward the decoys.

In seconds, they're directly overhead. "Now!" Ragland shouts. Shotguns boom in a quick barrage, and geese start falling. They hit the ground with loud whumps. One, two, three. In seconds, it's over.

Our guides walk out to gather the geese. The hunters stay to chide each other on shots missed. The excitement has stirred our blood. We're ready for another flurry.

The winter staging of snow geese on southeast Arkansas's Grand Prairie is one of the most imposing wildlife spectacles in the world. I happened to meet Leonard Lee Rue III in Stuttgart one winter day a few years ago. Rue, considered by many to be the world's premier wildlife photographer, had come to Stuttgart to photograph snow geese.

"I never imagined there would be so many," he told me. "I've photographed snow geese throughout their range, and never have I seen flocks as large as these. It's an amazing spectacle, seeing a single field covered with tens of thousands of geese."

At first one thinks of it only as a phenomenon of numbers. It's been possible in recent years to see as many as a hundred thousand snow geese within a few miles of Stuttgart. What I always find most memorable, however, is the roar of wings and the clamor of voices when a flock is startled. There's a sudden deafening din like a 747 getting airborne, then a ringing cacophony reminiscent of the high-pitched prattle a thousand women might make if gathered in a single room. It is a sound like no other, a wild melody that clutches at your heart and holds you spellbound no matter how many times you hear it.

The synchronicity of their movements is unforgettable, too: skeins of white, some two miles long, highlighted against bluebird skies or black thunderheads as the birds ride the towering wash of winter winds. Birds explode from a field with frenzied wingbeats, then stretch out full length, airborne, rank on rank, as if the whole flock had been cleanly wedged from the earth's surface. Mere inches separate the individuals, yet one never touches another. Several thousand bank smoothly against a head wind as though they were feathers on the wing of a single bird.

Snow geese once were much less common, but populations began mushrooming in the 1990s as winter wheat plantings expanded in Arkansas. The influx of snows came shortly after the growth in wheat farming. Biologists now worry that snow geese are so numerous they're destroying breeding-ground habitat in the far north. Certainly they're beginning to worry Arkansas wheat farmers. In response, the Game and

Fish Commission is continually liberalizing snow goose bag limits and extending the season for hunting them.

Despite the tremendous growth in Arkansas's goose populations in recent years, relatively few ardent goose hunters live in the state. Some duck hunters have switched part of their attention to geese, but it's still a fledgling sport here, and for the most part, the vast flocks of snow geese go about their daily business with little attention from hunters.

Jim Spencer, an information officer with the Game and Fish Commission and assistant editor of *Arkansas Wildlife*, says there are four primary reasons for the general lack of goose hunting activity in Arkansas.

"First, it's a relatively new opportunity," Spencer reports. "Wintering goose populations have increased dramatically in the recent past, and hunters are still behind the curve.

"Second, there are few wildlife management areas with suitable goose habitat. Most wintering goose usage occurs on private farmland in the Delta. Hunter access to the birds is more difficult than, say, to mallards on a WMA."

The third reason why not many Arkansas waterfowlers are serious about goose hunting is that it's one heck of a lot of trouble, Spencer says. "It's not much of a trick to slip down a canal bank and ambush a flock of feeding or loafing geese, but that's not a very sporting way of hunting them either. If you do it right, with a large spread of decoys set out before first light in the area you've scouted, a goose hunt represents a considerable investment of time and sweat."

Reason number four is tied to the general reluctance of the human animal to try something new. "Goose hunting in Arkansas is still an infant sport," says Spencer, "and even though many hunters have given goose hunting some thought, few of them feel they have enough know-how to even give it a try."

One way to avoid these problems is to hire a guide for goose hunting. Knowledgeable guides are seasoned hunters with hundreds of hours experience. They aren't "behind the curve" like many novice hunters. Guides lease large tracts of land where geese are likely to be feeding during the winter hunting season, so there's no problem with access either.

Amazingly large flocks of snow geese winter in Arkansas.

Best of all, perhaps, guides do all the work. You needn't worry about spending scores of hours scouting, doing the legwork to gain hunting permission from landowners, setting out and retrieving decoys, and other such practices associated with goose hunting. For a reasonable fee, reputable guides will do all this and clean and pack your birds, too.

If you go it alone, without a guide, you'll have plenty of work ahead of you. For decoys, many hunters use white trash bags filled with rice straw or white rags staked down with wooden pegs. Spreads of five hundred or more aren't unusual, and most hunters supplement the makeshift decoys with a few wind socks, silhouettes, shells, and full-bodied decoys.

Arrive at your hunting area well before daylight, and hunt with several partners to hasten placement of decoys. Don't bunch the decoys too tightly. A spacing of five to ten feet is about right. This gives the appearance of a relaxed feeding flock and provides space between decoys for an approaching flock to land.

When properly camouflaged, it's also possible to simply lay in the decoys without being detected. In snow goose decoy spreads, hunters often wear a white smock, coveralls, or old sheet and become, in effect, part of the decoy spread. Hunters should be positioned to shoot toward the downwind side of decoys because this is the direction from which geese generally come.

And what can you expect once you've made all these preparations? Aldo Leopold said it better than I when he wrote: "What is a wild goose worth? I have a ticket to the symphony. It was not cheap. The dollars were well spent, but I would forego the experience for the sight of the big gander that sailed honking into my decoys at daybreak this morning . . . I saw him, I heard the wind whistle through his set wings as he came honking out of the gray west, and I felt him so that even now I tingle at the recollection. I doubt that this very gander has given ten other men a symphony ticket's worth of thrills."

Leopold had it right. Goose hunting offers special thrills unduplicated in the broad spectrum of hunting opportunities Arkansans have at their disposal. Try it this season.

Specialize for Specklebellies

Most Arkansas goose hunters focus their attention on the flocks of snow geese and Canadas wintering in the state. Some wing shooters, however, also have discovered the challenge and excitement of hunting greater white-fronted geese.

Hunters know the white-front as "specklebelly," a reference to the broken black barring on the breast of a mature bird. The name "white-front" notes the white patch or "front" encircling the bill of adult birds. They are medium-sized geese, most weighing four to six pounds, rather slender and agile on the wing. While Canada geese glide down like huge bombers to a landing, white-fronts often careen out of the sky, sideslipping or butterflying down in a near vertical descent. Their voice is distinctive: high-pitched and melodious, like laughter.

Major waves of white-fronts wing into Arkansas in November from breeding grounds in arctic Canada and Alaska. Small flocks sometimes are seen in Oklahoma, Mississippi, Alabama, and Atlantic coastal states, but the largest wintering flocks are in natural wetlands and agricultural lands of Louisiana, southeast Texas, and southeast Arkansas. The mid-continent population—birds using the Central and Mississippi flyways—has grown in recent years, with visual estimates of 700,000. Since 1962, hunters have retrieved an annual average of 81,000.

As geese go, white-fronts are wary birds—more difficult to approach closely, less tolerant of human intrusions. They somehow seem "wilder" than other geese, and thus are among the most highly prized members of their clan.

Hunting geese of any sort is a lot of trouble, and because they are less common and more wary than Canadas or snows, white-fronts present a special challenge. Begin preparing well before the season. Secure permission to hunt on farms you suspect geese will use during the coming winter. Many Arkansas farmers lease their fields for hunting or hunt the land themselves. But geese sometimes damage winter wheat crops, and there are plenty of landowners who allow respectable sportsmen to goose hunt if plans are laid well before the season.

It's best to obtain permission to hunt several fields if possible, because there's no way to know where geese will be from day to day

during the hunting season. Fortunately, specklebellies are fairly predictable, wintering in the same areas year after year. A flock in a particular area last winter will usually be in the same vicinity this year and next year, too, if habitat conditions remain the same. If you located flocks of white-fronts last winter, try to obtain permission to hunt some of the fields where you found them.

When the season opens, it's time to figure out where the geese are. If you're lucky, a flock or two will be feeding in areas where you already have permission to hunt. If not, get back to work. Find out who owns land the birds are using, and see if they'll grant permission for a hunt. Then return well before daybreak to set up.

Study the movement patterns of the geese throughout the season, identifying feeding places, loafing areas, roosting sites, and flyways between each. Specklebellies select feeding fields at random, but once they start using a field, they generally continue coming back until the food supply is exhausted. If you had no luck hunting them on one area, you may get a better chance when they move to a new feeding site. Or, if they fly over or near your hunting sites when traveling between roosting and feeding areas, you may be able to lure them to your hunting area using decoys and calling.

Because white-fronts usually are found with flocks of snow geese, most hunters use the same decoys and decoy spreads used for snows. White-fronts tend to gather in small groups at the edge of snow goose flocks, so any decoys that look like white-fronts should be positioned to imitate that behavior.

Some hunters dig knee-deep pits in the field, big enough to put their feet in while sitting comfortably on the ground. Dirt is piled on the downwind side (the side from which geese will approach), and when geese drop into the spread, the hunters lean forward, using the dirt mounds for concealment. Check with the landowner before digging holes and always fill them after the hunt.

Specklebellies have a unique call different from Canadas or snows. Hearing this call helps attract them to decoys spreads, so it's wise to obtain and study an audio tape or videotape that teaches the proper sounds to use.

White-fronted geese are considered a special prize by Natural State waterfowlers.

One call to use is the two-note yodel, made by saying "*wa-wa, wa-wa...*" into the call. Both high-pitched and low-pitched yodels are used as a hail call to draw the birds' attention when a distant flock first comes within hearing range. When a flock gets close, switch to the feeding call, which is made by grunting "*kuluck*" into the tube. Continue calling until the moment you shoot.

A successful specklebelly hunt provides the makings for one of the most delectable wild-game meals you've ever eaten. The meat is considered by many to be superior in taste to Canadas or snow geese. Pluck and draw the birds, stuff with your favorite stuffing mix, and roast in the oven eighteen to twenty minutes per pound at 325 degrees. The resulting meal will be a fitting end to all those hours of effort you put into the hunt.

PREDATORS

Bobcat Action

He arrived like a ghost. One second there was nothing; the next he was there.

I was hunting squirrels in woods behind my east Arkansas home. Chickadees and kinglets buzzed in the trees. A pileated woodpecker flew past, the brilliant red of her long rakish crest gleaming like flame. I found a mossy seat beneath a giant beech, drew a bellows squirrel call from my pocket and tapped on its rubber end. Fifty yards away, a fox squirrel responded.

The russet squirrel sidled down the hickory and cut loose with a string of profanities, lashing the air with its expressive tail. I sat, watching its humorous antics, and pondered the best way to approach it for a shot.

Beneath the squirrel's tree, something moved. The woods were open, but I could not discern what it was that had caught my eye. I squinted. I stared. But nothing was there.

I looked again at the squirrel. It had stopped barking and was stretched tight against the bark, its large black eyes locked on the ground below.

I looked again beneath the tree. A large bobcat sat there. He was looking up at the fox squirrel, licking his muttonchop whiskers.

Though I had been focused intently on my surroundings, the big cat's approach had entirely escaped me. He was a phantom. His sudden presence startled me.

The squirrel was startled, too. He quickly ascertained his position on the lower end of the food chain and raced for a hole high above. The bobcat made a half-hearted leap for it, then started off as if the squirrel had never been there.

I tapped again on the squirrel call. The cat turned and captured me in its gaze. I remember most his luminous eyes, two pools of liquid gold. He looked into the depths of my soul, then turned away, and was gone.

I saw that beautiful animal several more times over the years. His home range and mine overlapped. Often he hunted mice by the edge of my garden. Sometimes, pulling into the driveway at night, I glimpsed

The bobcat's furtiveness makes it challenging to hunt.

his glowing eyes in the brushy woodland edge. I sat and watched for him on occasion, but even when he appeared, it was only for a moment. One second he was there, then he melted into the landscape. His camouflage was perfect. Even when in plain view, he could wholly escape my searching eyes.

I never hunted that bobcat. He was too close to home, too much a part of my inner circle. I have hunted others of his kind, though, and learned through the years that bobcats are perhaps the most challenging to hunt of all our wild creatures. No wild turkey was ever harder to call. No deer possesses more elusiveness and adaptability. No bear is more reclusive. No fox or coyote is more finely attuned to its environment.

The bobcat's amazing instincts and adaptability have served it well. Like many large predators, it was persecuted as vermin for decades. In 1727, Massachusetts placed a bounty on bobcats. In 1973 bobcat bounties were still paid throughout Maine, Minnesota, Missouri, New Hampshire, Vermont, and Utah. At that time, bounties were paid in some counties of fourteen other states. Predator control programs focused on its eradication. But the fierce bobcat, prolific and resourceful, matched the success of the coyote in its efforts to circumvent man. It is probably more common today than it was during colonial times. The U.S. Fish and Wildlife Service places the U.S. bobcat population at 725,000 to one million adult animals.

One key to the bobcat's success is the animal's mastery of habitats. The species ranges through portions of all forty eight contiguous states, plus southern Canada and northern Mexico, inhabiting boreal coniferous and mixed forests in the north, bottomland hardwood forests and coastal swamps in the southeast, semi-desert and scrubland in the southwest, and densely populated suburbs in the northeast. Only large intensively cultivated areas appear to be unsuitable habitat. Bobcats live in all counties in Arkansas.

Diet is another ingredient in the bobcat's recipe for adaptive expertise. Rabbits, hares, and small rodents compose the bulk of their food in most areas, but bobcats are opportunists and will eat grasshoppers, crayfish, raccoons, prairie dogs, porcupines, bats, peccaries, snakes, and birds. They are known to take domestic cats, carrion; and fruit, and male bobcats sometimes kill deer when winter snow makes running difficult. Diets vary by region and season.

Bobcat survival also hinges on the animal's uncanny ability to stay out of sight—and trouble. Bobcats are natural scouts and spies. They have senses that are wonderfully acute, and a nature that is all suspicion. They believe in being neither seen nor heard; and they have every art of precaution that the most accomplished spy could ever think of.

Add to this the fact that bobcats rarely prey on poultry or livestock. They mind their own business as far as human matters are concerned; thus they are seldom persecuted as pest species. This, too, enhances their prosperity. Bobcats are now the widest-ranging, most-common wild felid in the world.

Few people consider the bobcat a varmint any more. We realize the vital role these beautiful predators play in the balance of nature. We know they provide a necessary check on rodent and rabbit populations, which make up over half their usual diet. And we know that proper management creates a surplus of animals that can be taken by hunters and trappers without affecting the overall population. Hunting and trapping are allowed in at least thirty-seven states, including Arkansas.

"If you've ever hunted wild turkeys, you can understand why some of us have a passion for hunting bobcats," says John Heuston of Little Rock, Arkansas. "The same attractions are present—the difficulty, the challenge. Bobcats are very cautious. They're well camouflaged and very hard to spot. When you're calling, they don't come running right up to you like a fox does, or sometimes a coyote. They slip up on you. A caller may find one practically in his lap before he knows it's there. That's part of the excitement of hunting this amazing animal."

Heuston, an expert predator caller and hunter, has pursued bobcats for decades, from the high peaks of the Ozark Mountains to swampy bottoms along the Mississippi River. He begins each hunting season by scouting the territory he intends to hunt.

"Once good hunting territory is located through scouting or tips from farmers, rural mail carriers and others who spend a lot of time outdoors, you should map out a route that allows stands or hides every half mile or so," he notes. "The more stands, the greater your chance of success. You may make ten or fifteen stops and never see a bobcat, or you may make one or two and have no trouble finding a cat. You just don't know, however, so you want to be sure you have several different places you can try when you're out there hunting."

Heuston usually hunts on large public-owned wildlife management areas.

"I drive the back roads through an area and try to find places that look good to me," he says. "I'm primarily looking for habitat, the same kind of areas where you might find rabbits. If you have good rabbit cover—edge areas, brushy thickets, successional clearcuts, places like that—you have good cat cover. Bobcats will be where they can catch rabbits if they can."

The basis of Heuston's hunting technique is appealing to the bobcat's instinct to eat rabbits by using a call that imitates a rabbit's distress cries. When a predator catches a rabbit, the normally silent rabbit shrieks in fear and pain. It does the same when caught in a trap or fence or when accidentally injured. Bobcats know this sound and respond to it, looking for an easy meal.

"There are many companies making mouth-blown predator calls, and though each call may have a slightly different pitch or sound, all of them will attract bobcats," says Heuston. "I use only the closed-reed barrel-type rabbit calls. But open-reed calls that make a high-pitched mouse squeal can also be effective.

"Camouflage clothing is very important," he continues. "You're going up against one of the sharpest-eyed creatures there is, and the more you camouflage yourself the better. You'll have to hunt when it's legal, but bobcats can be called year-round, and don't seem to respond any better during one month or another. You want to be at your hunting area when the sun rises, and the best hunting will continue until ten o'clock in the morning or so. Up in the day, bobcats generally settle down and hole up somewhere. But they'll be active again at dusk and into the night."

Calling is best when there's little or no wind, one reason to recommend the first light of day, normally a period of calm. If there's significant air current, the call carries farthest in the direction, downwind, where you don't want it to go. Your best insurance is to have the prevailing wind at the back of your quarry rather than yours, blowing your scent away from the animal's keen nose.

"When you get to your hunting area, pull your vehicle off to the side of the road, and when you get out, be sure you don't slam the doors, don't talk to one another and don't smoke," Heuston says. "You want to get sixty to one hundred yards away from your vehicle, and you slip in there like you're stalking a deer. Get to your stand quickly but as quietly as possible.

"Sometimes I sit to call, and sometimes I stand, depending on the terrain. If it's brushy and you sit down, you may not be able to see anything. So sometimes I back up into bush or a cedar tree or something else that breaks my outline. A deer stand makes a great place to call from. I have a friend who hunts with his son. They carry a treestand, then he'll get up in a tree and his son will lay down at the bottom of the tree. The son lays flat on his back and calls. He can't see what's coming, but his father can. And he can watch his dad up there in the tree, and when he sees his actions, he knows what to expect."

When you begin calling, don't let your enthusiasm destroy the reality of the drama you're attempting to create.

"You start calling quietly then put a little more blood into it with each call," says Heuston. You want to sound like a rabbit that's been caught in a fence or by another predator. Start your series real low, and if that doesn't bring results then you can kick the volume up. Some guys believe in calling continuously, and others do series of thirty-second calls with pauses in between to look around and see what's coming.

"A fox or coyote will generally respond within five to fifteen minutes. But a bobcat may take thirty minutes or more. I'll usually stay at each stand close to half an hour. If nothing has come up, then I'll move on to the next spot. If a cat does show, I have my gun at the ready and make my shot—if I can. If I miss or spook the animal, I know I can come back and try him again. Coyotes are call-shy. If you miss one the first time, he may never respond to a call again. But bobcats aren't that way. A bobcat never seems to associate the sound of calling with the hunter. He's thinking 'What's that fat guy doing between me and my rabbit?' Miss him the first time, and you can call him back again and again.

"Predator calling is not for the casual hunter," Heuston states. "Don't expect to fill up the back of your pickup with varmints. You're an amateur 'rabbit' operating in a world of polished professionals who stay alive by not making mistakes. Arguably, no form of hunting is more demanding of skill, dedication, shooting ability and patience than bobcat calling. None. But that's what makes it so interesting."

The Arkansas Coyote: Nobody's Fool

In the Arkansas outdoors, there are many wildlife symphonies to warm the heart—the melodious calling of geese winging their way across the Delta, the primitive hooting of owls in black forests, the staccato chattering of squirrels playing tag in the treetops. For me, though, there's no more charming wilderness melody than the howling chorus of coyotes. Though I've heard their sonorous music on dozens of dark nights, it never fails to make the hair on the back of my neck stand up as I listen in wide-mouthed awe.

Though coyotes now reside in every county in Arkansas, they've been here a relatively short time. Few, if any, coyotes were here when the earliest settlers arrived, and before 1950, these grand masters of adaptation were found only in the state's most western portions. As agricultural practices changed and more open lands were created, coyotes extended their range. They reached the central part of the state by the early 1950s and reached the Mississippi River by 1964. Today, coyotes thrive alongside human habitation and actually can be found right in urban neighborhoods.

Coyotes are good news, bad news critters. The good news is coyotes play an important role in balancing populations of mice, rats, and other pesky wildlife. And as scavengers on dead animals, they help clean up woods and fields. Bad news is coyotes cause serious damage to livestock and melon crops in some areas. Poultry, hogs, sheep, goats, and young calves are common domestic prey, and at times, coyotes take fawns, young turkeys, and other wild game.

Some people think all coyotes should be killed on sight; others think they should be totally protected. The best management probably lies somewhere in-between. Coyotes, like deer and rabbits, are a renewable wildlife resource, and surplus animals can, and should, be taken by hunters and trappers under set seasons and regulations.

When compared to squirrels, deer, ducks, and other wildlife, coyotes are relatively unpopular as game animals. From 1976 through 1985, only three thousand to fifteen thousand Arkansas coyotes were harvested annually by hunters and trappers combined.

As coyote populations have grown over the years, however, there seems to be increasing interest in their pursuit. And this heightened interest means coyotes have changed also. Coyotes are more cunning and secretive in their ways than only ten or twenty years ago. Therefore the hunter has had to improve his skills and hone his efforts in order to be successful. Let's look at some of the how-tos and where-tos employed by today's successful coyote hunters.

The first step in coyote hunting is locating an area likely to harbor coyotes. According to a publication on the coyote's life history published by the Arkansas Game and Fish Commission, "Coyotes favor brushy fields with persimmon trees, blackberry thickets and tall weeds. They are abundant along forest edges near pastures and crop lands and are often found around clearings where trees have been harvested." The publication goes on to say, "A concentration of one coyote per two to four square miles is typical density for most of Arkansas; highest concentrations around poultry dumps or other sources of food may number two to three per square mile."

This tells the coyote hunter two things. Good coyote hunting is likely to be found around brushy fields, forest edges, and commercial clearcuts. And except around poultry dumps and other high concentration areas, success will come only by moving from one likely hunting area to another to compensate for the coyote's low population density.

The most effective lures for coyotes are sounds of their natural prey in distress. Calls that produce the squalling sounds of a dying rabbit are most popular, and these are available in basically two types—the newer battery-powered tape-player models and the traditional mouth-blown hand calls. A staggering variety of these two basic call types are available, with new models being introduced almost each year. But the type of call you select is not as important as what you do with it. Any type of predator call will work in practiced hands.

Though battery-powered calls offer several advantages, most hunters still prefer the satisfaction and enjoyment gained from outwitting a coyote using a mouth-blown call. Proper style and technique can be easily learned by listening to one of the many excellent tapes (cassette and video) available on the market today.

Begin calling with loud volume, but not for long. From then on, call sporadically at low volume as this makes the coyote less wary and more intrigued. If you don't get a quick response—say in twenty minutes or less—move to a different location and try again.

When you arrive at a hunting site, exit your vehicle in total silence and move some distance away. Position yourself below the skyline when in hilly country. Coyotes have keen eyesight and notice obvious changes in the landscape. Never call with the sky silhouetting you.

When you commence calling, remain as motionless as possible, as movement is immediately noticed by most predators. Consistent results dictate wearing camouflage clothing—jacket, pants, hat, head net, and gloves. It doesn't hurt to wear camo boots, too, and to wrap your gun in camo tape or a camo gun sock. All clothing should be made of soft, quiet material. And to combat the coyote's extraordinary sense of smell, it's wise to use some type of hunting scent to mask your human odor.

In more open terrain where it's difficult to conceal yourself, you can use camouflage netting to build makeshift blinds at each location you hunt. Drape the cloth over a bush in front of you or behind if your background is partially open. A netting backdrop breaks your outline, and your camouflage costume blends in to disguise the dreaded human silhouette.

A coyote hunter in the Razorback State has a wide choice of places to hunt. The Game and Fish Commission's network of ninety-two wildlife management areas contains hundreds of thousands of acres, much of which is prime coyote territory. In addition, several national wildlife refuges permit coyote hunting by permit, and excellent hunting also is available on Arkansas's three national forests, especially around the edges of clearcuts and woodlands. The state's innumerable small private holdings also provide good hunting for landowners and others who have permission to hunt.

According to the Game and Fish Commission, most of the state's coyotes are harvested in the Ozark Mountains and the Arkansas River Valley. Good prospects for coyote hunting in these regions include Hobbs State Management Area near Beaver Lake, Madison County WMA north of Huntsville, Sylamore WMA north of Mountain View, and Galla Creek WMA south of Atkins.

The agricultural delta area of eastern Arkansas also has a large population of coyotes. Several major and minor stream bottoms wind through the croplands in this flat region, and these are good coyote areas. Public lands open to predator hunters include St. Francis National Forest WMA in Lee and Phillips Counties and Wattensaw and Dagmar WMAs in Prairie and Monroe Counties.

In central Arkansas, Camp Robinson WMA is a good bet, and in the west, Fort Chaffee WMA has an abundance of old farms and fields that make ideal coyote habitat. Good possibilities for the Ouachita Mountain region include Winona WMA near Paron and Lake Greeson WMA near Daisy, and in south Arkansas, try Poison Springs WMA northwest of Camden and Hope WMA near Hope.

The coyote is thriving throughout Arkansas. But abundance does not necessarily equate with hunting success. The coyote is nobody's fool, and successfully hunting this adaptable predator is an extreme challenge. Nevertheless, that's part of the thrill, and no one said it would be easy. Once you call a coyote and savor the excitement, you'll want to go calling every chance you get.

Hunting Arkansas Bobwhites

We may never see the glory days of bobwhite quail hunting our fathers and grandfathers experienced earlier this century. Habitat loss has taken a heavy toll, and days when you could park on a hilltop and find eight or nine coveys within sight of the vehicle are long since past.

Quail hunting still attracts numerous devotees, nevertheless. Even now, there's good quail hunting found statewide if you take time to seek it out. And the elements of the hunt—camaraderie, fresh air, gaunt pointers, sporty wing shooting—retain their obsessive allure. When a racing setter suddenly skids to a halt, twisted into a "C" by a scent no human can savor, every muscle quivering like a plucked bowstring, the drama of hunter and hunted unfolds, and you find yourself embraced by a feeling of intense gratitude for the given grace of such moments.

A SOUTHERN TRADITION

Though bobwhites range throughout the eastern and central United States, bobwhite hunting belongs to the South with all its color and boundless hospitality. Quail are simply "birds" to Southern shooters, and the mention of "bird hunting" conjures up visions of plantation houses, sprawling sedge fields, and a brace of slat-ribbed pointers sailing across the countryside. Some even hear strains of gospel music filtering up from the fields beyond the barn.

Though we wish it were otherwise, for most of us, quail hunting bears little resemblance to this idyllic setting. Old Shep replaces the pedigree pointers, and we're much more likely to hunt on Uncle Jack's back-forty than some high-dollar shooting resort or fancy plantation.

This isn't noted to discourage would-be quail hunters, however, but rather to keep them from being unduly influenced by the classic picture of the aristocrat atop his horse watching blue-blooded pointing dogs working before the handler on an opulent plantation. Quail hunting can be as simple or as sophisticated as you want—or can afford—to

---

For many bobwhite fans, a quail hunt just wouldn't be the same without a good pointing dog along.

make it. Expensive dogs, riding horses, and English doubles aren't required to savor its many pleasures.

A 1985 Arkansas Game and Fish Commission survey (the most recent conducted) found that approximately thirty-six thousand hunters pursued quail during the 1984–85 season. Of these, about half hunted with dogs, half without. Private industrial lands were hunted most often, followed closely by public lands and private non-industrial lands. The average hunter was thirty-six years old and harvested twenty-two quail that season.

These statistics tell how many Arkansans hunt quail and where and how. But they offer little of use to beginning hunters. Let's take a closer look at quail hunting tactics and equipment and some of the best locales for pursuing these little buzzbombs.

THE SEARCH

At one time, prime quail habitat was found throughout Arkansas. Unfortunately, modern land use practices have eliminated many good quail areas, and extensive scouting plays an increasingly important role in most hunters' success.

In his book, *Quail Hunting in America,* author Tom Huggler explores the search for quail. "Identifying prime habitat and then hunting it effectively is the key to becoming a primary, rather than incidental, hunter of quail," he says. "The ability is something not easily explained. It is something you do, almost intuitively, and it comes from a combination of hundreds—maybe thousands—of mental photographs of what productive habitat looks like. You gain that knowledge by hunting countless covers that do not hold birds and by remembering those that do.

"Looking for the right habitat at the right time," he says, "is the place to start."

Bobwhites rarely are found in the middle of a crop field or in heavy woods. Instead, they favor edge cover, where two habitat types intersect. This might be a brushy fencerow running through a crop field, a briar patch at a pasture's edge or brush piles adjacent a small woodlot. Look for roosting areas such as heavy brush and native grass fields, escape shelter like hardwood thickets and shrubby property lines, and feeding areas where bobwhites can find a variety of grains, wild seeds, legumes, forbs, and insects. Finding appropriate cover with plentiful edge is the key to locating quail.

Some of today's best hunting is on public wildlife management areas. Intensive management efforts by the Arkansas Game and Fish Commission produce superb quail habitat, where diligent hunters may jump several coveys a day. On Wattensaw WMA near Hazen, for instance, numerous old fields are managed for quail by controlled burning and planting food plots of sunflowers, corn, and other quail foods. Four- to five-acre timber cuts create more edge areas and new-growth plants important to quail. Quail have responded well, and Wattensaw's population is one of the highest in the state.

Hope WMA in southwest Arkansas also is managed with quail in mind. Fields are divided by buffer strips of sumac, autumn olive, and other food and cover plants. Alternate strips in fields are mowed each autumn to keep fresh material on the ground for quail. Timber stands are thinned to keep them open, thus creating more ground-level forage plants. Controlled burning also is an important part of the quail management program.

Other top quail hunting wildlife management areas include Camp Robinson, Blue Mountain, Gulf Mountain, and Winona. But public hunting opportunities aren't limited to these areas alone. With a little extra effort, you can find decent public quail hunting on nearly every wildlife management area, national forest, and national wildlife refuge in Arkansas.

A lot of Arkansas's best quail hunting is on private land, and fortunately, many landowners still will allow you to hunt their land if you ask permission and show good manners. If possible, make contacts in person, well before the season starts. Don't be abrupt. Take time out to talk, and offer to lend a hand with some chores.

If your request is granted, invite the owner along, and if he can't go, share some dressed birds with him. Ask questions that show you're a responsible hunter. Are there livestock around? Areas off limits? Gates to latch? Keep your hunting party small, and don't march in dressed like Rambo ready to bombard the enemy.

Here's another tip: always send a thank-you note and some small token of your appreciation following each trip. When you knock on the door next fall, you'll be remembered.

DOGS AND GUNS

Quail hunting and dogs are nearly synonymous, and serious hunters soon conclude they can't do without a good pointing dog. As one hunter so aptly put it, "Going bird hunting without a dog is like using a strainer for a dipper. You can try as hard as you want, but you don't get jackspit out of it."

Quail sit tight, and a dogless hunter could walk past many coveys a day without flushing a single bird. A good pointing dog pinpoints birds and allows you to prepare for the heart-stopping flush. It also is important to recover every bird we kill, and a good dog helps us fulfill that obligation.

Probably the best reason for owning a dog, though, is the singular beauty of a magnificent bird dog on point. Seeing a class gun dog exercise its instincts is the only reason many quail hunters venture afield. Killing birds is secondary to the experience. It's dog work, atmosphere, and companionship that make the hunt.

Pointers, setters, and some spaniel breeds, especially the Brittany, are the dogs of choice. They've been bred through many generations to find these little birds, and that's what they do, better than any animals on earth. Experienced breeders and trainers across the state can help you select and train a dog suited to your needs and income.

When quail hunting, quick shooting at short ranges is typical, so a light, fast-handling shotgun using a reasonable charge of fine shot is preferred by most hunters. The twenty and twelve are the most popular gauges because of ammunition availability. And because most quail are hit within twenty or thirty yards, an improved cylinder or modified choke usually is selected for sufficient shot dispersal. Number 7-1/2 or 8 shot provides the dense shot pattern needed to effect a clean kill on these small birds.

As for other equipment, keep it light for the most enjoyment from the sport. Many upland hunters wear "brushbuster" pants to turn briars and a game vest to carry birds. Wearing bright colors allows your partner to spot you easily. Quail calls help pinpoint birds from a broken covey. Other extras are nice, but they're far less important than knowing your game and how to hunt it.

TIPS FOR SUCCESS

Quail have an extensive repertoire of evasive maneuvers. Here are a few tips that can help you bag today's savvy birds.

- Hunt "pocket cover." Big is not always best. Don't overlook small spots of cover such as weed patches, crop field corners, plum thickets, and abandoned homesteads.
- Try hit-and-run tactics. Leapfrog from one prime covert to another without wasting time on large barren areas between potential hotspots.
- Hunt early and late except during bad weather. Quail usually move between roosting and feeding areas near dawn and dusk. Hunting then can pay big dividends. During inclement weather, however, quail leave the roost later, and midday hunting may be more productive.
- Check the crops of harvested birds. Knowing what quail are feeding on can lead you to first-rate hunting.
- Plan early-season hunts. By late-season, natural mortality has reduced quail populations, and the dog-wise birds remaining seek dense security cover. The best hunting usually is early in the season when young, naive birds are numerous and easily found.
- Pace yourself. If you push yourself or your dog too fast, you'll miss many birds.

COVEY BREAKS AND POINTING DOGS

A kid in overalls walks out the kitchen door, grabs an old single-shot twenty-gauge as he goes, whistles up an old setter from under the porch and heads for the old field out back. The eager dog knows what's expected of him and soon locks up on a covey hidden in the brush. Now the lad faces his own small moment of truth. His throat is parched, his chest feels wrapped in rubber bands, his heart slams in his ears. He puts a shell in his gun and walks past the motionless hunting machine that has done its job and now waits for the boy to do his.

The boy doesn't feel his feet scuffing through the weeds, but he can smell the dust. From the corner of his eye, he glimpses a movement. There they go! A thousand of 'em all directions! Everything's a flurry of sound, dust, and motion, but the lad finds his mark and then . . . it's over.

The boy smiles as the dog retrieves the bird. He smoothes the quail's feathers, sticks it in his pocket, reloads the little shotgun, and looks out across the field where the setter already is searching out a single.

Why do quail hold such a special place in the hearts of hunters? If you have to ask, you just ain't been there.

Leapfrog Quail Hunting

A few decades ago, large unbroken tracts of prime quail habitat were found throughout Arkansas. Hunters could drive to the country, put out a bird dog or two, and expect to find several coveys of bobwhites while still within sight of the truck.

Unfortunately, hunting like this is nothing more than a dream in most parts of the Natural State today. Modern land use practices have ravaged many good quail areas, and those remaining are often smaller, more remote, and harbor fewer birds. This means the modern quail hunter must be precisely what the word "hunter" implies. He must be willing to ferret out small "pockets" of quail cover with potential for good shooting, then spend the day moving from one pocket to another to find birds.

The productive quail pocket may be nothing more than a patch of broomsedge edging a pine thicket, the overgrown banks of a farm irrigation ditch, or a forest margin where beggar's-lice fight sweetgums for living space. Many hunters by-pass these spots because they look too small or unlikely. But the good "pocket" hunter takes nothing for granted. He frequently travels rural byways, investigating every tidbit of cover that might hide a covey of birds and marking its location on a map for later reference.

He marks the weedy fence corner where cocks were heard calling, the old homestead where he flushed two coveys, and all the little strips and patches of cover that show promise as quail hotspots. Then, when the magic day rolls around, the wrinkled map is pulled from the glove box, and he picks a half-dozen or so spots he can hunt by leap-frogging from one to another and another and another. At some sites, he comes up birdless. But others harbor a covey or two, and the pocket hunter is sure of getting a little shooting at several stops. He takes one or two birds, or maybe none, then moves on to the next spot, taking care not to over-shoot the coveys.

The edges of small forest clearcuts are worth working, especially during the first few years of succession. Forgotten orchards and abandoned homesteads always should be investigated. Powerline rights of way are promising, and on small hillsides where pockets of blackberry brambles are murderous, bobwhites take up residence.

Other excellent but often overlooked quail pockets include islands of woods between big fields, wildlife management area food plots, plum and dogwood thickets, brush-choked fencerows, grassy terraces, property lines of multiflora rose or autumn olive, and field corners out of reach of the combine.

Some pockets are in suburbs in vacant fields, undeveloped subdivisions and around abandoned buildings. Safety is paramount when hunting these areas, and discharging firearms may even be illegal. Check state game laws and local ordinances first, and always secure landowner permission before hunting private lands.

If you like, you can hunt small pockets without using dogs. Lacking a canine companion, you visit a spot, tramp around, and hope for action. At flush, you're always off balance, the sun is in your eyes, and there's too much cover to get off a good shot. Worse yet, the jump shooter probably walks by ten birds for every one a good dog would locate.

Ideally, you should have a close-working pointing dog that moves at a slow to moderate pace. Because there usually there is not much acreage to cover, a fast, wide-ranging dog isn't needed. In fact, he's a problem because he'll soon be on other property.

In small pockets, it's best to release only one dog. The other dogs stay in the truck and get their chances farther down the line. If you hit a sizeable area, twenty acres or more, you may want to turn out two dogs.

The flanker strategy is good for working borders of pocket cover. One man follows the dog, if it's a pointing breed, and the other walks along the edge, waiting for a clean shot at any bobwhites bursting out of the low canopy. If a flushing dog is used, it's best to send the dog in and remain outside. Some quail may zigzag away at low altitude in the brush, but a fair percentage will present a good target.

Despite how you hunt—with a dog or walking 'em up—picking pockets is a top-notch way to bag modern-day quail. There are multitudes of overlooked pockets that harbor one, two, or three coveys at a time, and the birds will be there if they don't get too much pressure. You take one today and another will be there tomorrow and still another the day after tomorrow.

Bet the bundle on a single locale, and you may go home empty-handed.

Modern quail hunters often leapfrog from one small area of cover to another in their search for bobwhites.

The Canecutter Challenge

A rabbit is a rabbit is a rabbit. Right? Well, that's what many Arkansas small-game hunters think.

The innocents who accept this philosophy, however, probably spend all their rabbit-hunting time chasing cottontails because, when a hunter has pursued the swamp rabbit, the cottontail's bottomland cousin, he puts that thought out of his mind forever. When he has hunted both species, he realizes that saying there's no difference in swamp rabbits and cottontails is like saying there's no difference between beagles and St. Bernards because they're both dogs.

They're kinfolks, all right. But cottontails and swamp rabbits are two distinctly different animals.

Arkansawyers call the swamp rabbit "swamper" or sometimes "canecutter" because of its fondness for young switch-cane shoots. Swampers resemble cottontails, sure enough. Long ears, powerful legs, brown fur, powder-puff tail—all the classic cottontail traits are present. The differences, nevertheless, are profound.

The most obvious variation is size. A run-of-the-mill swamp rabbit is nearly twice as big as a typical cottontail. A cottontail usually weighs two or three pounds, while a swamper tips the scales at four to eight. Yet, the swamper isn't just an overgrown cottontail.

For one thing, the swamper, unlike B'rer Cottontail, is a swimmer. Not just a "dogpaddle across the river to escape the dogs" kind of swimmer. The swamper is more like a furry frog. It doesn't hesitate to swim a creek or slough to get from this point to that or to throw dogs off its track. And when hotly pursued, it not only swims, it dives. A swamper pressured by dogs may plunge in and hide under a wad of roots or beneath a logjam with only the tip of its nose above the water. When you put your beagles on the trail of this critter, you'd better outfit them with snorkels and swim fins.

Cottontails and canecutters differ in running style, too. Unlike cottontails, which usually run short, predictable circles that quickly bring them back to the hunter, swampers often take the dogs completely out of

Swamp rabbits lead beagles on much longer chases than their cottontail cousins.

earshot, running a long, tortuous course that bends and twists through every slough, brush pile, and thicket in the bottoms. A 'cutter may circle the same path twice, unseen by the hunters. Then, just when they've figured out how to intercept the rabbit . . . presto! Ol' Water Bunny charts a new course and heads straight for the Canadian border.

Swampers climb, too. They can outrun and outswim almost any beagle, but given a choice, they'll escape without a large expenditure of energy. If there's a hollow tree within a mile, a swamper climb inside, out of reach, quicker than you can say "raccoon."

Super-bunny? You'll have to decide for yourself. It's possible, being the swamper junkie I am, that I'm a bit prejudiced.

Still, I've been hunting swampers for thirty years. And during that same time, I've spent countless hours hunting doves, ducks, squirrels, quail, and cottontails. As far as I'm concerned, if it's challenge and excitement you're after, no other small-game hunting sport can hold a candle to chasing swampers with dogs.

If you're a small-game enthusiast, and for some reason you haven't managed a trip afield in search of canecutters, I suggest you finagle an invite as soon as you can. Until you do, you'll never know the gut-wrenching excitement, the hard-core challenges, and the ultimate thrill of small-game hunting at its best.

Fortunately, there still are plenty of good places to pursue swampers in Arkansas. In fact, east Arkansas provides some of the best swamp rabbit hunting in the eastern United States. With a little effort, you should be able to locate several areas with healthy swamper populations.

Unlike cottontails, which usually live in dryer upland habitat, swamp rabbits require wetlands to thrive. You'll occasionally bag a cottontail in swamper territory, but the reverse rarely is true. Swampers live out their lives in half-flooded timberlands and swamp thickets where a good pair of hip boots are must-have gear. Although a lot of southeast Arkansas bottomland has been cleared for farmland, enough tracts remain to keep a swamper fan busy for years.

Some of the best swamper territory is along the White River from Augusta to the Mississippi River. Three public hunting areas along this stretch have good swamp rabbit populations. Henry Gray/Hurricane Lake Wildlife Management Area covers 17,524 acres of prime swamper habitat just southeast of Bald Knob. Wattensaw Wildlife Management

Area, a 19,184-acre area near Hazen, is bounded by the White River and Wattensaw Bayou, both of which provide flooded bottoms attractive to swampers. White River National Wildlife Refuge encompasses 160,000 acres of superb swamper habitat along more than ninety miles of the White River.

Other southeast river bottoms also support thriving public-lands swamper populations. On the Cache River south of Augusta, hunters find good swamper hunting on 6,284-acre Rex Hancock/Black Swamp Wildlife Management Area. Dagmar Wildlife Management Area covers 9,720 acres of swamp rabbit territory on Bayou de View west of Brinkley. Bayou Meto Wildlife Management Area, a blue-ribbon swamper hotspot, provides 32,250 acres of public hunting land southwest of Stuttgart.

Other good bottomland swamper areas open to the public in this region include 65,000-acre Felsenthal National Wildlife Refuge in the Saline-Ouachita river bottoms near Crossett, 6,100-acre Overflow National Wildlife Refuge west of Wilmot, and 8,904-acre Cut-Off Creek Wildlife Management Area southwest of Dermott.

There's plenty of good swamper hunting found on private lands in the southeast as well. And because most landowners don't prize swampers like deer or ducks, it's not hard for a courteous hunter to strike up an acquaintance with a landowner who'll grant permission to hunt canecutters on his back forty. Some of the best private-lands swamper havens are those along the St. Francis River, the L'Anguille River, Bayou Bartholomew, and LaGrue Bayou.

One enjoyable, though difficult, swamper hunt I experienced took place one January in a swath of bottomlands tucked along the L'Anguille River in St. Francis County. Two friends, Karl Maslowski and Mike Stough of Cincinnati, had driven down from Ohio for an Arkansas swamper hunt. I'd managed to coax Ed Middleton, a devoted swamp rabbit hunter from Colt, to serve as our guide. We also were joined by two Wynne residents—Shelton Ellis, Ed's frequent rabbit hunting companion, and my longtime hunting partner, Lewis Peeler.

Ed Middleton probably knows as much about hunting swamp rabbits as any hunter in east Arkansas. He has an in-depth knowledge of swamper behavior gained by spending long hours in the bottoms, rubbing a whiskered chin with a callused hand as he studies the swampers running before his beagles. It is a knowledge that has produced a special knack for interpreting the baying of the dogs and the course of the rabbit, and then, when all is right, positioning himself to intercept the swamper within shooting distance.

It's Ed's guests, however, who do most of the shooting. A gracious host, I've seen Ed pass up several easy shots so one of his newfound friends could bag a swamper.

You watch Ed Middleton slip through the bottoms, and you know the man is more than a visitor here. He's as much a part of the swamp as the rabbits he chases. He's at home here, and it's obvious he has a special love for these east Arkansas bottoms.

Ed's dogs are special, too. They have to be, for it takes more than an ordinary beagle to win a game of "Hares and Hounds" with these bunnies. Pete, a long-legged hound mix, is the strike dog. If a swamper's anywhere near, his dustbuster nose will home in on the scent, and soon the chase is on. Lady, a petite little bitch, keeps the pack on track with her keen trailing ability and dogged determination. Rascal and Scrapper keep running rabbits from making good their escape. They know every swamper trick in the book, and no amount of swimming, circling, or other elusive behavior will keep them from their appointed rounds.

Our L'Anguille swamper hunt started out with a bang, despite the fact that an unusually bad storm had dumped a foot of snow two weeks earlier. A hard crust had formed on the white woodland carpet that still remained. We were hardly in the woods when Pete laid his nose on a big 'cutter holding tight in its form in a patch of honeysuckle.

Booooroooo! Booooroooo! The chase was on, and the hunters quickly scattered to cover all possible escape routes.

Good fortune was smiling on me. I was standing alone at the edge of the dirt road running through our hunting area, when the big swamper came loping my way.

At first, I thought this was a different rabbit than the one the dogs were running. The 'cutter was moving slowly for an animal being trailed by a pack of beagles, and I could still hear the dogs far off in the distance. Nevertheless, I aimed and fired two heavy loads of number fours as the swamper crossed the road. To my dismay, the rabbit never broke stride and was soon out of sight in the thickets. I feared my shooting abilities might now come under some rather embarrassing scrutiny.

I soon discovered this was indeed the swamper the dogs were trailing. The vociferous pack drew near and crossed the road on the rabbit's path. But they were hardly out of sight when the hullabaloo stopped.

As it turns out, I hadn't missed. Shelton had just walked up when Pete came out of the woods carrying the swamper. Pretty as you please, he laid it at Shelton's feet, then turned, nose to the ground, and headed back into the woods. A dead rabbit doesn't hold Pete's interest very long.

Although the icy ground made it difficult, the dogs performed extremely well that frigid January morning. Twice, they managed to flush a swamper, and both times the chase lasted well over an hour. We paired up, listening and waiting, trying to predict the course the rabbits would follow. But it was all to no avail. The swampers figured our every move. If we zigged, they zigged. If we covered this corner, they crossed at that corner. We started discussing the possibility that swampers have built-in radar.

It was nearly noon when we jumped our second swamper. We were walking across a broad expanse of open woods on our way back to the trucks for lunch. And there, where you'd least expect it, a swamper came barreling out from under a log. Karl fired, then Mike, then me, then Ed, then Mike again. But the 'cutter kept running, apparently impervious to our barrage of lead.

The dogs followed the rabbit into a honeysuckle thicket, and soon after, Pete emerged with the big swamper buck held gently in his jaws. Dropping the rabbit at Ed's feet, Pete looked us over as if to say, "It's about time, guys. Whatcha been waitin' on all day?"

Back at the truck, Lew warmed up some delectable soup and fried peach pies. Tailgate lunches have become a tradition on our swamper hunts, and half the fun of coming is sitting around the truck filling our bellies and reminiscing about hunts gone by.

"I wish we'd done better," Ed said wistfully. "I've seen times when the dogs would run ten or twelve swampers in a morning. But with all this snow and ice on the ground, the rabbits aren't moving much, and it's hard for the dogs to find them."

"You know, Ed," Mike said. "I wish we'd done better, too. But I can honestly say I don't know when I've enjoyed a hunt any more. Some guys measure the success of their hunts by how many animals they shoot. But to me, there's more to it than that. It's the chance to get out and enjoy the fresh air, a chance to make new friends who treasure the outdoors as much as you do. In that respect, I don't see how our trip could have been any better."

Karl was sneaking another peach pie into his pocket. "Hell, guys," he said. "The day's not over yet. If you fellows are finished talking, maybe we can get back to hunting."

The dogs were already back in the bottoms, looking for another swamper. Shelton blew on his cow-horn dog call and a long, mellow sonance embraced the woods. "Come on, Pete," he shouted. "It's time to move on."

"I know just the place," Lew said. "Remember that spot up the road we hunted a few years ago, Keith? I'll bet we can find some swampers over there."

It's a demanding sport, this swamper hunting. You wear yourself out fighting through the brush, then you freeze your butt off waiting for the rabbit to make his circle. You watch and wait and plan, and then, just when everything seems right, everything goes wrong. It's frustrating and tiring. But if you have the patience, if you're not one of those guys who measures the success of the hunt by the number of rabbits bagged, then maybe, just maybe, you ought to give swamper hunting a try. The rewards you'll reap will make all the effort worthwhile.

Rabbit Tactics: Lewis Peeler Style

When you walk into Lewis Peeler's insurance office in Wynne, Arkansas, one of the first things you'll notice is a collection of photos proudly displayed on the wall behind his desk. In one photo, Lewis is sitting atop a cooler watching the sky for another dove to add to the harvested birds piled around his feet. In another, Lewis is grinning ear to ear as he holds up a stringer of big slab crappie caught in Louisiana. There's a photo of Lewis squirrel hunting and another of him holding up a dandy largemouth. One shows Lew yanking a stringer of big bream out of Lake Des Arc and still another shows him landing a jumbo channel cat. It's an impressive pictorial record of this man's exploits in the out-of-doors.

If you were to ask Lewis to pick his favorite photos, though, he'd undoubtedly point to two rabbit hunting shots. In one, Lewis is standing ankle-deep in a bottomland slough, almost hidden in a thicket of saplings and vines. At his side is a handsome lemon-colored beagle named Reb, and Lew is praising the dog for helping him bag the swamp rabbit dangling from his hand.

The second photo was taken at the end of a successful Cross County cottontail hunt. Lewis and a hunting partner are sitting on the tailgate of a pickup, their shotguns laid atop a dog box in the truck bed. A small beagle is resting her feet on the tailgate, sniffing a cottontail Lew's buddy is holding. Beagle Reb is perched on the tailgate between the two men, and Lewis is rubbing his head again, clearly pleased with the dog's performance.

When it comes to hunting and fishing, Lewis Peeler has many interests. But having known the man for thirty-four years, I can tell you without hesitation his real passion is rabbit hunting. Stick Lewis Peeler in a briar patch (no pun intended), and he's as happy as a toddler in a mud puddle. Accompany him to the bottoms for a swamper hunt, and his enthusiasm becomes infectious. Rabbit hunting is his way to unwind, and though I've hunted with dozens of ardent rabbit hunting enthusiasts, I've never met a man who enjoys the sport any more than Lewis.

"One important thing to learn about hunting rabbits with dogs," Lewis says, "is not to rush your dogs. If you have a good dog, he'll get in there and work out all the good places where rabbits will hide. But

if you stay too close to your dog, he'll tend to go over the cover too fast and move on. Dogs often gauge their pace by your actions, and if you want to go on, they will, too. It's best to stay back and give them time to work the cover out and get their noses into everything."

Lewis notes it's just as important to sit tight once the chase is on. "After the dogs jump a rabbit, many people follow them to try to head the rabbit off," he says. "The best thing to do, though, is to move to the area where they jumped the rabbit, and pick a good place where you can see well. Then just wait for the rabbit to circle back. To me, that's the most enjoyable part of rabbit hunting, waiting there and listening to the chase. Why chase the rabbit down? That's why you have dogs."

Over the past two decades, good rabbit cover has become increasingly difficult to find in the east Arkansas Delta, Peeler's favored hunting area. Small family farms that once were common have been replaced by huge agricultural conglomerates that cultivate thousands of acres. Brushy fencerows and other prime cottontail cover have been cleared to make room for more cropland, and most of the wetlands where swamp rabbits thrive have been drained and cleared for planting. Lewis thinks rabbits are adapting to the change, and hunters may have to change their tactics to be successful.

"A lot of places where they used to farm small plots of ground are gone now," he says. "And a lot of the fencerows and other edge areas rabbits like are gone, too, because those small areas have either been cleared up entirely or because they've grown up in tall cover that's not good for rabbits. Hunting was better when those small areas were cultivated. For instance, right behind my house, we used to cultivate a lot of little terraces, and when we were farming, we had more rabbits than we do now when everything's grown up in tall cover. Hunting was better when we had more fencerows."

The result of all this, Lewis thinks, is a change in rabbits' activity patterns. "At one time, You could hunt about any time of day and kick up rabbits," he says, "but now it doesn't seem that way. Now it seems the best hunting is early in the morning and late in the afternoon. I don't have any scientific explanations for why this is happening, but I think it's got a lot to do with increased hunting pressure and loss of

---

Lewis Peeler praises his dogs, Reb and Bear, after a successful swamp rabbit chase.

habitat. Maybe the rabbits are adapting to it and doing like deer—feeding early and getting back into cover. But whatever the reason, the best hunting now seems to be early and late in the day."

Lewis also has noticed rabbits prefer more remote patches of cover than they once did. Some hunts now take him far off the road where few other sportsmen venture. That's one of the keys to his success.

"Seems like a lot of rabbits I find nowadays are back in isolated areas away from roads and houses, little out-of-the-way places that are hard to get to," he says. "One place like that that comes to mind is a spot where I hunted a few years ago. We were hunting grown-up banks on a series of irrigation ditches, and we walked way back off the road to a small patch of cover where probably no one had ever hunted much. That little spot was just wrapped up in rabbits, and hunting without dogs, six of us bagged forty-seven rabbits.

"It pays to keep an eye out for those places other hunters tend to overlook. It may be a mile from the road, and you may have to walk across open muddy fields to get to it, but those are some of the best rabbit hunting spots you can find."

Cottontails are his bread-and-butter game, but Lewis spends a lot of time hunting bottomland swamp rabbits. "The first rule of swamper hunting is to carry a good heavy load of shells, heavy load 4s or 6s," he says. "Swampers are bigger and tougher than cottontails and harder to hunt. Carry a good pair of rubber boots, too, and be patient. Swampers usually run bigger circles than cottontails, especially if you have fast dogs. In fact, your dogs may go out of earshot before they turn the swamper back. It's exciting hunting, but you have to patient to be successful."

One thing that makes Lewis a first-rate hunter is his willingness to share what he knows with others. Don't ask him to reveal the locations of his best rabbit coverts because I've requested he keep those secret for my visits. But if you want to talk hunting or fishing, just drop in his office in Wynne and ask him about the photos hanging on the wall. It's a sure bet you'll enjoy the visit.

Rabbits without Rover

There are basically two ways to hunt rabbits—with dogs or without. Devout dog men wouldn't think of hunting without their canine pals. But many hunters simply don't have the time, financing, or inclination to manage a well-trained pack of beagles.

Where does that leave the dogless hunter? In pretty good shape, really, so long as the hunter is willing to work for his hasenpfeffer. Where rabbits are plentiful, a canine-less cottontail hunt can provide lots of action-packed excitement. But the dogless hunter can't sit on a stump and await the singing announcement of an incoming rabbit. His success, or failure, relies on his own legwork and effort and not on that of a pack of beagles.

Hunting rabbits without dogs can be productive any time, early or late in the season. In fall and early winter, hunting pressure, natural predation, and weather have yet to thin the population. Rabbits are more numerous and easier to find. During late winter, rabbits are fewer, but they're more concentrated, too, avoiding cold winter weather by hiding in the thickest cover. A hunter willing to brave the brambles can enjoy fast-paced jump-shooting, even on the coldest days.

The first order of business is identifying a good hunting area. When walking 'em up, this means finding an area that is fairly small or confined so there's a better chance of flushing rabbits into the open for an easy shot, and one that's seldom hunted so rabbits are more likely to be plentiful. Look for isolated patches and strips of cover not easily accessible by other hunters, and try to find several such places you can hunt during a day afield. By "spot hunting"—covering one fencerow or brush patch in an hour or so, then driving on to another potential hotspot—you'll locate more rabbits and boost your chances for finding consistent action.

When there are two or more people in your "no-Rover" hunting party, try hunting long narrow strips of cover—brushy fencerows, lines of tree-shrouded thickets between crop fields, abandoned railroad rights-of-way, cover-choked ditches, and such. One or two hunters walk through the middle, kicking spots of cover that may hide rabbits. The others walk

the outside edges, standing ready to pick off retreating rabbits that hightail it out one side.

A variation of this technique uses blockers and drivers. One or more gunners wait on stand while others attempt to flush and drive rabbits toward them by beating the cover on foot. The drivers have the hardest going, but periodically, drivers and blockers switch places so everyone gets in on the action. Blockers must be good snap shooters. They'll probably have some rip-snorting action for a moment or two as cottontails sprint past them.

Safety must be foremost on everyone's mind. A strict set of rules governs every drive. 1) Only blockers carry guns. 2) To increase visibility to one another, everyone wears the same hunter-orange bodywear and hats required for deer hunting. 3) No shots are taken in anyone else's direction. 4) No one shoots until their target is positively identified. 5) Blockers remain in their assigned position until the drive is over. 6) Drivers follow their assigned route and end up where they're supposed to be. Everyone on a drive should know where his hunting buddies are at all times.

So everyone knows what's expected of them, it's a good idea to map out your hunting strategy before each drive. The person who best knows the lay of the land should be the drive boss, and everyone follows his or her instructions precisely. Using a map, a pencil and paper, or just a stick in the dirt, the drive boss illustrates exactly where the blockers will be positioned and where the drivers will work. At the completion of each drive, everyone assembles, and the hunters reorganize for the next drive.

Next to safety, the single most important aspect of a successful cottontail drive is proper deployment of the blockers. Hunters must be positioned where they can cover the rabbits' escape routes.

To best accomplish this, confine your hunting to narrow patches of cover with well-defined borders created by open fields, streams, and other features. Position blockers at one end or near small breaks or bottlenecks in the cover. The best areas are open enough so the blocker has a good shot at crossing rabbits, but not so barren or wide that rabbits will avoid crossing them.

A productive rabbit hunt doesn't require the presence of hunting dogs.

Blockers shouldn't be positioned at the center of the bottleneck or opening, nor should they face the drivers. First, this isn't safe. Second, approaching rabbits will see the blockers immediately. Instead, blockers should stand off to the side so shots will be angled away from the drivers. This also permits fleeing rabbits to follow familiar escape routes without detecting the blockers.

Although four or five people can be used in a properly orchestrated drive, in most areas with small to moderate patches of cover, two or three hunters are plenty. The two-hunter approach worked fine on one memorable hunting trip with my buddy Jim Low.

We were hunting a long narrow strip of thickets, with a field of standing cotton on one side and an open plowed field on the other. Jim had hunted here before and knew flushed rabbits invariably would head straight down the strip of cover, then break to the right and cross into the cotton field. Knowing that gave us the upper hand.

The cover strip was about a quarter-mile long, so instead of driving the whole patch at once, we divided it into sections. One of us took a position up ahead in the open turnrow between the cotton field and the thicket. The other stomped through the brush to flush hiding rabbits. There were plenty of cottontails, and most headed across the turnrow and into the cotton field just as Jim predicted. In two and a half hours, we managed to bag eight rabbits—not too bad for walking them up.

When present, piles of brush and timber also merit the attention of hunters working without dogs. These woody heaps attract plenty of rabbits and concentrate them in a very small area, a key advantage for the jump-shooter. Some hunters make their own brush piles by placing a loose covering of brush over a framework of heavy branches, then come back to hunt them after they've "seasoned out" for a few months. Others hunt brush piles left by timber cutters and farmers clearing their land.

The best way to hunt a brush pile is to circle it first, trying to identify the most likely exit a cottontail will use. Look for trails through adjacent cover, large openings in the brush, or anything that gives a clue as to how the rabbit will react to your intrusion. Then position one or two hunters where there's a good view of the exit, and let another stomp through, without a gun, from the other side. Be ready. This is fast, sporty gunning, and many great wingshots and high scorers on sporting clays fields don't fare too well during their first encounters with brush pile cottontails.

One casual yet challenging method of hunting rabbits is stalking them, one on one, hunter against animal. Rabbits are adept at hiding, so the hunter must use a healthy measure of cunning to score consistently when using this technique.

Much of what I know about stalking rabbits I learned from an older friend named Tommy. When I started hunting with him, I had an inclination to run full speed ahead, believing the more cover I stormed through, the more rabbits I was likely to see. Tommy, on the other hand, just poked along, rarely kicking the brush at all, but looking, always looking, canvassing every bit of cover through which he walked. His slow pace aggravated me to no end, as did his tendency to carry his gun draped over an elbow, muzzle pointing at the ground a few feet ahead of his rubber knee boots, a carry from which it would obviously take half a minute to get into action. The efficient hunter, I thought, always carried his shotgun in both hands, muzzle up, ready to be thrown to the shoulder in a split instant to send a deadly shot charge on its way. Tommy didn't match my mental image of an efficient hunter.

All of which shows how young and ignorant I was. While I was rushing around, stomping through every inch of cover, Tommy was *hunting*. He carefully perused everything around him, looking into thickets and briar patches, under brush piles, between the roots of trees. And after a while, it dawned on me that he was seeing more rabbits with his casual approach that I was with my incessant hurrying. "Hold up, boy," he'd say, pointing a finger into a thicket. "See his eye shining against the leaves?" Eventually I'd see the bright little dot of black, out of place in the crisscross of cover. Then magically, the rabbit's whole body would appear, and I'd stand there and wonder why I couldn't see one like that myself.

Thinking back, I'm sure there were many times when my helter-skelter hunting method took me right past many rabbits that sat tight, relying on their excellent camouflage to hide them. Tommy, of course, saw most of them. He looked everywhere and missed very little. And when he finished hunting a brushy draw or fencerow, there was no sense in anyone else going through it.

In the years since I hunted with Tommy, I've learned much more about hunting rabbits without dogs. I've learned, for instance, that rabbits' soft fur does little to turn the cold, and on sunny winter days, they'll sit in a spot out of the wind where they can warm themselves in direct sunlight. Knowing this helps when I'm stalking rabbits on frigid days late in the season.

I've learned that if a rabbit isn't spooked too bad, a sharp whistle may stop it in its tracks, giving me an added few seconds to make a clean shot.

I've learned that rabbits in isolated patches of cover will try to sneak around behind me rather than cross open ground. Others sit tight till I pass, then squirt out behind. Glancing over my shoulder now and then while hunting helps me bag some of these renegades before they escape.

I've learned to wear heavy clothing when hunting without dogs to keep from turning myself into a lump of hamburger when thrashing through the stickers.

And best of all, I think, I've learned that hunting rabbits without dogs can be just as much fun as hunting them with a pack of beagles. Happiness, my friend, is small-game hunting, no matter how you serve it up.

SQUIRRELS

Crowley's Crackers

I found the stand of creek-bottom hickories while looking at some topo maps of St. Francis National Forest one September. I'd spent several days fishing on Bear Creek Lake, and looking for a change of pace, I decided to check out some of the area's excellent squirrel hunting possibilities.

I settled on a swath of timber running along a little creek between Forest Road 1901 and the St. Francis River. I pulled into the area at daybreak, parked beside the gravel road and followed a trail into the timber. As I approached the river, I stumbled across a grove of hickories loaded with nuts. I knew they were loaded because I heard the pitter-patter of nut cuttings raining on the forest floor. Several treetop squirrels were cracking nuts.

Stalking slowly through the woods, I managed to move into position without alerting them to my presence, and just minutes later I had the makings of a squirrel breakfast in my game bag. Before 9:00 A.M., I had harvested an eight-squirrel limit and was headed back to camp.

Some of the best squirrel hunting in eastern Arkansas is along the devil's backbone of territory called Crowley's Ridge. Stretching 210 miles from southeast Missouri to near Helena, Arkansas, this timbered ridge rises abruptly two hundred to four hundred feet above the otherwise flat agricultural delta. Most land in this oasis of hardwoods is privately owned, but many landowners will grant permission to hunt squirrels if you ask. For hunters who would rather stick to public lands, though, St. Francis National Forest near the ridge's southern end is the ticket to good squirrel hunting.

AMERICA'S SMALLEST NATIONAL FOREST

St. Francis NF covers just 21,202 acres, making it our nation's smallest national forest. Located between Marianna and West Helena in Lee and Phillips Counties, the entire national forest is cooperatively managed as a wildlife management area by the Arkansas Game and Fish Commission. The forest is about a one-hour drive southwest of

Stream bottoms in St. Francis National Forest harbor healthy squirrel populations.

Memphis and two hours east of Little Rock. Access is by Arkansas Highway 44 from Marianna and Arkansas Highway 242 from Helena. Good Forest Service roads run through the area's interior.

St. Francis NF takes its name from the St. Francis River, which forms a portion of the eastern boundary. The Mississippi River also abuts the forest, near the southeast corner, and a short stretch of the L'Anguille River just above its confluence with the St. Francis forms the forest's northeast boundary.

Two other large water bodies also are found here. Bear Creek Lake is a favorite spot for visitors who enjoy fishing, swimming, boating, picnicking, and camping. It's considered by many to be the best redear sunfish lake in Arkansas, with lots of these "shellcrackers" exceeding a pound in weight. Largemouth bass, catfish, and crappie also are plentiful. This 625-acre lake is atop Crowley's Ridge in the north end of the national forest and has five developed recreation sites on its shore.

Storm Creek Lake covers 420 acres near the southern tip of the national forest, a few miles north of West Helena. It also has outdoor recreation facilities and supports thriving populations of largemouths, bream, crappie, and catfish, with a bonus complement of hybrid striped bass. Along the fifty-mile shoreline are many beautiful stands of mixed hardwoods.

SQUIRREL HUNTING BASICS

Hardwood-covered "hogbacks" and "hollows" blanket most of the St. Francis area. But the easternmost edge of the national forest is primarily flat, low, big-river bottomlands. It's almost a sure bet that one area or the other—uplands or bottoms—will offer good squirrel hunting possibilities sometime during the season.

On weekdays in early autumn, you'll seldom see another hunter in most locations within the national forest. Even on weekends, if you're willing to hike away from the roads, you can find plenty of territory where you can pursue squirrels in relative solitude.

Gray squirrels and fox squirrels both live in the St. Francis, but gray squirrels are more abundant. The gray squirrel weighs three-fourths to one-and-a-half pounds. The fox squirrel is generally larger, weighing up to three pounds. Both species may occupy the same tract of woods, but fox squirrels typically are found in more open woods, usually near the forest edge. Gray squirrels prefer dense stands of trees in deeper woods. In St. Francis NF, I've found fox squirrels are most common along the rivers and around the lakes.

The species also differ in their activity periods. Gray squirrels are most active at first light; fox squirrels arise a bit later. Hunters should be in gray squirrel woods at dawn and hunt the first two hours for best results. The third hour is somewhat productive, but midday is usually unproductive. A little activity can be expected most of the afternoon, but there's no worthwhile peak.

When hunting strictly for fox squirrels, you can stay in bed an hour later and find best results the second and third hours after sunrise. The first hour is OK, but again, afternoon activity is minimal. Because fox and gray squirrels both are common in St. Francis NF, you can find excellent hunting throughout the first three hours of the day.

PLENTIFUL FOOD EQUALS PLENTIFUL SQUIRRELS

Finding squirrels here is primarily a matter of finding the right foods. They move from one food source to another as different foods come in and go out. For instance, during the earliest part of the season, squirrels often feed on dogwood drupes, mulberries, hackberries, tulip-tree cones, and other soft mast. When they're feeding on soft mast, hunting can be tricky. The trees that produce soft mast aren't as abundant as oaks, hickories, and other nut producers, so if squirrels are concentrated where soft mast is abundant, they may be difficult to pinpoint. In this situation, it's also darn near impossible to locate Ol' Nutcracker by sound. Nice thing is, if you do some pre-season scouting to find soft-mast-producing trees, you may find numerous squirrels in a small area, even in a single tree, come opening day.

As the season progresses, black gum fruits, maple seeds, and hickories come in, and the squirrels move to them. Finally, when acorns are ready, squirrels head for the oaks. When you hit this stage in the game, your quarry may again be difficult to pinpoint, because white oak trees are scattered throughout the entire national forest. When squirrels are eating acorns, they'll be scattered, too, forcing the hunter to keep on the move.

BEECH TREE BUSHYTAILS

I haven't mentioned beech trees yet, because they offer unique hunting opportunities. Covered in smooth gray bark, these beautiful trees occur throughout much of St. Francis NF. When they produce nuts, squirrel hunting in tracts of beech trees is little short of phenomenal.

Beeches are especially attractive to early-season squirrels, and if you can pinpoint healthy stands, be sure to check them for squirrels early on. They produce hard, spiny burs containing two or three small, sweet-meated, triangular nuts. Beechnuts are tiny, averaging about sixteen hundred to the pound. But they're like candy to squirrels. When the nut crop is good (good beechnut crops are produced at two- to three-year intervals), squirrels flock to stands of beech.

Beechnuts require one growing season to mature, and many are ripe by September. Seed fall begins after the first heavy frosts have caused the burs to open. But by that time, squirrels may have stripped the trees bare of nuts. The best hunting for beechnut bushytails is usually in September or October when the seeds first ripen.

In addition to food, beech trees also provide den sites for squirrels. The spreading crown of a single old beech may have dozens of holes where squirrels can find shelter. Use binoculars to locate active den holes worn smooth by squirrels, and be ready when they emerge to feed.

The important thing to remember is that St. Francis squirrels migrate from one area to another during squirrel season. Try to learn where different food-providing trees are located and when the foods squirrels prefer are likely to come in. Knowing this, you can find squirrels.

EARLY-SEASON HUNTING

If you have a choice, hunt for St. Francis squirrels during the early weeks of squirrel season. Early-season hunting conditions are more favorable than conditions encountered after the leaves have fallen. Squirrels are less wary during the season's first few weeks, and there are plenty of young, foolish squirrels around. Leafy branches restrict the squirrel's vision, allowing for closer, easier stalks, and because nuts are still clinging to branches, squirrels are moving more in the trees overhead, making them easier to see and hear. You're also less likely to encounter the deer hunters who flock to St. Francis NF later in the year.

Bushytail fans who take advantage of these favorable circumstances enjoy some of the best squirrel-hunting action the season can offer.

Stalking is a technique ready-made for the early-season squirrel hunter. Squirrels aren't as wary of hunters then, and leaves are still on the trees, allowing the hunter to approach more stealthily. Late in the season, when leaves have fallen, squirrels can be difficult to stalk because they can see movement on the ground for longer distances. Stalking is one-on-one—the squirrel's keen senses and treetop vantage against the hunter's furtiveness and patience.

Tree-bark and leafy camouflage patterns do wonders to conceal you from wary squirrels, but safety aspects also should be considered. When you're leaning against a tree, another hunter could mistake any slight movement for a squirrel. It happens with tragic regularity, and in Arkansas, "victim mistaken for squirrel" is one of the leading causes of hunting accidents. Be cautious, and wear fluorescent orange clothing when appropriate.

As you move through the woods, watch the ground so you can ease forward with the least possible noise. Stop every ten or twenty yards to carefully scan the trees before moving another few yards and repeating the process. Motion is what you should look for. A shaking branch is the most common clue you'll see, but you might see the squirrel itself as it runs down a limb.

Another trick is to hunt toward the sun when you have the option. It sounds like stupid advice, but don't knock it until you've tried it. It's much easier to spot movement in branches when those branches are silhouetted against the sun. The secret is to stand so you have a tree trunk or clump of leaves shielding your eyes from the direct glare.

The single most important thing a squirrel stalker can learn is patience. Don't get in a hurry, because you won't see many squirrels if you do. The slower you go, the better your chances are apt to be.

HUNTING THE LAKE SHORES

I first started noticing the abundance of squirrels in St. Francis National Forest while fishing on Bear Creek Lake. One autumn day following a period of summer drought, I counted more than thirty squirrels feeding and drinking along the banks.

Though Bear Creek Lake only covers 625 acres, it has a very

irregular shape. There are literally scores of small coves and fingers of water, giving Bear Creek more than sixty miles of shoreline. Storm Creek is likewise configured, with fifty miles of shoreline.

Both lakes are skirted by stands of big oaks, hickories, beeches, and other mast-producing hardwoods. Because the soil near the lakes stays fairly moist year-round, mast crops like acorns and hickory nuts are more reliable, with good crops produced almost every year. On the other hand, drier areas of the national forest may have poor mast crops during years with little rain. Consequently, squirrels are likely to be abundant year after year near the lakes. And during periods of prolonged dryness, they may migrate from other areas of the forest to stands of trees along the lake shores. Savvy hunters can cash in on this bushytail bonanza.

There are many cabins and summer homes around Bear Creek Lake, so observe all safety precautions when hunting. Hunting is not allowed around homes, cabins, or near recreation sites, but there are still plenty of places where you can beach a boat and take a short stroll through the woods to hunt squirrels. Storm Creek has fewer developments, but observe the same precautions when hunting there.

SHOTGUNS OR RIFLES?

Shotguns and rifles are both popular for taking St. Francis squirrels. There are avid proponents for each weapon, but if you're like me, it doesn't matter which you use. If you take a shotgun, every squirrel you see will be out in the open but a hundred yards away. Take a rifle, and they'll be running like blue blazes overhead in thick foliage. For safety reasons, however, always use shotguns when in the general vicinity of camping areas and cabins.

Some hunters prefer using a shotgun because this weapon allows a quick, clean kill when squirrels are racing from one leafy branch to another at close distances. This is a commonly encountered situation, especially when stalking early in the season. Others prefer the longer shooting range and quietness afforded by a 22-caliber rifle. Leafy branches aren't a hindrance, they say, so long as you move quietly and scan the woods carefully for sitting squirrels.

Both types of guns perform well in the hands of a capable hunter, and when you boil it all down, the proper gun is whatever brings the most confidence to the hunter. Whether you shoot a rifle or a shotgun, you'll win some and lose some. That's the nature of hunting.

ACCESS INFORMATION

Access into St. Francis NF is via two Forest Service roads. Forest Route 1900 runs past both lakes. The north end is reached off Highway 44 south of Marianna at the Maple Flat Recreation Area on Bear Creek Lake. The road then continues through the forest to a point on Highway 44 one mile north of West Helena. Forest Route 1901 traverses the entire eastern border of the national forest and also is reached off Highway 44.

A Fishy Way to Squirrel Hunt

There he was, big as life, running down the riverbank like a rufous-coated mink—slipping, darting, and slithering over, under, and around every little hurdle. Then, as suddenly as he appeared, he was gone.

"Where'd he go?" Gregg Patterson whispered, a puzzled look furrowing his brow.

"I'm not sure," I responded, "but he's bound to show himself sooner or later. There aren't too many places he can hide around here."

The trees edging the river were sparse—a big elm, a couple of small oaks, a thin band of locusts running along a small creek spilling into the larger stream. The object of our abbreviated discussion, a big fox squirrel, had exited the scene via a thick tangle of vines and shrubs blanketing the ground beneath them.

A rustle stirred the leaves overhead. Branches bent earthward under a too-heavy weight. A patch of russet passed through the greenery, then a long orange tail. Our quarry was striking out for safer ground.

Silence is essential for success, so with hand signals, we synchronized our movements. An index finger was pressed to lips and nose—*Ssshhh!*—then the same finger pointed upstream. There. Over there.

I dipped a paddle in the water, and the canoe pivoted around. Patterson used more sign language—a palm outstretched, pumping back and forth. Close enough.

I followed Patterson's gaze into the treetops, shielding my eyes from the glare of the morning sun, straining, squinting, looking for a knot on the tree that was not a knot, or a telltale wisp of chestnut fur caught in the breeze—anything that might give the squirrel away.

Bad news, these guys, the squirrel must have thought. It moved again, and I saw it, sidling around the tree trunk, trying to avoid our scrutiny. Patterson saw it, too, and waved me forward. Easy now, easy, just a little closer. Don't drag the bottom of the canoe on those rocks.

Patterson raised the shotgun, fluidly, silently, pressing the knuckles of his trigger hand against his cheek. But no, not yet. The squirrel moved again. The gun came down. More signals. More movement. Good. Right here. That's it. Now stop.

The gun came up again. This time it stayed up. I plugged my ears with stubby fingers, squinting my eyes into crow's-feet. The shot was not unexpected but it rattled me nevertheless.

There was success, though. The shot was true, and Patterson scurried up the bank to retrieve his kill.

"Crafty devils, aren't they," he said smiling, stroking the animal's thick reddish pelt.

"Yeah, but that's what makes them so fun," I answered. "Let's see if any of his cousins are running around here."

River floating is one of the best of all ways to hunt squirrels. Aside from sandwiching two pleasant sports—boating and hunting—together, float-hunting has many other advantages.

First, a river float-hunt allows you to visit remote areas away from the crowds. Because access is somewhat restricted, hunting is kept to a minimum, and top quality shooting results.

Second, the silent water stalk by canoe or johnboat puts squirrels in the bag. Riverbank squirrels seldom are wary of hunters in boats, and floating eliminates the sounds produced by even the most careful stalker. A quiet approach by water usually fools them.

Hardwood river bottoms produce lots of squirrels because they have more dependable crops of acorns, hickory nuts, and other mast. Mast failure usually is associated with drought. But because streamsides are less affected by dryness, food supplies are more reliable, and consequently, squirrels usually are plentiful year after year.

River hunting also is peaceful, relaxing, and rewarding. The constantly changing scenery adds to the adventure.

PLANNING

Floating for squirrels, like any other hunt, requires proper planning. And like most outdoor adventures, the planning is enjoyable.

Step one is locating a stream that flows through good squirrel habitat—mature woodlands made up of oaks, hickories, and other mast-producing hardwoods. Try to select one that flows through a national forest, wildlife management area, or other public land where you can hunt without worrying about trespassing problems.

It doesn't matter if the stream you choose is a small mountain creek, a large bottomland river, or something in-between, but remember, the

slower the stream, the better the floating technique works. Fast-running whitewater rivers just aren't safe or practical when you're planning to shoot from the water. The best streams are rated Class I or II on the international scale of difficulty—moving water with few or no rapids and obstructions so little maneuvering is necessary.

Unless you can motor back to your launch site, you also should select a stream with bridges or road access at convenient put-in and take-out points. A five- to ten-mile stretch is usually ideal for a one-day float-hunt, but the distance you should plan to travel depends on the speed of stream flow, the amount of hunting time you have, and whether or not you plan to camp. Arrange shuttle service with a local outfitter several weeks in advance, or plan on hunting with a partner and driving two vehicles to the river.

SQUIRREL BOATS AND OTHER EQUIPMENT

Canoes are the boats of choice for most on-the-water squirrel hunters because they're quiet and easy to maneuver on gentle streams and can be launched and taken out with minimum effort. If low-water conditions make portaging necessary, the canoe shines. There's one big disadvantage, however, especially with shorter models, and that's instability. Canoes can be easily tipped when not handled properly or when negotiating tricky water. Novices should learn basic canoeing skills and canoeing safety before harnessing the boat to hunting methods.

Johnboats provide a more stable alternative and work superbly on bottomland streams where portaging seldom is necessary. They provide a low silhouette for that "part-of-the-river" appearance so important in this brand of hunting, and can be easily maneuvered using a small trolling motor or by sculling from the front seat. Carpeting, car mats, or portable foam mats placed in the floor reduce the unforgivable noise problems associated with aluminum hulls. (The same is true for canoes.)

Rubber inflatable boats also make good squirrel-hunting crafts. They're stable and make good shooting platforms. More surface drag makes them float slower than canoes or johnboats, a definite advantage

A river float can take hunters to backcountry hunting areas where squirrels are plentiful and hunters scarce.

on faster flowing streams. On sluggish waters, however, inflatables barely move, making heavy paddling or rowing a necessity.

A dull finish on your boat can greatly improve your success. Squirrels can be taken from a bright red or silver canoe, for instance, but you'll take more from a craft painted brown or green. Some hunters break the outline of their craft by camouflaging it with netting like that used in duck and turkey blinds.

The equipment you carry should include at least two paddles, life jackets for each person (which should be worn at all times), a small cooler for lunch and squirrels, one rifle or shotgun, ammunition, camouflage clothing, raingear, hip boots or waders (if you want to keep your feet dry), and a dip net with a long handle. Only one gun is needed because it's safer if one person shoots while the other maneuvers the boat. A long-handled dip net helps retrieve squirrels that fall in the water.

TECHNIQUE

The solo hunter can be successful if he is patient and careful, but most savvy float hunters prefer working in pairs. One paddles the boat while the other shoots, and they trade places periodically, allowing each to get in on the action. The boat is maneuvered slowly and smoothly to avoid any unnecessary rocking and frightening the game. On slow-moving waters, even novice boaters can hold the boat steady to allow for clean shots with either shotgun or rifle.

The twelve- or twenty-gauge shotgun offers an advantage in bouncy, moderate current where snap shots may be the best you'll get. A .22 rifle, on the other hand, works great on gentle pools and doesn't spook downstream squirrels to the extent a shotgun does. Choosing one or the other is mostly a matter of personal taste and shooting ability. Some hunters carry both to cover all possibilities.

Safety is paramount. Ammunition is never chambered until a squirrel is spotted and the boat is in a stable position.

Hunters should be afloat at daybreak because the action starts at dawn. On small waters, start hunting from the middle of the stream. Check for noise or movement on both sides, in the trees, and on the ground. When a squirrel is pinpointed, move close to the bank so you're not as obvious in your approach.

On wide rivers, stay close to one shore or the other while spotting squirrels. Some hunters try to cover both banks and find themselves suddenly out of range of either. Squirrels are gone before an approach can be made.

Travel slowly, drifting with the current and steering with a paddle. Keep movements and noise to a minimum. If you're silent and still, most squirrels will react as if you're nothing more than a log floating downstream. It's not unusual to drift within twenty yards of a bushytail cutting nuts in a tree or drinking at the water's edge. Most will show no fear, and that is their downfall.

Pick your shots carefully. If you can be certain of your target and make a clean kill from your boat, do so. There are times, however, when it's more prudent to go ashore and move in closer for the kill.

If you've traveled a long stretch of river without seeing a squirrel, tie or anchor your boat and spend some time looking and listening. Squirrels may be away from the outer edges of cover where they're not easily seen, requiring a more attentive approach for locating them.

If the float takes you into a nice section of woods with an active squirrel population, you may want to secure your boat and hunt along the stream. One of the primary advantages of float-hunting is gaining access to roadless backcountry other hunters rarely visit. Top-quality shooting results. Of course, if there's any doubt about land ownership or access, keep out. Landowners get understandably touchy about strangers stalking their woods without permission.

Check game laws closely before undertaking this method, to be sure you know all restrictions. Federal waterfowl regulations also should be examined. During seasons for ducks, geese, and coots, you'll have to hunt with steel shot only, and during these times, it's illegal to hunt from a motor boat unless the motor has been completely shut off. Float-hunting with rifles or pistols is unlawful during waterfowl seasons.

What constitutes a successful river squirrel hunt? For some, it is nothing less than a limit of squirrels. But for most of us, just being there is a triumph.

As we drift along in the current, we find peace, relaxation, and relief from all the weary realities that bind our hearts and minds. And if we bag a few squirrels along the way, that's just an extra gift.

Outfoxing Ol' Foxy

The beautiful fox squirrel is one of the most challenging, fun-to-hunt game animals in Arkansas. Now you see him; now you don't. This little treetop Houdini is a master of the disappearing act.

While his gray squirrel kinfolks depend on nimble, fleet feet to elude their pursuers, the fox squirrel plays a different game. Being heavier, he's not as agile a treetop dancer as the gray and is much more prone to do his foraging on the ground. Flush him from his feeding quarters, and he's rather casual about getting away.

Instead of running up the nearest tree and rushing skyward like the gray squirrel, leaping from treetop to treetop, ol' Foxy scampers up a tree and almost defiantly challenges anyone to find him. The bushytail sprawls out on a limb in an effort to make himself inconspicuous, or he may curl up inside a hollowed fork. Often he'll sidle around the trunk to keep out of the hunter's sight. The fox squirrel's bag of tricks contains even more challenging ruses, and all are effective.

The fox squirrel is the largest tree squirrel in North America. A mature male might weigh more than two pounds and measure twenty-eight inches from the tip of the nose to the tip of the tail. Mature grays won't be more than a couple feet long or much over a pound in weight. Its size makes the fox squirrel a hunting prize.

The "fox" part of the name was derived from the animal's typical coloration. The upper body is usually a variegated brownish black tinted with yellowish-orange. The paws, face, belly, and tail, however, usually are a brilliant shade of rufous orange, reminding some of a fox's coloration. There are many other color patterns, as well, ranging from solid black to strawberry blond, with numerous shades in between.

The lethargic fox squirrel is a late riser and feeds and retires earlier in the afternoon than gray squirrels. Grays are usually busy at the crack of dawn, from first light through the first two hours of the morning. Fox squirrels typically don't start moving until the second hour after sunrise and don't retreat until after the third hour. There may be a small amount of activity at dawn, but it's usually minimal.

A second, yet smaller, peak of activity occurs in late afternoon. For gray squirrels, this usually coincides with the last hour before darkness.

Fox squirrels, on the other hand, like to get out and about a bit earlier in the afternoon and will be tucked snugly away in a nest or den tree well before the sun goes down.

Foxes and grays also differ somewhat in their selection of home sites. The fox squirrel prefers a more park-like habitat than the gray, usually living in more open timber, along forest edges or in small stands of large trees. The gray is by nature a denizen of the deep woods, preferring dense stands of trees over an open forest floor.

This doesn't always hold true, of course. Fox squirrels sometimes are bagged in the middle of huge, compact tracts of woodlands, and grays may be found in sparse trees growing along fencerows. Nevertheless, the pattern holds true more often than not, and if you're hunting specifically for fox squirrels, you'll want to concentrate your efforts in their preferred open-timber–forest-edge habitat.

There are other living requirements you also should know. While fox squirrels eat a wide variety of foods, everything from birds' eggs and insects to tree buds and mushrooms, their mainstay is mast—almost any kind of nut. White oak acorns and hickory nuts probably top all choices, if available, but black walnuts, sweet pecans, red oak acorns, pignuts, beechnuts, hazelnuts, and other varieties also are relished.

Field corn is considered a special treat, through all stages of its development—milk stage to hard corn. Consequently, a tract of hardwood timber adjacent a corn field is likely to contain numerous fat fox squirrels. You also may find these bushytails feeding on hackberries, wild grapes, wild cherries, mulberries, and other fruits.

Hunting for fox squirrels, specifically, can be a real challenge for Arkansas sportsmen. In some respects, hunters must be more alert and stealthy than when hunting grays. With grays, you can stalk slowly or sit still and watch for shaking branches that indicate a squirrel is scampering through the trees. Fox squirrels are slower and more prone to remain in one spot for longer periods. The limbs they travel most often are usually larger and less likely to shake. The hunter, then, practically has to discern the outline of a stationary fox squirrel from that of a stationary limb.

Some say fox squirrels are less wary of intruders in their woods than grays. But the way they react to perceived threats makes them more difficult to hunt. Instead of fleeing through the canopy and offering the

quick-moving shotgunner a good target, fox squirrels are apt to dart into a hole or simply disappear against a branch.

Most folks go after fox squirrels just like hunting grays. They find fresh cuttings on the ground or a den tree or nest, then sit down nearby and wait for the squirrel to show itself. If you're not endowed with enough patience for this tactic, you can stalk the critters, moving slowly through the woods, watching the trees and ground for signs of activity. Be sure to watch the ground because this is where moving fox squirrels are most apt to be.

A good pattern is to walk ten steps, then stop beside a tree, look your surroundings over carefully for five minutes or so, then, if you haven't sighted anything, move ahead another ten steps and repeat the process. Listen attentively at each stop. Sometimes the only indication that a fox squirrel is in the vicinity is the sound of nut cuttings pitter-pattering on the forest floor.

If the woodland understory is dry, it may be best to sit while hunting, moving only occasionally. Fox squirrels have a keen sense of hearing, and leaves or twigs crunching underfoot will send them scurrying for a hidey-hole. This dry woods technique may not be necessary, though, if you can find a small stream or creek running through the area. Savvy fox squirrel hunters often score by wading a creek or carefully picking their way along the damp banks.

Several different color phases of fox squirrels can be found in Arkansas, and if you want to add extra challenge to your hunting, it might be an interesting hobby to collect, and have mounted, as many of these as possible.

Some woods I've hunted in southeast Arkansas have sizeable populations of solid black squirrels. For instance, on a weekend deer hunting trip in White River National Wildlife Refuge near DeWitt, I counted three coal-black bushytails. I'm told that Felsenthal National Wildlife Refuge near Crossett, Arkansas, also has a higher-than-average number of black squirrels in its woods, and I've seen them in other areas, too, including Henry Gray/Hurricane Lake Wildlife Management Area near Bald Knob, and Bayou Meto WMA, the world-renowned duck hunting tract near Stuttgart.

The fox squirrel is a handsome prize for those who enjoy a challenging small-game hunt.

Many people mistake these black limb-chickens for an entirely different squirrel species. That's understandable because they have such an unusual appearance. They actually are a dark (melanistic) color phase of the fox squirrel. The fox squirrel's scientific name, *Sciurus niger,* means black squirrel, a reflection of this characteristic. These strikingly beautiful animals probably gain a foothold in certain areas when an aberration in genes in several squirrel families results in one or more young that are black. These then slowly build up a population in which a dominant black-coloration gene persists.

Other unusual color patterns may be found as well. Some fox squirrels appear multicolored, with black on the back and orange or buff underparts. The most beautiful I've seen were entirely black except for a brilliant orange tail.

Some have prominent yellow washes under the legs and on parts of the back and tail. Occasionally, you'll find one that resembles a cross between a fox squirrel and a gray squirrel, with white underparts and a rich intermingling of chestnut and gray over the rest of the body. You might even happen upon a pure white squirrel. These are rare, but not unheard of, and some are true albinos with pink eyes and skin. Some mammalogists claim there is more variation in color among fox squirrels than among any other wild mammals on the continent.

Fox squirrels and gray squirrels are equally delectable table fare. So it may seem a bit silly to pursue fox squirrels alone, especially in woods harboring both species. The thing is, squirrel hunting, like any other sport, can get a bit monotonous at times. And the only way to break the monotony is to add a little extra challenge. Singling out fox squirrels does just that, making your squirrel hunting jaunts even more enjoyable.

Peak Hunting for Bushytails

With a name like Hickory Nut Mountain, I figured I couldn't go wrong. Where there are hickory trees, there are squirrels. So I ventured to this landmark in Ouachita National Forest for a hunt.

I decided to confine my activity to a circle of land at the foot of the mountain. A small creek meandered through the area, and because roads surrounded the location, I didn't have to worry about getting lost in the pre-dawn darkness. The creek bottom would likely have plenty of hardwoods and plenty of squirrels.

I pulled into the area at daybreak, parked at the side of the gravel road just above the creek and looked out across a beautiful scene. The morning sun was breaking over the mountains, illuminating the golden foliage of a thousand hickory trees. The entire forest was bathed in a yellow glow, dew was falling off the trees, and a clear, cold creek cascaded over weather-worn rocks in a valley lined with galleries of hardwoods that seemed high enough to touch the clouds. The autumn colors were at their richest, and gentle weather made for a perfect outing.

I padded quietly along an old logging road, and soon found a stump on which to rest my backside. I'd just sat down when I spied a pair of gray squirrels feeding in an old maple, just out of range. Working slowly through the woods, I managed to creep into position without alerting them to my presence, and just minutes later I had the first squirrel of a limit in my game bag.

The mountains of Arkansas are squirrel hunters' heaven. Not only do they harbor tremendous numbers of bushytails, they also provide exquisite scenery. It's easy to understand why some refer to the Ozarks and Ouachitas as "God's country."

Best of all, there are thousands of locations like Hickory Nut Mountain where hunters can find great public squirrel hunting in a resplendent setting far from the maddening crowds. On weekdays during autumn, you'll seldom ever see another hunter in most locations. Even on weekends, if you're willing to hike or canoe in, you can find plenty of territory where you can pursue squirrels in relative solitude.

The reason the Ozarks and Ouachitas have so many squirrels is because of the abundant mast-producing hardwoods that provide a

plentiful supply of foods. The Ozarks in northern Arkansas are covered primarily with upland hardwoods. Shortleaf pine is the main timber type on the drier, south-facing slopes of the Ouachitas, but there are plenty of upland oak-hickory forests on the moister north-facing slopes and along creek and river drainages. When mast crops are good, hunters can look forward to some fine squirrel hunting.

If you're hunting in mountains for the first time, get your hands on a set of maps that shows public land boundaries, creeks, streams, and backcountry roads. In the Ouachitas, squirrels tend to be concentrated near some body of water such as a creek, river, pond, or lake. These are the areas most likely to have hardwoods producing consistently good crops of acorns, hickory nuts, beechnuts, and other squirrel favorites. Squirrels can be found just about anywhere in the Ozarks, but again, they tend to concentrate in areas close to a good water supply.

Wildlife management areas managed by the Arkansas Game and Fish Commission provide some of the state's best mountain squirrel hunting. In the Ozarks region, White Rock, Piney Creeks, and Sylamore Wildlife Management Areas are among the best. Prime areas in the Ouachitas include the Muddy Creek and Caney Creek management areas.

White Rock Wildlife Management Area encompasses 280,000 acres and is within easy driving distance of Fayetteville, Fort Smith, and Clarksville. Stretching across five northwestern counties, it is capable of absorbing large numbers of hunters. With a pretty good network of roads, hunters tend to spread out rather than concentrate as is the case in many smaller areas. Many sections of this rugged area are reached only by hiking in, so there are numerous sections that are rarely hunted.

Finding squirrels on White Rock, or any area for that matter, is a matter of finding the right foods. They move from one food source to another as different foods come in and go out. Try to learn where different food-providing trees are located and when they come in. Knowing this, you usually can find squirrels.

A few of the best squirrel-hunting areas on White Rock area are the Big Flat area northwest of Horsehead Lake in Johnson County, the area around Baldwin Creek near St. Paul, and the Delaney Creek

---

Team hunting in mountainous regions can encourage wary squirrels to reveal themselves.

drainage in the north-central part of the management area. Other good areas are around Hurricane Creek, Frog's Bayou, and Indian Creek.

Piney Creeks WMA covers 180,000 acres within the Ozark National Forest north of Russellville and south of Harrison. Squirrel hunting is normally good to excellent. Hunters should look on north- or east-facing slopes for stands of mature hardwoods—above twelve inches in diameter—for squirrel concentrations.

Scouting also is important here. Squirrel hunting is best in big stands of hardwoods, but look for special locations in these woods. Look for edges where one type of woods border another. Pockets of hardwoods in pines are prime squirrel areas. Old logging roads running through the woods also are good.

Although squirrels come from practically every hill and valley in Piney Creeks, a few places are consistently good. The three major drainages on the area—Big Piney Creek, Little Piney Creek, and the North Fork of Illinois Bayou—all have good concentrations of squirrels. Other good locations include the Pilot Rock area in the west-central portion between Big and Little Piney, the areas around the community of Treat, and on woodland adjacent the Parker Ridge Forest Service Road on the western edge.

Sylamore Wildlife Management Area, covering 150,000 acres north of Mountain View, is another popular Ozark squirrel hunting area. As in most upland locations, squirrel populations rise and fall in cycles on this area, but timbered mountains and valleys usually have huntable numbers.

Sylamore is bounded on the east and north by White River and on the west by Buffalo River and Big Creek. Sylamore Creek, the area's namesake, flows southeastward across the area and into the White River. Springs and creeks also are abundant, so water is not a factor limiting mast production during normal years. The preponderance of upland hardwoods is composed primarily of oaks and hickories, with a heavy complement of lesser fruit-bearing as well as nut-bearing trees and shrubs that supplement the major mast-producing species.

A hunter can go after squirrels anytime and in any weather situation and have a chance, but certain conditions make squirrels more active or the hunting conditions more ideal. For instance, if the woods are dry, it's harder to hunt. You might want to ease into an area where the squirrels ought to be feeding then sit and let things settle down for a while. During warm, sunny weather, dawn to mid-morning and late-afternoon periods are best. But if the day is overcast or if a light rain is falling, you can hunt all day, picking up a squirrel here and there. Perhaps the best time of all is when a brisk rain suddenly stops and the sun pops out.

Covering 146,206 acres fifteen miles southwest of Danville in Yell, Montgomery, and Scott Counties, Muddy Creek Wildlife Management Area provides Ouachita Mountain squirrel hunting at its best. Squirrel hunters sometimes shy away from the area because of the preponderance of pine timber. But hunters who concentrate their search in creek bottoms and along slopes with oak and hickory trees shouldn't have any trouble bagging a limit of bushytails.

If you find Muddy Creek squirrels feeding in several specific spots rather than being dispersed throughout a big spread of hardwoods, its often best to get hidden and ambush squirrels as they steal out in search of breakfast. A squirrel's eyes are conditioned to movement, and it's not frightened by something that doesn't move. Let *it* move around and make the mistakes.

If, however, you find the squirrels loose and scattered, a few here and a few there, it will pay to still-hunt, catfooting quietly through the woods, being alert for movement and sounds.

Caney Creek Wildlife Management Area southeast of Mena is another area for the hunter who likes to avoid the crowds. It's remote, rugged terrain, and part of it has been officially designated a wilderness area where no vehicular traffic is permitted.

Squirrel hunting is good on Caney Creek's eighty-five thousand acres, with the bushytails thriving in an area with more hardwood timber than in most of the Ouachita Mountains. Here, it may be wise to team up with a partner when hunting.

Team tactics are best employed by just two hunters. One hunter works his way along a hardwood ridge, staying just below the ridgetop so he's not silhouetted against the sky. He moves up slowly, stalking a hundred yards or so and taking a stand with his back against a tree. His partner then works his way through the draw below, watching for squirrels and keeping keenly aware of his buddy's position. Safety should be foremost in both hunter's minds.

The high man is at eye level with squirrels his friend might scare up, a definite advantage. Bushytails fleeing from the man below will move uphill, high into the trees in an instinctive urge to escape possible danger. The low man will bag many of the squirrels before they see him. Those that spot him first and try to make good their escape usually can be taken by the ridge man if he remains unseen and alert. The ridge man moves up again and the process is repeated when the man below draws near.

For a real mountain squirrel-hunting treat, consider floating one of the streams running through lands open to public hunting. Since water and the trees around it are consistent attractions to squirrels, it's logical to combine the pleasures of boating, squirrel hunting, and maybe some fishing as well, on the same float trip. It's a bit illogical, perhaps, that so few sportsmen try it.

Two of the best streams for enjoyable float tripping are Illinois Bayou and the Little Missouri River.

Three sections of Illinois Bayou run through prime squirrel-hunting territory in the Ozark National Forest. A ten-mile float on the North Fork from Dry Creek put-in (Forest Road 1310) to the Forest Road 1001 takeout is delightful, with medium to difficult rapids, great scenery, a wonderful sense of solitude, and plenty of squirrels.

The Bayou's Middle Fork offers an exciting, two-mile float from the Snow Creek put-in (two miles up Forest Road 1312 off Arkansas Highway 27) to the Bayou Bluff Recreation Area just below the junction of the Middle and East Forks. This section is seldom far from roads, yet it also offers a sense of remoteness and some truly fine squirrel hunting.

When water is up, a good float also can be had on the East Fork. The twelve-mile journey from Forest Road 1301 to the Bayou Bluff campground is steep and wild, passing through the middle of the 10,700-acre East Fork Wilderness Area. This isn't a float for novices, but there are plenty of quiet pools for enjoying a fishing break and ample access for a hike-in squirrel hunt on the steep, oak- and hickory-covered hillsides.

The lower portion of the Little Missouri River from Arkansas Highway 84 west of Langley to the headwaters of Lake Greeson runs largely through timber company lands open to squirrel hunting. Beech and mulberry trees are abundant along this stretch, and when the trees are full of berries in spring or nuts in fall, it's possible to take a limit of squirrels from a single tree.

Floating conditions are best when one to two feet of water cover the old low-water bridge just below the Highway 84 bridge. This ten-mile stretch is interrupted more often by pools and is less difficult to run than the water above, but it's still recommended only for intermediate or better boaters. Take out at the Star of the West Use Area where the Little Missouri empties into Lake Greeson.

When float hunting, it's best to move along one bank or the other, taking advantage of overhanging cover and staying within shotgun range of the trees. Move slowly and stop when you get into a squirrelly-looking area. Occasionally it may be necessary to tie up and spend some time looking and listening.

If you float into a section of woods with an active squirrel population, don't hesitate to pull the canoe up on a gravel bar to do some old-fashioned stalking. But don't forget to tie your craft to something solid. Many floaters make a long hike out when the river steals their canoe.

Pardon the pun, but if you want to get in on the real "peak" hunting for Arkansas bushytails, head for the mountains. Squirrels are abundant, the scenery can't be beat, and the upcoming season could be the best we've had in years. Don't miss it.

WHITE-TAILED DEER

Wilderness Whitetails

Wilderness. For a small yet growing number of Arkansas deer hunters, this word means more than any other. It's a word that conjures visions of untamed lands where peace and solitude are a tangible part of the outdoor experience. It's a word that brings reminders of hiking and canoeing to backcountry camps, exploring vast tracts of unspoiled woodlands and hunting deer that seldom cross the path of man. As the bits and pieces of true wilderness continue to dwindle, more and more of us seek out the remaining remnants, looking for quarters where we can break from civilization and completely immerse ourselves in the ancient rhythms of nature.

Unfortunately, large swaths of unfettered backcountry are becoming scarce. What outdoorsman has not experienced the disappointment of returning to a favored hunting spot only to find it forever altered? Perhaps a "No Trespassing" sign has gone up, or land development is taking place. As our human population grows, such experiences increase, leading many of us to think that our children and grandchildren may be unable to enjoy wild lands isolated from development and exploitation.

To assure that wilderness areas are protected for future generations, Congress, in 1964, passed the Wilderness Act. In the act, wilderness is defined as "an area where the earth and its community of life are untrammeled by man, where man himself is a visitor who does not remain ... without permanent improvements or human habitation ... which generally appears to have been affected primarily by the forces of nature ... has outstanding opportunities for solitude ... has at least five thousand acres of land ... and may also contain ecological, geological and other features of scientific, educational, scenic, or historical value."

The number of designated wilderness areas continues to grow. When the Wilderness Act was first passed, fifty-four wilderness areas totaling about nine million acres were established throughout the country. Today, the National Wilderness Preservation System contains almost 106 million acres of designated wilderness at 644 locations.

Arkansas encompasses twelve wilderness areas covering more than 150,000 acres. Five of these areas are within Ouachita National Forest—

Roadless wilderness areas offer special rewards for the deer hunter.

Black Fork Mountain, 8,430 acres; Caney Creek, 14,460 acres; Dry Creek, 6,310 acres; Flatside, 9,507 acres; and Poteau Mountain, 11,299 acres. The Ozark National Forest contains five more wilderness areas—East Fork, 10,688 acres; Hurricane Creek, 15,427 acres; Leatherwood, 16,980 acres; and Upper Buffalo, 12,035. The state's largest wilderness, Buffalo National River, covers 34,933 acres and is managed by the National Park Service. Big Lake Wilderness in Big Lake National Wildlife Refuge is the smallest at 2,143 acres. It is managed by the U.S. Fish and Wildlife Service.

Management objectives for the wilderness system are drawn from the Wilderness Act. These objectives include to perpetuate for present and future generations a long-lasting system of high-quality wilderness that represents natural ecosystems; to provide opportunities for public use and enjoyment of the wilderness resource; to allow plants and animals indigenous to the area to develop through natural processes; to maintain watersheds and airsheds in a healthy condition; to protect endangered or threatened plant and animal species; and to maintain the primitive character of wilderness as a benchmark for ecological studies.

To hunt deer in a wilderness area is an experience like none other. But not all hunters are suited to it. Most are still inclined to enjoy their deer hunting in areas readily accessible by car, truck, or all-terrain vehicle. Modern comforts are a prerequisite for gratification, and camp would not be complete without a recreational vehicle or large tent, a four-burner stove, padded cots, lawn chairs, and other conveniences.

Today, however, hunting wilderness whitetails holds a special mystique for more than just a few deer hunters. Wilderness hunting seems to cast a spell on almost everyone who tries it, and even unsuccessful hunters treasure the special fascination of trekking through huge roadless tracts of land for white-tailed deer. They fully understand that chances of connecting on a big buck are slim at best, but they return year after year to give it their best.

Wilderness areas in Arkansas encompass thousands of acres of prime whitetail territory. These wild islands in the sea of civilization are remote enough to offer solace and solitude to hunters. They offer enough elbow room to isolate the visitor from the anxieties of modern life. On a wilderness trek, you can look over your shoulder to say good-bye to the world's troubles and turn around to welcome the womb of the backcountry.

Hunting wilderness whitetails isn't entirely carefree, though. These pristine tracts of land are open only to those willing to overcome the distance and rugged terrain with their nomad home on their back. Austerity is a prerequisite, for everything the hunter needs to survive and pursue his quarry must be packed in on foot or horseback. How far you penetrate the wilderness depends on how well you can carry and use your limited allotment of equipment. Wilderness deer hunting doesn't begin at dawn, break at noon, and end at dusk. It is a total sporting existence lasting every minute of every day and night spent in the wilds.

The U.S. Forest Service offers this reminder to wilderness explorers: "As a visitor to the wilderness areas, you should be aware that you are entering a primitive environment where you will be faced with the challenge of being entirely self-sufficient for whatever time you plan to remain there. There are no shelters, campgrounds, tables, fire grates, water spigots, or detailed trail signs. You will be either afoot or on horseback, because no motorized vehicles are permitted in these areas. You will meet and live with nature on its own terms, and become familiar with the sometimes scary feeling of being completely on your own far from the nearest trace of civilization. Even though trails in the wilderness are not marked, you will probably be able to locate and follow the most popular trails. A few trail signs, foot bridges and other basic facilities may exist, but only where they are essential for safety of the hiker or protection of the wilderness itself. Enjoy the wilderness areas. They are maintained so that they can be enjoyed for the next visitor, for many generations to come."

For most, the rewards of a wilderness hunting experience far exceed the investments. Bill Jones of North Little Rock, Arkansas, is one such hunter. During eleven years pursuing backcountry whitetails, he has visited five wilderness areas in the Arkansas mountains, backpacking in and camping for periods up to nine days. The allure of these natural sanctuaries keeps drawing him back.

"When I'm walking into a wilderness area, I can feel the stress draining away from me," Jones says. "You may spend a whole day and not ever see another individual. The only noise you hear, other than woodland sounds, might be the low drone of an airplane. It's quiet. You don't have someone ripping and roaring around in a vehicle. You don't have someone running a bunch of dogs through your place. If you run into someone, you know he's a real woodsman. The folks who are trigger happy, shooting at sounds, things like that, are left behind, because they won't get more than a hundred yards from the truck. You're able to regenerate your values, to contemplate the reason for your existence. It's almost a religious experience."

Preparedness, says Jones, is an important key to enjoying the wilderness experience. He notes that hunters should be in top physical condition and should be well versed in first aid, map and compass reading, outdoor cookery, and backpacking.

"You may be four miles or more from the nearest road," he says. "You've got to know your stuff. You can't just go in there and do it. There are no telephones, no vehicles, nobody to take care of you. So you must know all your camping skills and be able to take care of health and safety on your own. Getting lost is the most likely thing to happen, so be sure you're an accomplished map reader. Leave a map with family or friends so someone knows where you are and when you're expected to return."

"Prepare for the worst and hope for the best," is the motto of many wilderness hunters. You should take proper rain gear and survival gear. Even though you're in the South, weather can be severe at times. You might leave with the weather being good, then get into a full-blown thunderstorm. Prepare for those situations, and hope you never have to use some of your gear.

Hunters should be prepared in other ways, too. "My partner killed a nice deer," one wilderness visitor told me, "and we had to make two trips to pack it and our gear out of the wilderness area. We field-dressed the deer, quartered it and buried everything we weren't going to haul out. Then, after packing our gear out, we came back and packed out the deer quarters. Wilderness areas cover some rough terrain, and it will be tough going if you kill a deer."

The chances of bagging a sizeable whitetail are excellent on many Arkansas wilderness areas. Some hunters believe wilderness areas consist only of old growth or mature timber, not the kind of place for whitetail hunting. But most Arkansas wilderness areas aren't old growth. They have openings beneficial to deer, and hunting pressure is less on these sites than it is on more accessible areas. Bucks live longer, and you see bigger deer.

For some people, though, bagging a deer is secondary to the aesthetics of a wilderness hunt. "The group I go with has hunted on Arkansas's Leatherwood Wilderness Area for ten or eleven seasons, and we've only killed three deer," Bill Jones says. "But we keep going back because of the way it makes you feel. I realize once I'm out there how important my wife and my family are to me. In fact, I realize how important everything around me is. I think, what in the world would I do without modern rain gear? How do you suppose an Indian would have lived through that rainstorm in a buffalo robe? It puts things in perspective.

"As you get to the last night," Jones continues, "you sit around the campfire, and you know tomorrow you've got to load up and go back to the real world. It gets a little bit emotional sometimes, because you know you will not have this experience again. Each and every one of these trips is entirely, totally, one hundred percent different. And you realize this is something that's in your past now. It'll never happen again.

"You don't want to leave. You get everything gathered up, and you huff and puff and sweat as you carry your gear back to the vehicle. Then, when you get close to the road, you hear a car coming up. It kind of tightens you up just a little bit. It pulls your drawstring just a little bit tighter. And before you've even left, you're already thinking about the next trip."

Crossing the boundary from civilized living to true wilderness leaves an indelible mark upon the hunter's soul. Contentment never comes easy again. It exists only in the backwoods away from the tyranny of telephones, schedules, and pressing responsibility, in a place where the odds are real, and the necessities of life—shelter, food and drink—are no longer guaranteed.

Why wilderness? Writer/naturalist Sigurd Olsen summed it up in a voice that is still clearly heard. "Ask the men who have known it and who have made it part of their lives. They might not be able to explain, but your very question will kindle a light in eyes that have reflected the camp fires of a continent, eyes that have known the glory of dawns and sunsets and nights under the stars. Wilderness to them is real and this they do know; when the pressure becomes more than they can stand, somewhere back of beyond, where roads and steel and towns are still forgotten, they will find release."

Farmland Deer, Arkansas Style

It's late in the season. Frigid temperatures and dreary weather have set in, and you're just about ready to hang up your gun and bow for the season. You haven't yet bagged that trophy deer you've dreamed about all year, and the chances of a successful conclusion to the season are getting slimmer as each day rolls by. Right?

Well, just because the season is wearing down, you shouldn't throw in the towel yet. Many hunters mistakenly believe if they don't harvest a good buck during opening week, they might as well give up. Nothing could be farther from the truth. Your chances of a nice deer aren't much worse now than before. In fact, they could be better.

It's true most deer are taken during the first week of the season; most of these are quickly harvested because they're younger, less experienced animals. That's one reason why eight out of ten yearlings are bagged during the earliest part of the season.

Plenty of deer, including some big bucks, are still out there. They're smarter and much more difficult to bag, but as the season progresses, your chances of nailing a trophy buck actually increase, not decrease. You can be successful if you change your tactics to fit the behavior of late-season whitetails.

One important facet of late-season hunting is hunting the right area. Arkansas encompasses a lot of varied hunting terrain. You can hunt mountains or swamps, pine woods or oak/hickory forests, dry rocky slopes, or damp creek bottoms. All these areas have healthy populations of deer, but during the late part of the season, if it's big deer you're after, you'd be wise to hunt farmlands.

Why do agricultural lands rate higher than other habitats? Several reasons come to mind.

First, agricultural foods are very important in the deer's diet, especially during the hard months of winter. A study conducted along the Mississippi River found that five of the ten preferred deer foods were crops raised by farmers. These were winter wheat, corn, alfalfa, grass, and lespedeza.

George Hobson of Marion poses with the record whitetail he killed on a St. Francis County wheat farm in 1987.

Farm crops also have a relatively high protein content and tend to produce deer that are bigger, healthier, and fatter than woodland deer. A whitetail thriving on corn, soybeans, alfalfa and other farm crops can stay in good physical condition year-round. Woodland deer, on the other hand, may run into hard times, especially if the mast crop is poor.

In wooded areas, deer primarily rely on mast and browse for food. There are fluctuations in mast crops from year to year, and in some years, shortages of acorns and other important mast crops can force deer from their normal home range to areas where food is more plentiful. As often as not, deer move into winter wheat fields or other farmlands where food is plentiful. I once counted over one hundred deer on a forty-acre winter wheat field one January afternoon. Most of these exceptional gatherings take place—at least during daylight hours—toward the end of hunting season when fewer hunters are in the field.

Studies have found that deer concentrations can be up to ten times higher in the immediate vicinity of agricultural crops than in the more remote wooded areas. These same studies reveal that the deer disperse when the food is gone. But in many areas of Arkansas, winter wheat, waste grain, and other farm foods are available to deer throughout the season. In farming areas, deer may remain concentrated on agricultural lands well past the end of hunting season.

Some of Arkansas's all-time biggest bucks were taken in farm country:

- the George Hobson Buck, killed on a St. Francis County wheat farm, 1987, scored 208 5/8 points;
- the Clem Bilgisher Buck, picked up on a row-crop farm near Boydel, 1959, 206 1/8 points;
- the Roger Hansell Buck, killed on a farm in Arkansas County, 1992, 178 1/8 points;
- the Van Sturdivant Buck, killed on a Chicot County farm, 1951, 173 2/8 points;
- the Jimmy Brown Buck, killed adjacent a Chicot County wheat field, 1991, 173 2/8 points.

And many more. Another good reason to hunt farmlands.

FINDING A FARM TO HUNT

The largest deer are almost always farm-raised. That is, they live near farms and visit the farmer's fields. Quite often they join right in with the cows and feed alongside them. The sweeter the grass, the more they eat and the healthier they get.

Usually this doesn't bother the farmer too much, because there's plenty of grass to go around. But the deer don't stop there. Almost all other farm products appeal to deer. Soybeans and corn are big winners. Green vegetables are delights. Hay fields attract deer, as do patches of lespedeza and alfalfa. The *piece de resistance* is fruit. Peach, grape, and apple orchards may attract heavy concentrations of deer. Because damage caused by deer often is extensive and expensive, most farmers welcome hunters who exhibit responsible behavior.

When looking for farmland to hunt, check with your local wildlife officer. These professionals often know landowners who are experiencing serious crop damage caused by overabundant whitetails. On a farm I hunted in south Arkansas, the landowner showed me acres of freshly sprouted soybeans that had been nipped off close to the ground by feeding deer. Damage by deer was so great, the farmer received a deer depredation permit from the local wildlife officer that allowed him to shoot several deer to help minimize crop destruction. The owner, eager to reduce his financial losses, was more than happy to allow me to hunt deer on his land several days each season.

Orchard owners often experience similar problems. Deer can wipe out a grove of small fruit trees. Befriending farmers trying to reduce deer damage is one of the best ways to pinpoint farm-country whitetail hotspots.

ETIQUETTE IS IMPORTANT

Serious whitetail hunters know it's best to start the search for a hunting area well before the season. When seeking private lands hunting opportunities, don't drive up to the door on the first day and ask if you can hunt the woods behind a farmer's house. Visit the landowner well in advance of the season. Quite often, if you can prove you're a responsible hunter, you can get permission to hunt, perhaps even on land that is posted.

That visiting hunters should treat a farmer's property with respect goes without saying, but don't overlook other courtesies that will help assure you'll be welcomed back when hunting season rolls around again. Time and time again, I've heard farmers complain that hunters never think of them until deer season. A Christmas gift, birthday card, some flowers for the wife, a present for the kids, or an offer to help with farm work all do a great deal for cultivating good hunter-farmer relations.

Share your success with the farmer, too. Most landowners who welcome you on their property also take an interest in the hunt. Even if he doesn't want any of the venison (make sure to offer a share anyway), he's probably watched your deer while working his land. It's part of the farm, and sharing your success with the landowner makes him feel appreciated.

WHERE TO HUNT

Deer densities vary from region to region within Arkansas, and overall hunter success differs greatly depending on the particular area hunted. The amount of farmland and type of farmland also differ considerably.

The Delta Region in eastern Arkansas contains a higher percentage of farm acres than other regions of the state. Soybeans, corn, winter wheat, and other deer foods are abundant here, and a most larger Arkansas bucks killed during the last decade have come from this region.

Kenn Young and Dan Doughty, in their book *Monster Whitetails of Arkansas,* explain the link between Delta farmlands and big Natural State deer. "Much of this area is agricultural, so row crops provide ample food high in mineral content. If you were to look at the monster bucks killed nationwide during the past ten years (1985–1994), you would find more and more are coming from just such cropland areas. The reason is basic; the same minerals put into the soil to grow crops, and transferred to the plants, are the same ones that grow superior deer. Also, a majority of the land within the area consists of large farming operations. This means the land is private, and access is limited at best. While frustrating to hunters, it serves to give the resident bucks time to gain that part of the big buck equation most often missing: age. With that addition, all the factors in big buck production are present, and the delta becomes the one section of Arkansas where all the big buck equation elements (genetics, food and age) are most common."

Young and Doughty also note that "a plat map, good manners and planning ahead will still go a long ways toward finding you a place to hunt" in the Delta.

The rugged parts of the Ozark Mountains are ill-suited to row-crop farming. Fruits, particularly grapes and apples, are important in some areas, and pasture acreage usually exceeds cropland. In winter, deer depend heavily on acorns and other hard mast for food, but if nut crops are sub-par, they yard up on every small patch of farm food they can find. Successful hunters look for out-of-the-way food plots, corn fields, lespedeza patches, and other winter food sources where deer are likely to gather.

Woodlands are extensive and cropland limited in the Ouachita Mountain Region. A large portion of this region lies within the Ouachita National Forest or is owned by private timber interests. Much of the remaining land is in pasture, and hay is the major crop, followed by corn. A hunter who scouts and finds a small grain field or other bit of farmland can increase the odds for killing a nice animal.

The Arkansas River Valley supports a large agriculture industry. Soybeans, corn, winter wheat, oats, and other favored deer foods are abundant in the lower lands, and there is considerable emphasis on commercial, sometimes winter-grown, vegetables such as spinach and green beans in the western part of the region. There's excellent trophy deer potential on private farmlands within the region, and on Holla Bend National Wildlife Refuge near Russellville, 2,463 acres are planted in crops each year. Whitetails consume the farm foods produced and find refuge in the cover of bottomland woods. This area supports a thriving, healthy deer population.

The Gulf Coastal Plain in south Arkansas is known as the state's "deer factory." Overall deer numbers are far higher here than in other areas of the state, so if your focus is simply on killing a deer, any deer, then the Coastal Plain is where to go. An out-of-balance buck-doe ratio and widespread overpopulation lessens the chance of bagging a trophy here, but amidst the large commercial pine plantations are thousands of acres of farmland where deer are abundant.

HOW TO HUNT FARMLAND

In January, after the rut, bucks regain their strength by resting long hours and feeding on food sources convenient to their bedding areas. But winter is coming on, and the bucks feel the need to nourish themselves in preparation for the hard times ahead. Gradually, their daily routine shifts. They venture out farther and farther from their core areas in search of quality food. If preferred agricultural crops are in the area, most bucks eventually will end up feeding there.

In pressured areas, emphasis should be placed on hunting trails between bedding areas and crop fields. To determine the location of bedding areas, look for and follow well-used trails leading away from the perimeter of a crop field. It's best to enter these areas alone and quietly. When you begin to hit really dense cover, you're probably entering the bedding areas, especially if you jump some deer while scouting. It's not a good idea to push the deer because it might spook them from the area. So when you jump a deer, back up and leave.

How close you set up to a bedding area should be determined by when you'll be hunting. If you plan to hunt mornings only, stay close to the bedding area. That way you can catch deer when they're coming back from feeding areas. If you set up too close to feeding areas in the morning, you'll only see deer when it's too dark to shoot.

If you plan to hunt only in late afternoon, stay a little closer to the feeding areas. Don't hunt right on the edge of the field though, because you'll probably only see deer after shooting hours are over. Set up somewhere between the bedding and feeding areas, and you can catch the deer when they're coming out for their evening meal.

If, like many hunters, you prefer to hunt on the edge of a farm field rather than in the woods, select a spot for your stand that is near a main deer route to or from the field. Your first scouting trip around the edge of a grain or alfalfa field may reveal enough deer tracks to give you the shakes. But don't let this confuse you. Careful scouting will reveal a main route for entering and leaving the field.

It's also best to choose a stand offering good cover going to and from your vehicle, so farmland deer won't be as likely to notice your entry and exit.

Still-hunting also can be effective if conditions are right, but deer are spooky late in the season and difficult to sneak up on. Hunt to the last legal minute of the day and be in position in the morning before first light. Try to find bottlenecks or some physical feature that helps funnel a buck your way. Things are tough during the late season, so use every advantage you can.

When you do find an area to hunt, it's a mistake to think that taking farmland deer is easy. Whitetails haunting agricultural areas can be much harder to collect than their cousins in wilder territory. Nevertheless, hunters who invest heavily in preseason scouting to learn the day-to-day habits of their quarry can enjoy a bountiful harvest on these often overlooked deer lands.

Woodland hunting always will be the mainstay for most whitetail fans, but if you're seeking a new tack to spice up your outings this year, give farmland deer hunting a try. Prime farm country offers some of Arkansas's best hunting for big, healthy deer.

Hunting the Rut

The stories continued far into the night. The topic of discussion was the deer rut and the incredible behavior changes displayed by whitetail bucks during the rutting season.

"It was the damnedest thing I ever saw," said one hunter. "I was sitting on my stand and heard a noise off to my left. When I turned to look, there were six deer standing in the clearing. Five bucks were following a single doe. They were so spellbound by that doe in heat, they wouldn't have noticed the Wabash Cannonball coming through the woods.

"Weren't none of the bucks anything to brag about," he continued. "The biggest was only a six-point. But we needed meat for the freezer, so I decided I'd bag my limit if I could. I got lucky. Two shots, and two bucks fell."

The hunter continued. "The four deer that hadn't been shot trotted away when I fired. But before I'd left my stand, that doe and three bucks circled back and were standing out in the open, not twenty yards away. I couldn't believe it. Heck, one buck I'd shot was still kicking on the ground. The others were so desperate for female companionship, they were completely oblivious to the threat of death. It was like they'd never heard me fire my gun."

Certainly, this man's story illustrates an extreme example of a buck's oft-times erratic rutting behavior. But during that evening in deer camp, I heard many more astounding tales about rutting bucks. One hunter told of shooting a ten-pointer trailing a doe. To his surprise, another buck—an eight-pointer—appeared in the same spot seconds later. It, too, was killed, and as the hunter walked to his kill, another eight-pointer exited the woods from the same direction as the first two. Had the hunter been so inclined, he said, he could have bagged this deer as well.

I can't vouch for the authenticity of these two stories, but I've had my own weird encounters with rut-crazed whitetails. One incident occurred in east Arkansas on a cold December morning. I was walking to a photo blind at dawn when a doe bounced out of the timber into the field beside me. I stepped behind a tree and stopped to watch. She stopped twenty yards away and looked over her shoulder, training her ears behind her. She seemed totally unaware of my presence.

A ten-point buck now appeared, upper lip curled to catch the doe's scent. The doe wheeled away back into the woods. The buck turned, too, but remained in view. I slowly raised my camera. The buck, about thirty steps away, suddenly turned and faced me, only a small sapling between us.

Snorting and pawing the ground, the buck puzzled me out, then advanced. I suddenly realized the whitetail's spinal hair was erect and its ears laid back, signs I interpreted to mean battle stations. I placed a bigger tree between us and yelled "Scat!"

The buck's posture and expression reminded me of a drunk trying to force his alcohol-addled senses back to reality. But he didn't flee when I shouted. Instead, he approached even closer, eyeballed me very coolly, then much to my delight, he turned and walked away. Once, he looked back. His body language seemed to say, "Fellow, if it wouldn't keep this sweetheart waiting, I'd add injury to insult."

Again, this is an extreme example of erratic rutting season behavior. But it further illustrates the fact that a buck seeking a mate may undergo dramatic behavior changes, thereby increasing the hunter's chances of bagging a trophy. Rutting season is the one time a wise old buck is likely to slip up and give a hunter a shot at him.

Still, this vital period in a buck's life cycle continues to be shrouded in mystery and misunderstanding. Arkansas hunters talk about the rut all the time, but few really understand the biological processes involved—factors setting the rut in motion, the precise time of year this usually occurs, the effects changing environmental conditions have on the rut, and how the rut influences a buck's day-to-day movements.

Fewer still realize that much of this information might still be unknown were it not for Steve N. Wilson, former director of the Arkansas Game and Fish Commission. Wilson conducted detailed studies of the reproductive biology of Arkansas deer while a graduate student at the University of Arkansas in Fayetteville. The fact that he spent four years conducting field studies on deer reproduction qualifies him as an expert on rutting whitetails.

In an interview I conducted, Wilson was quick to point out that

knowledge of a rutting buck's day-to-day behavior is a distinct advantage in bringing home venison. He's convinced that bagging a deer, during the rut or otherwise, is a product of dedication, not chance, and the still-hunter in particular can benefit tremendously by studying buck behavior during the rut.

Wilson notes the best deer hunters he knows have a good understanding of whitetail behavior characteristics. "I'd guess three-fourths of Arkansas's deer hunters, maybe more, have no idea what's happening during the rut," he said. "They don't know what's going on between bucks and does, or more importantly, what's going on between bucks frequenting the same area.

"Many have no concept of home range, the distances deer travel and their activity areas," he continued. "They never ask themselves, 'What does a scrape mean in terms of all the other bucks in an area? What does it mean to that individual buck? Are there primary and secondary scrapes? How are they used, and how do they come into play?'

"An understanding of the basic biology of rutting deer," he says, "can make a man a much better hunter. It makes a difference in the deer hunter's attitude—his concept of success and anticipation. If he knows how deer react under a certain set of circumstances, then he's more willing to sit in a stand longer, and, consequently, his chances of success are far greater."

The first key to understanding rutting behavior is learning what factors set the rut in motion and the time of year this usually occurs. Many hunters have misconceptions about this. Some think the rut is brought on by changing weather. Others believe moon phases are responsible.

In reality, the rutting season is tied to photoperiodism, or light periods. The onset of the rut is determined by days getting shorter. Decreasing daylight signals the buck's glands to produce male hormones that initiate the breeding process. To a lesser extent, genetics and nutrition also influence the rut's progression.

Because day length shortens first in northern latitudes, the rut begins first in northern areas and progresses southward. This is borne

---

During rutting season, whitetail bucks throw caution to the wind, making them easier targets for savvy hunters.

out by the results of the four-year deer reproduction study published by Steve Wilson and his college professor, John Sealander, in 1971.

Wilson and Sealander's study centered on determining precise estimates of conception and fawning dates by analyzing reproductive systems of harvested does. In doing this, they determined mean conception dates for does in northern, central, and southern areas of Arkansas.

According to Wilson, the mean conception dates coincide with the peak of the rut in each region. Bearing that in mind, the Wilson/Sealander study determined November 13 was the peak of the rut in north Arkansas, which includes the Ozark Mountain region and the northern Delta region. The entire range of breeding (the earliest and latest conception dates) was October 21 to December 17.

The peak of the rut in the central area, primarily the Ouachita Mountains and the central Delta area, occurred on December 9, almost four weeks later than in the northern area. Bucks in this area were breeding does from November 2 to January 1.

In the Gulf Coastal Plain and Delta of south Arkansas, findings were similar to those for the central area. The rut peaked on December 5, but conception dates ranged from October 25 to February 6.

A key point more observant hunters already have noticed is that the actual breeding period increases from north to south. Breeding occurs for at least a fifty-seven-day period in the north, sixty days in central Arkansas, and seventy-three days in the south. On a broader scale, this is further demonstrated in studies that have shown the rut in Michigan, far to the north, occurs mostly in a 14-day period. In southern Florida, deer may breed year-round.

Add to this the fact that bucks are in the rut four to six weeks before they actually begin courting receptive does, and for a similar period after the actual breeding season, and you can see that the actual rut extends over an even greater time period.

Wilson mentions that the results of his deer reproduction study were important to game managers in setting proper season dates. "I think the most significant thing our study determined," he noted, "was that the Arkansas Game and Fish Commission was, and still is, setting deer seasons to coincide with rutting season when hunters have the best chance of success."

Although rutting dates given are probably typical for an "average" year in Arkansas, factors such as weather can influence the amount of rutting activity. For instance, Wilson reports that when bucks are fully in the rut, a cold snap can trigger increased buck activity. Likewise, a period of unseasonably warm weather can bring rutting behavior to a near standstill.

Many hunters believe that rutting bucks are constantly moving, often traveling many miles in pursuit of receptive does and often leaving their normal home range. Thus, these folks believe it's impossible to hunt a particular buck during the rut—a trophy deer for instance—because he won't be using just one certain area.

It's true bucks exhibit an increase in activity during the rut. Bedding becomes less frequent and occurs only for brief periods. Yet while a buck may be constantly moving, his movement is typically confined to the territory he's established as his home range.

A whitetail tends to use the same range for all its activities year after year. And his range usually is smaller than most hunters believe. Studies show most bucks spend their entire lives within an area less than a thousand acres in size, usually one hundred fifty to five hundred acres.

In areas such as Arkansas's Coastal Plain region where deer densities are high, home ranges generally are smaller than in other areas. Where populations are lower, in the Ozarks for instance, home range size increases.

What does this mean for the hunter? For those hunting high deer-density areas, chances of bagging a rutting buck are probably greater because that deer will be visiting the same area more often due to the smaller size of his home range. Of course, whether or not you shoot one depends on your discovery of the area he's most likely to visit on a regular basis. In the case of a rutting buck, this usually is a scrape.

Scrapes are circular ground clearings, one to three feet in diameter, that a buck uses to inform a doe he's available. Usually a buck makes several scrapes in his territory. He paws away all ground covering, urinates on the spot, and chews the branch that typically overhangs the spot. He then rubs his face against the branch to impart scent from his head glands there.

Look for scrapes in or near established trails, particularly along ridgetops, logging roads, flats along streams, and adjacent woodland fences. In any such location, a line of frayed rubbing trees is a clue not only to a buck's whereabouts but also to the whereabouts of his scrapes.

Often found just a few feet from a scrape, a rubbing tree, or just "rub," is a small sapling used by a buck to polish his antlers and scent-mark his home range. The bark usually is scarred along a section one to four feet from the ground. The greatest concentration of rubs is made where a buck's private trail meets the main trail used by several deer. Usually, the larger the rubbing tree is in diameter, the larger the buck that made it.

Some rubs rarely are used, so try to make your stand downwind from a rub and scrape close together, an almost sure indication a buck will revisit the site. Hunt only fresh scrapes, those still damp, musky, and free of forest litter.

Unless he's been shot, a buck generally will return to his scrape at least once daily. But exactly when and how often he'll show up is unpredictable. After dark is his favorite time, but it's not uncommon for a buck to make his rounds at dawn, dusk, or even midday hours. So be on your stand early, and stay there throughout the day. The key to success is patience and a thorough understanding of what the deer is likely to do.

Remember that success comes to those who work hardest. Like Steve Wilson says, bagging a deer is a product of dedication, not chance. Thus it doesn't usually bestow itself on those who merely wish for it.

If you want to bag a nice deer this season, learn the habits of the game you seek. That's the foundation essential to consistent deer hunting success. Do your homework, and the rutting season could be the time you finally bag that buck of a lifetime.

Big Bucks on "The Refuge"

They were a trio any deer hunter would have traded his favorite gun to see just once: three massive bucks with record-book racks thicker than an ax handle at the base. They sported beams that swept wide above the ears then curved back upward to heavy, white points gleaming in the afternoon sun.

Feeding with the impressive trio was the biggest flock of wild turkeys I had ever seen. Thirty-eight birds in all, including six gobblers with lengthy beards. That sight is forever etched upon my mind.

I have visited White River National Wildlife Refuge every winter since 1976, and on every trip I've made during those twenty-five years, I've seen at least one, and as many as fifty, nice white-tailed deer bucks. In 1977, it was a heavy-beamed eight-pointer that walked within ten feet of me. In 1979, I tallied twelve bucks with eight-point racks or better before noon. One was a twelve-point, a once-in-a-lifetime wallhanger with long, high tines and massive antlers that, on a side view, appeared to extend beyond the end of his nose.

Nineteen eighty-seven was the year friends and I watched a monstrous ten-point buck parade across a levee a quarter mile away. This was, we agreed, an animal that exceeded three hundred pounds. The next year brought more thrills as we counted over one hundred whitetails feeding in a single field during a period of high water. Within that group, we used a spotting scope to pick out no fewer than eight bucks from six to ten points each. All were huge, healthy animals.

I know White River has more than its share of wallhanger whitetails because I've seen them with my own eyes. If I draw a hunting permit this year, I'll be back again to hunt them, as I have for many years. Like the hundreds of other hunters who visit each year, I'm lured by the promise of a truly trophy whitetail—something a cut above the average "nice" rack. I know there are darn few places in Arkansas where I have as good a chance to find one.

White River National Wildlife Refuge lies within Desha, Monroe, Phillips and Arkansas Counties in southeast Arkansas, above the confluence of the Mississippi and White Rivers. The area is administered by the U.S. Fish and Wildlife Service, having been established in 1935,

primarily for the preservation of waterfowl habitat. The refuge ranges from two and a half to six miles wide and extends along the lower White River for about ninety miles. More than 350 natural lakes punctuate a bottomland landscape interlaced with bayous, chutes, and channels that connect with the river. During high-water years, well over half of the refuge may be covered by river overflows.

The 160,000 acres making up White River National Wildlife Refuge offer an ideal breeding ground for big buck deer. Around 154,000 of those acres are covered by hardwood timber—bitter and sweet pecan; overcup, red and willow oaks; ash, maple, elm, sycamore, sweet gum; and others. Through an active timber management program, inferior trees are removed, and growth of good mast-producing species is accelerated. This also allows sunlight to come through in abundance. The bare soil exposed by logging is a receptive seed bed, and grasses and woody plants grow to form a dense understory, providing food and cover for deer. Lakes, sloughs, and streams winding through the tall timber combine with adjacent farms to produce critical "edge" habitat favorable to whitetails.

All this makes the big bucks grow fat and healthy, and today, White River National Wildlife Refuge supports a thriving, healthy deer population that is closely monitored and hunted accordingly.

White River has quite a reputation for big deer. The area has consistently yielded quality deer for several decades now, and it's not uncommon to find young bucks with out-sized racks. This is due, in large part, to the excellent habitat produced by the region's rich soil. In addition, the refuge carries fewer deer per square mile than other parts of south and southeast Arkansas, hunter numbers are closely regulated, and the terrain is somewhat difficult to hunt, facts that allow some bucks to age enough to reach their full potential.

The trained professionals on the refuge staff have played an extremely important role in producing a quality deer herd. There are few other places in Arkansas where the principles of sound deer management are followed more intensively. Comprehensive data collected on each year's harvest provide invaluable information on sex ratios, age

---

A fertile environment and good deer management combine to produce huge bucks on White River National Wildlife Refuge.

structure, and growth rates of the herd. Those data are studied each year and provide the basis for setting season dates and hunting regulations for the refuge.

All things considered, Arkansas deer hunters are extremely fortunate to have White River National Wildlife Refuge in their midst. Few places in the nation offer the kind of quality deer hunting available here. And with the continued concern for proper wildlife management on the part of refuge personnel, the fertile bottomlands along the White River should continue to produce some of Arkansas's biggest whitetail bucks for many generations to come.

Hunting the Legendary Razorback

Besides being the mascot of the University of Arkansas football team and the unofficial symbol of Arkansas, the razorback hog has long been considered a sporty hunting adversary. Perhaps the hunting of these fierce animals, a pastime with deep roots in our history, convinced Arkansans the razorback was a fitting symbol. Consider this "Graphic Description of a Hog Hunt Through Rough Forests" taken from the July 30, 1887, edition of the *Arkansas Gazette*.

> Perhaps the most exciting sport in this country is hunting the wild hog.
>
> These beasts no more resemble the stately porkers of the north than a wild Indian resembles an alderman. With their long, lean black bodies, their horrible heads and curved tusks they are about as ugly as the boars which tear the dogs in Rubens' pictures. Panthers run from them, and hunters, daring to attack the wounded hogs on foot, have been killed by them. Indeed, the planter himself once had a narrow escape. He had shot a boar which his dogs had caught, and dying though the creature was, he was tearing the dogs to pieces. The planter jumped to the ground, and stabbed the boar. The boar turned on him and he is not likely to be nearer death until the hour he dies. "Just then," he said, "I saw V——'s horse's head. He had his gun up but he was afraid to fire for fear of hitting me. I tell you I yelled for him to fire. 'I'm gone if you don't,' says I. So he fired and the old fellow rolled over."
>
> On the hunt which we attended a boar charged on one of the horses with such impetus that he brought the horse to his knees; in that position the rider shot the boar dead. Capture these beasts, and they will not make a sound, only gnash their teeth and die fighting.

According to the unidentified writer, the hogs were hunted in bottomland canebrakes. Each hunter rode a horse, so they might keep up with the dogs as they chased the quarry, and stay above reach of their

---

A razorback tusker like this is perhaps the most appropriate of all trophies for the Arkansas hunter.

savage quarry. The writer then describes at length his first hog hunt, which he says he was "not likely to forget . . ."

> The dogs ranged ahead and soon they had started the boars in half a dozen different directions . . . the planter spurred old whitey on and he kept the lead. A rattling volley of barks pierced by a howl. "The hog's at bay," said the planter; "he's killing the dogs."
>
> A strange noise like castanets clashes through the medley of barks and yelps; it is the boar gnashing his teeth.
>
> In a second we are on him, a huge monster in the trampled space, tossing the dogs right and left on his tusks, cutting them horribly. The planter lifts his gun . . .
>
> All at once we see a dog sprawling in the air and the old white horse rears, nearly unseating the planter. The planter springs off and fires in the cane. A horrible black head bounds up and falls over, shot so truly that it doesn't stir.
>
> The rest of the day was only repetition . . . To feel once more that fresh wild thrill I'd give—but who can live life over.

I remember well the first wild hog I ever saw. It was in the bed of a pickup truck driven by an old man named Jahu Todd. Mr. Todd was an expert hunter, and while pursuing whitetails in the Ozarks, he had killed this huge boar, which weighed in the neighborhood of five hundred pounds. It was an imposing beast, impressive in size and features. Although massive, it was muscular and lean-looking, low at the flanks and higher at the shoulders. The head was as big as a whiskey keg, and its long wrinkled snout was still covered with dirt from rooting in the woods. It was covered from head to hocks with dense, wiry, black hair, which was longest and thickest along the spine. Looking upon that sharp, thin mane, I could perceive first-hand how Arkansas's legendary razorbacks earned their name.

The beast's most impressive features were its tusks, or "tushes" as Mr. Todd and my friends called them. The two largest pushed back the lips and swept upward in almost circular fashion to a point above the snout. Each was as big around as a man's thumb, and about six or eight inches long. I remember running a finger along the outer edges, which proved to be sharp as knives. Two smaller tusks grew above these, their purpose being to safeguard and sharpen the lower set, those honed bottom tusks being the instruments a boar employs to deal with the world.

With one quick swipe, he can disembowel a dog, and enough hunters have received severe lacerations in hog attacks to prove their danger to humans to well.

A more wicked set of dentures I have never seen.

One estimate from the Arkansas Game and Fish Commission places indicates there are fifty thousand to seventy thousand feral hogs in the state today. Most are descendants of domestic hogs that escaped or were turned out to range freely generations ago. In decades past, folks often released pigs to feed off the forest. The razorbacks had the run of the woods most of the year and got fat on mast. In autumn, they were penned and fed corn to sweeten the meat. When winter came, they were butchered to furnish an ample supply of ham, shoulders, middlings, sausage, and lard to run the family until the next hog-killing time.

This was a good system for many years, but with changing farm practices, fence laws were enacted forcing owners to keep their livestock under control. There was no way to capture all the free-ranging hogs, however, and many adapted to life in the wild.

Feral hogs now inhabit fifty-two of the state's seventy-five counties. Most are in south Arkansas. (Ironically, feral hogs do not inhabit Washington County, the home of the University of Arkansas Razorbacks.)

These thousands of rooting hogs cause many problems. They destroy terrestrial and aquatic vegetation, ruin water holes used by other wildlife, and destroy nests of ground-nesting birds. Acorns, an important food for many species of native wildlife, compose a significant portion of their diet. Feral hogs often damage row crops, and frequently carry diseases, such as brucellosis and trichinosis, which can be transmitted to domestic stock and even humans.

Despite the many problems caused by feral hogs, it was against Arkansas law to hunt stray or free-roaming hogs until recent years. A law passed in the 1840s, which remained in effect until 1999, said, "no person shall use, work, or exercise any acts of ownership over any animal taken up by him until he shall give notice thereof to the county clerk." (The person capturing the animal could, however, "ride the animal to the county court for the purpose of giving notice to the clerk.") If the clerk found marks or brands upon the animal, he examined the State Brand Book to determine the owner, and the impounder had to notify the owner of having "taken up" the animal. If no marks of ownership were found, the hog would be displayed on the courthouse lawn for up to thirty days to let the landowner claim it. If no one claimed ownership, then the hog could be turned over to the finder.

Violation of this law was considered theft of property, a Class D felony. And sometimes those who violated it were shot by angry livestock owners. Cleveland County municipal judge Sanford Beshear Jr., in a 1989 letter to the Game and Fish Commission, noted "As recently as 1974, people have been shot in Cleveland County for shooting the hogs of another."

In order to resolve such problems and help rid Arkansas of these destructive animals, the state formed the Feral Hog Task Force in the late 1990s, a group consisting of twenty-three government organizations and private corporations. As a result of their efforts, a law was enacted by the legislature in 1999 that makes it easier to hunt these beasts. That law takes away the presumption that a wild hog has an owner, and defines a feral hog as one roaming on property without the landowner's permission. The law didn't create a hog-hunting season but allows hunting for them year-round on private property (with legal access and landowner permission) and allows their hunting on public lands during other game seasons if the weapon used is legal for the season open at the time.

The 1999 law also makes it illegal to release hogs on public land. This practice has become increasingly troublesome as the popularity of hog hunting has grown in recent years.

Someone once said that hunting bears with a willow switch is a lot like hunting razorbacks, regardless of the method. "Only a damn fool without a lick of sense would do either." But if you're still determined to bag a wild hog, here are some tips to help you achieve that goal.

Good hog-hunting locales can be difficult to pinpoint. A classified newspaper ad and phone calls to state and county officials often will lead to landowners eager to rid their property of destructive hogs. Visiting with managers of wildlife management areas and national wildlife refuges may produce similar results.

On-the-ground scouting also helps you zero in on hogs. Turned earth and leaves where hogs have been rooting for food are the most obvious sign of activity. Look, too, for tracks and trails. Hog tracks are similar to deer tracks but more rounded. Their trails often form tunnels in thick underbrush. Bedding areas range from elaborate grass nests built by sows to raise their young to simple depressions dug in the ground, usually surrounded by brush or a fallen tree. During cold weather, beds tend to be on south-facing slopes.

Wallowing areas also may be found on scouting forays. Hogs wallow in mud to cool themselves and rid their bodies of insects. Their wallows usually are by seeps and springs or around lakes, ponds, and sloughs. After wallowing, a hog rubs itself on nearby trees, leaving more clues to its presence. You can determine the hog's size by how high off the ground the mud is.

Listening for hogs just before daylight, as one might listen for a gobbling spring turkey, can help in pinpointing your quarry. Hogs are noisy when feeding, and you often can hear their squealing and grunting. Many still hunters employ this method, moving close to hogs prior to daylight.

If you become a hard-core hog hunter, you will discover you must try every legal and fair-chase means at hand because you never know what will work next, or at what precise moment a razorback will decide to do . . . *God-knows-what.*

We do know wild hogs are tough, and a high-powered gun, .270 or larger, is recommended for killing them. Adults average one hundred to two hundred pounds, and have been known to exceed five hundred, so sheer size dictates a big firearm. Also, under the hide of older boars is an inch-thick "shield" of keratin, the stuff of hooves and horns. It extends on either side of him from his shoulders to his last ribs, and shields his vital organs from the tusks of other boars when he fights. It is said this shield is strong enough to stop not only tusks, but light bullets or arrows as well. Try plugging a boar with the wrong firearm, and you may do nothing more than anger him, and wind up ground to sausage in the process.

Hogs have a keen sense of smell. Hearing is their next defense, but this sense isn't as sharp as a deer's. Hogs have poor eyesight. By staying downwind and moving slowly, you sometimes can stalk within close range of hogs when pursuing them on foot.

Among the best hunting locales are densely vegetated wet areas. Hogs move out of bedding areas in thickets during late afternoon or at night to feed. Using corn for bait is an effective way to take them. Stand hunting in feeding areas near dawn and dusk also works well if hogs haven't been overly disturbed.

Conducting a walking drive is another way to hunt razorbacks. The key, as in any drive, is using the terrain to your advantage so the hogs only have a single escape route. Drivers walk through an area where hogs are bedding, creating noises to spook the hogs ahead of them. Shooters position themselves along the escape route. To be safe and effective, an in-depth planning session should be conducted prior to the drive to explain safety precautions and the positioning of shooters and drivers.

Although wild hogs are shy and secretive by nature, never forget they can be unpredictable and dangerous if cornered or crowded. They're incredibly quick—nothing "lumbering" about them in any respect—and they can be on you with amazing speed. In a fracas, they're living buzz saws, slashing man or beast with their meat-hook tusks. As one hunter put it, when you hunt hogs "you better wear your tree-climbing britches." Always keep your distance, and if you believe you've killed one, make absolutely sure by putting an "insurance round" through the head.

In many respects, Arkansas's wild hogs live up to the razorback's legendary status. They're intelligent, hardy, ferocious animals, and there's just *something* about hunting them, something that draws out the daredevil in hunters. They are, certainly, a fitting symbol for our state.

On Being a Turkey Hunter

My good friend Jim Spencer, a turkey hunting addict, once wrote, "Where turkey hunting is concerned, there are no lukewarm feelings. Either you is or you ain't."

Unfortunately for those of you who *is,* I *ain't,* which accounts for the paltry number of chapters in this book that are devoted to turkey hunting.

I have hunted Arkansas's wild turkeys on numerous occasions. One day, I even managed to kill one—a fall bird called into range by my buddy Jim. I even have, by myself, called a wild turkey into shooting range. It was a huge gobbler, strutting and drumming in all his spring glory, with a beard that must have been ten inches long. I admit I had an adrenaline rush as I worked that bird, and the moment might have been even more exciting had I been carrying a gun and been able to shoot that big tom. But I wasn't, and I didn't. I was just out for a walk in the woods, and had stuck a diaphragm caller in my pocket in case I heard a bird gobbling.

I can't totally explain my lack of enthusiasm for turkey hunting, but I think it springs largely from my penchant for more action-oriented hunts. I love hunting rabbits with beagles because there are lots of chases, lots of shooting, and you're allowed to talk. I like duck hunting because I can watch the birds as they work to the callers, there's usually lots of shooting, and when the ducks aren't working, you're allowed to talk. I like hunting woodcocks and chasing squirrels with hounds because there's usually lots of shooting and you're allowed to talk *all* the time.

Come to think of it, maybe I don't care for turkey hunting because you have to sit and be quiet; no talking allowed. And if you fire no more than a single shot, you can still say you've had a good day.

Jim Spencer says I'm simply sick. "You must be," he says, "to have gone turkey hunting as often as you have without being bitten by the bug." Yet Spencer admits that turkey hunting fever is an illness in itself. "The disease isn't fatal," he once wrote, "but it's seasonally debilitating . . . The only cure is prowling through mountains, swamps or piney woods

---

Success rarely comes easy for those who pursue the wild turkey.

during spring, eyes burning from lack of sleep, searching for a bird whose call sounds like a cross between a mugging and a train wreck. And when you find him, you then don't know how to deal with him."

He's right, of course. And reading those words, I am quite happy to remain unafflicted.

Now, all that being said, I hope you won't let my feelings keep you from going turkey hunting. If you're already a turkey hunter, you won't give a tinker's hoot what I have to say anyway. But if you're not turkey hunting yet, if you're still considering whether or not to give it a try, then remember, either you is a turkey hunter or you ain't, and you won't know for sure until you've tried. I am terribly unqualified to tell you how to do it, so instead, I will share some words of wisdom from fellow scribes who are infinitely more qualified to give you advice.

To begin, you should know exactly what you're getting into. Jim Miller, a wildlife specialist with the University of Arkansas Extension Service, put it bluntly in "Spring Sickness" published in the winter 1977 edition of *Arkansas Game and Fish Magazine.*

"Regarding the hunting of wild turkeys," he wrote, "it is probably the most physically demanding type of hunting available in Arkansas. To be successful, it requires being in the woods near good roosting areas at least thirty minutes before daylight, extensive foot travel to locate and to hunt the bird, calling throughout the day, and staying in the woods after dark in an attempt to hear birds fly or gobble to help select a good location for the next day's hunt."

Miller then lists six paths to success.

> 1. Do as much scouting as possible prior to opening day, especially listening for gobbling early in the morning.
> 2. Become a good hunter; know how to look for signs such as scratching, dust, tracks, etc.
> 3. Become confident in your calling ability. Listen to turkeys, records or tapes if you're not familiar.
> 4. Utilize camouflage clothing, including face mask and gloves.
> 5. Learn patience and when or how much to call.
> 6. Know how far your gun will effectively provide the dense pattern of shot necessary to cover the head and neck of a turkey.

"...most turkey hunters learn something every time they go hunting," he continues, "and the honest ones will admit to being unsuccessful on many hunts."

Gregg Patterson, another of my friends, and another excellent writer on the sport of turkey hunting, says that persistence is the successful turkey hunter's main weapon. ("Not for the Faint of Heart," *Arkansas Game and Fish Magazine,* March/April 1986).

"A dogged stubbornness to remain in the field and seriously scout and hunt, even when the weather, time of day and lack of visible or audible birds are seemingly against him, is an irreplaceable attribute," he wrote. "Turkeys have been, and will continue to be, called in and taken by the persistent hunter in rain, on windy days and in the middle of the day."

Patterson also notes that, "There's no substitute for the turkey hunter who can react to the hunting situation each bird presents. This type of hunting demands that the hunter possess a thorough knowledge of the wild turkey's habits and idiosyncrasies. The old 'sit under a tree, call a few times, and stay absolutely still' advice, more times than not, will make for a disappointed turkey hunter. Each turkey dictates what the hunter should do. The alert hunter keys in on what the bird is doing and then decides what strategy to take."

Jim Spencer gives some of the best turkey hunting pointers I've seen in "Words of Wisdom on a Grand Spring Sport" (*Arkansas Wildlife,* spring 1997). In this light-hearted look at the sport, he shares "some of the pitifully few things I've learned" while participating in this "confusing, frustrating, aggravating game." He gracefully consented to let me share some of these tidbits of wisdom here again.

> If you "roost" a turkey (that is, hear him fly up and/or gobble late in the afternoon on the day before you're planning to hunt), he will either change locations, develop lockjaw or be killed by a bobcat during the night.
>
> Never hunt within hearing distance of a stream you're not willing to wade or swim, unless you're heavily into beating yourself on the head with sticks and other forms of masochism. When you hunt close to one of these unwadable streams, every gobbler you hear will be on the other side, and there won't be a boat within five miles.
>
> The frequency of a turkey's gobbling is directly proportional to the number of competing hunters within range of his voice. Stated another way: if you are the only hunter within five miles of a turkey, he won't make a peep. If there are fifteen other eager

hunters on the same mountain with you and the bird, he'll gobble with every breath.

A turkey possesses the ability to see up, down and behind himself, all at the same time. It is a fallacy, however, that turkeys can see through rocks. Only Superman can do that. Instead, turkeys see around them.

Turkeys cannot hear your heart beating at forty yards, as some hunters claim. That's ridiculous; no bird can hear that well. Instead, they feel the pressure waves your pulse sends through the air.

Turkeys are allergic to many things, among the most noticeable of which are: movement; the sound of twigs breaking underfoot; shiny objects such as glasses or noses or the bead on the end of your gun barrel; and any object in their home range which has not been in the same spot for at least three years.

If there are three possible directions from which a turkey can approach your calling, and two of them afford good visibility, the turkey will always come in via the third route. That is, if he comes at all, which is highly unlikely.

Turkeys have the ability to turn invisible at will. How they achieve this I can't say, but I know it to be true. They vanish on me all the time.

Calling turkey gobblers is very simple; any cretin can do it. Making them come to the calling is what's hard.

There are five basic calls from which to choose: yelp, cluck, purr, cutt and cackle. All are equally effective in making a gobbler go the other way.

When you do succeed in calling a gobbler within gun range, nine times out of 10 he will (a) come up directly behind you and gobble in your ear, (b) come into view while your gun is still in your lap, (c) let you get your gun to your shoulder and then come into view 90 degrees away from where it's pointing, or (d) stay just out of sight under the crest of a hill and gobble and drum until some other hunter comes along and kills him or scares him away.

"We could go on and on with this," Spencer says. "My wisdom on the subject of turkeys is bottomless. But I don't want to tell you everything there is to know and thereby wreck your enjoyment of the sport.

"There are things a turkey hunter ought to learn on his own."

For advice on where to hunt wild turkeys in Arkansas, I've turned once again to Jim Spencer, who offered these suggestions:

Piney Creeks Wildlife Management Area. "This big, rugged area offers 180,000 acres to bump around in, most of it excellent turkey habitat."

Gene Rush Wildlife Management Area. "This area covers a little over 18,000 acres, encompassing some of the toughest, most beautiful country in the Ozarks. Ditto some of the best turkey hunting in the state, particularly on the north side of the area where the land starts falling away toward the Buffalo River."

White Rock Wildlife Management Area. This area, covers 280,000 acres of Ozark National Forest north of Ozark on both sides of the Pig Trail. It's as rugged as Piney Creeks and Gene Rush, but White Rock's mountains have better-defined benches, and getting around in this area is a little more manageable."

Sylamore Wildlife Management Area. "Occupying parts of Marion, Baxter, Searcy and Stone Counties, Sylamore's hills and hollows serve as home to a turkey population that's healthy and growing. With 150,000 acres of hunting available, Sylamore also offers a hunter the chance to find a place to call his own."

Mount Magazine Wildlife Management Area. "Rising improbably out of the Arkansas River Valley south of Clarksville, Mount Magazine and its three associated smaller mountains (Chickalah, Rich, and Huckleberry) form the highest land mass in the state. This 100,000 acres of public land also provides good habitat for a thriving turkey population. Again, we're talking about rough country here. But there are enough birds to make it worthwhile."

Holla Bend National Wildlife Refuge. "This 8,000-acre national wildlife refuge lies inside an old cut-off of the Arkansas River east of Dardanelle. It hosts a healthy turkey population and is open to archery hunting only. If you want to take a gobbler with a bow, this is probably the best place in the state to try your luck."

Muddy Creek Wildlife Management Area. "Because of its long-time reputation as the state's premier turkey hunting spot, this 146,000-acre area still catches a lot of hunting pressure. However, the pressure is probably lighter than twenty years ago. And now that the turkeys have made a comeback, it's a good bet for a hunt."

Winona Wildlife Management Area. "Because it's only thirty miles west of Little Rock, Winona catches more hunting pressure than Muddy

Creek. However, most of that pressure is on the east side of the 160,000-acre area, and hunters willing to drive clear around or through to the west side can still find fairly uncrowded hunting. There are plenty of turkeys to hunt, too."

Caney Creek Wildlife Management Area. "Caney Creek's birds aren't as numerous as Muddy Creek's or Winona's. Fortunately, there's not as much hunting pressure on this area as on the other two, so a hunter can usually find a bird to call his own somewhere on these 85,000 acres."

St. Francis Forest Wildlife Management Area. "At 21,000 acres, St. Francis is by far the smallest of the Forest Service wildlife management areas in the state. But don't let that dissuade you. The past several years have produced excellent hatches along Crowley's Ridge, and there are more birds in St. Francis Forest than anytime in the past decade."

In closing, I will leave you with the words of John Madson, a man whose writing I much admire. Prior to Madson's death a few years back, he often hunted spring turkeys in an Ozark Mountains camp with Jim Spencer and other wild turkey fanatics. Jim speaks fondly of Madson and the days he spent with him, and in 1994, Jim encouraged me to purchase a story Madson had written, and publish it in *Arkansas Wildlife*. That piece, "America's Big-Game Bird: An Historical Perspective," deserves a special place in the literature of turkey hunting.

I think Jim would agree that these three paragraphs from Madson's article are a fitting end to this chapter.

> Only in North America do certain camouflaged eccentrics sneak into the spring woods, bleary of eye and high of hope, to imitate the come-hither calls of a hen turkey. If all goes well, a lusty tom responds—gobbling, tail fanned, wingtips brushing the ground, the naked skin of his head and neck shifting from red to blue to white. About as often as not, however, His Royal Pomposity will 'hang up' just beyond gun range, strutting and gobbling and looking, as one hunter put it, 'Like a VW car with both doors hangin' open.'
>
> Something usually goes wrong. Some detail, some flaw in camouflage or position or timing, is perceived by the keenest eyes and most suspicious nature in the timber. The gobbling ends. There may be a sharp *pert!*, a sound of running, then nothing. Might as well pick up and move on.

No matter. Slaying a gobbler isn't the only reason for going into the spring turkey woods before first light. Being there at the very beginning of a spring morning is enough. I will never forget the turkeys I have talked with, but just as unforgettable is the strange luminous quality of dogwood blossoms in false dawn, and the cardinal flowers and little wild irises growing along Ozark creek branches.

Good luck on your hunt. I hope you discover you *is* a turkey hunter.

The Rabbit Man

In most respects, he was an uncommonly common man. But in the few short seasons I hunted with him, I found in the Rabbit Man a depth of character as rare and priceless as the most precious jewels.

I met him in the winter of 1987. "Let's get together this weekend and go rabbit hunting," my friend Lewis said. "One of my clients invited us. Sounds like he has some pretty good dogs. Says they had a real good hunt just a couple days ago."

And so it was that two days later, in the parking lot at his downtown office, Lewis introduced us, the Rabbit Man and me.

I knew from the start there was nothing pretentious about him. "Nice meetin' ya," he said extending a callused hand. "Now if we're done with the pleasantries, maybe we can get on about doing some huntin'."

Crotchety old cuss, I thought to myself. And, indeed, that morning, the Rabbit Man looked the part. He smiled very little, and his furrowed face was roughened by a three-day stubble of beard. He was a big man, but he looked haggard and old for his sixty-five years, like the pictures you see of old-timey farmers who lost it all in the Dust Bowl.

He dressed in typical hunter's garb—a plaid flannel shirt, brushbuster breeches with a swath of vinyl across the front of each leg, red suspenders where he hitched his thumbs, a camo hunting cap, a canvas coat, and rubber knee boots. A shiny, black-and-white animal horn with a pewter mouthpiece dangled from a piece of twine slung over one shoulder— a come-hither signal for his dogs. Encircling his right wrist was a copper bracelet, an amulet, he said, to ward off the arthritis that riddled his bones.

The picture stuck with me as we followed his pickup, driving to the bottoms. What makes this man tick? I wondered. Why did he invite us here?

Not far from the town of Colt, which is hard to find on most maps, a gravel road cuts into the middle reaches of the L'Anguille River, an

---

The Rabbit Man, Hugh "Ed" Middleton.

ancient stream that writhes across the east Arkansas delta like its namesake, the eel. Not far from that gravel road, down a muddy dirt path, is a little blackwater seep the locals call Lost Pond.

The name is befitting, for you might easily pass within a few yards of Lost Pond and never know it is there. That is part of its charm. For in its isolation, deep within this sea of bottomland hardwoods, this tiny pool rarely receives human visitors. Wood ducks come here to rest and feed. Deer drink from its cool, tannin-stained waters. The woodlands around it are eternally damp and thickly understoried, a haven for swamp rabbits and woodcocks and other wetland creatures.

It was here the Rabbit Man led us.

We parked the trucks just east of the Pond, and stepped onto a blanket of hard-crusted snow. The wind was nippy but refreshing, and I began to feel the twinge of heady anticipation that always precedes a good rabbit chase.

The Rabbit Man opened the wooden box in the bed of his pickup and turned out the dogs, whistling and bellowing to spur them on. Then, cradling our guns under our arms, we followed the snuffling pack of hounds into the heart of the Lost Pond woods.

I studied the old man as we walked, and remember, quite succinctly, how the curmudgeonly, wayworn facade faded away. He reminded me of a bruised child given a mother's kiss to make it all better. The sullen glower was replaced with a broad smile, and when we stopped, so as not to rush the dogs, the Rabbit Man began to talk.

"This here's God's country, son, or at least the closest I've ever come to it," he said, gesturing with a sweep of his outstretched hand. "Lotsa folks don't care much for it. Too muddy. Too many mosquitoes and snakes. But the swamp rabbits and cottontails like it plenty good. Lots of 'em, all through here. And me and my dogs . . . well, we kinda take a hankering to any place there's lots of rabbits."

He beamed as he talked, and I suddenly realized the grumpy disposition I had perceived at first had not been that at all. It was more a bit of agitated impatience, an old man eager to get out of the city and back to the special, out-of-the-way haven where he was happy and at ease.

We hunted for several hours—talking, listening, waiting, when a chase was on. The dogs bawled and yammered off in the distance, tracing huge ellipses, parabolas, and figure eights through the woods as they hounded the Lost Pond swampers.

The Rabbit Man could not see the dogs, but then again, he could. His gaze followed their every move, and now and again, he would relate what was happening out there beyond the trees.

"They've lost him," he would say when the woods fell silent. "But just you listen. Ol' Pete'll figure him out." Shortly, the clamor would start again, and the Rabbit Man would smile a knowing smile.

"Hear Scrapper and Rascal? They're bringing him around. Sounds like Lady fell back in with them, too. She got sidetracked for a minute, but she's back on the trail."

He knew what the dogs would do before they did it, and though the rabbits seemed totally unpredictable to me, never showing when I'd expect it, the Rabbit Man always inserted one of our hunting party in just the right place to cut short their escape. Only rarely did he step in himself to shoot, that privilege being appointed for his guests.

I watched him slip through the bottoms that day, like a will-o'-the-wisp—here now, then gone, silently and unexpectedly—and knew the man was more than a visitor in those bottoms. He was as much a part of the swamp as the rabbits he chased, at home, fully incorporated into the landscape.

I remembered a few lines I'd read once in a Barry Lopez story. "...To hunt means to have the land around you like clothing. To engage in a wordless dialogue with it . . . It means to release yourself from rational images of what something 'means' and to be concerned only that it 'is.'"

I could see that's how it was with the Rabbit Man. When he opened the dog box and set his hounds loose in the bottoms, he was at peace with the world. All the pains and worries melted away. It was enough just to be there. The reasons why mattered not.

Despite my initial misgivings, something special happened that day. A seed was planted, and over the next hunting season and the next and the next, it grew and blossomed into a deep, unexpected friendship. The long drive between our homes kept me from hunting with the Rabbit Man as much as I would have liked. But I found an excuse to go afield with him at least once or twice each season.

We were generations apart, but being in those Lost Pond bottoms had a magical way of erasing our many contrasts. We would listen to that glorious dog music and talk for hours about beagles and swamp rabbits, about good cooking and good women, hunts past and hunts to come, and other matters of mutual importance. There were always a few jokes he'd saved up special for the occasion, but they were tempered by bouts of pensiveness when the old man would speak of deep concerns.

Mostly he worried about the noose of agriculture tightening 'round the neck of his beloved bottomlands.

"It'll all be gone someday," he said, staring into the autumn woods. "Thirty years ago, when I first started hunting here, there was so much more. Tupelo trees six feet through the middle. Oaks you could have built a house in. Game everywhere, like you couldn't imagine.

"Now it's shrinking away. Cleared up for the plow. Given over to soybeans and rice. I hope I'm not around when it's all gone."

I always hated to see those days come to an end. But in a way, it's the endings I remember most.

"Hear those dogs, boy?" he'd always say, looking out over his beloved woods. "They're playing my song.

"I hate to call 'em in."

Then he'd pull that old animal horn out from under his coat, and placing it to his lips, he'd sound a note, long and mellow.

And so it was that glorious dog music would end.

The layers of character that made the Rabbit Man different from the many other rabbit hunters I have known cannot be reduced to a single proposition or a simple-minded set of clichés. Yet, were I forced to choose the one trait that set him apart from others, I would say it was the intense, unwavering love he had for the sport.

For most participants, rabbit hunting is only a casual diversion. Outings are sporadic and unplanned, usually on weekends late in the hunting year when other game is no longer in season. Some are serious about the sport, to the point of even keeping a few beagles for their occasional forays afield. And, no doubt, they savor the many pleasantries inherent in this popular sideline. But the fickle nature of their safaris precludes them from the unique group of which the Rabbit Man was a part.

For the Rabbit Man, you see, hunting rabbits was no mere passion. It was more of a vital function, like a heartbeat and breathing. Being in his favorite coverts, watching and listening to the hullabaloo of his dogs chasing a long-legged canecutter or cottontail, was a magical elixir that nourished and sustained him. And like an aged man who'd found the Fountain of Youth, he returned to partake of the potion again and again, as often as possible.

Had he been deprived of those outings, which were an almost daily event during rabbit season, I have no doubt he would have withered away long before I met him.

I've met others like the Rabbit Man, but they are a rare and dying breed, destined, I'm afraid, for unheralded extinction. It is an unfortunate fact that most hunters, even those of us who consider hunting an undying passion, can no longer devote ourselves to our pleasures in such an all-encompassing manner. Despite our preferences to the contrary, we find ourselves caught up in day-to-day affairs that demand an ever-increasing share of our time. And as we give ourselves over to business and family matters and other such importances, we surrender, without a struggle, to the notion that we are "doing what's right," that pleasures are to be indulged only after we finish our toil.

That is why, I suppose, I felt compelled to write this story about the Rabbit Man. In many ways, he was an uncommonly common man. But he also was a man who embraced his passion for the outdoors and made it a priority in his life. In that respect, he was part of a small and vanishing brotherhood. We should remember his kind, if only because most of us wish that we, too, could more often indulge our fancies.

Ed Middleton, the Rabbit Man, passed away on February 19, 1991. Though I thought about it several times, I did not hunt with him that season. It was the first time in several years we'd not managed a trip or two together. Too much to do at home and in the office. Too little time for "unimportant" stuff like rabbit hunting.

When I read about his passing in the obituaries, I wasn't really too shocked. The Rabbit Man had been getting slow of late, complaining more often about his arthritis and walking shorter distances before he had to stop and catch his breath.

I spoke to him once in January, listening to him complain about two new pups that wouldn't mind him. Pete had died the last season, and Scrapper, now toothless, was too old to chase rabbits any more. The young pups just couldn't fill the shoes of the old veterans.

When the news of his passing finally sank in, I sat on top of the dog house and wept for the first time in many years. The tears flowed for a long time, each one falling on the head of the little beagle pup I embraced.

As the sun fell behind the mountains, I turned the dog out and listened as she ran a cottontail across the hillsides.

Booorrooo! Booorrooo!

It was a harsh sound, primitive and untamed. But it fell on my ears like a choir of angels.

"Can you hear that, Rabbit Man?," I said, casting my eyes toward the orange sunset. "She's playing your song."

Off in the distance, I thought I heard the long sonorous note of an old animal horn. And I knew, somewhere, the Rabbit Man was listening.

Limbgripper Jim

I suppose there was a time when Limbgripper Jim enjoyed the killing. Most hunters do, and Jim hunts as much as any man.

The killing, however, is no longer important. I hunt with Jim every season but can't remember the last time I saw him carry a gun.

He called last winter. "I'd like to take you and your boys on a hunt this weekend," he said. "Meet me early Saturday, and we'll make a morning of it."

I agreed.

"Don't forget," he added. "Leave your gun at home. This hunt's for the boys."

At the appointed time and place, we met.

"Heel, Ranger," Jim says as we enter the woods. Ranger heels. Jim rubs the dog's ears, and looks into his eyes. "Now listen, ol' buddy," he says in a voice as slow and syrupy as sorghum molasses. "These boys here want to shoot some squirrels. When I say go, I want you to go find one, OK?"

The dog looks at Jim knowingly. He shivers impatiently but holds for the command.

"Now GO," Jim shouts. Ranger is off like a stone released from a catapult.

The treeing cur's performance is amazing. In two minutes he trees. Jim smiles as we near the place where Ranger waits, reared up on a big oak, barking.

Jim gathers the four boys around. "Now remember," he says. "Safety first. Watch your gun barrels. Keep your safety on until you see the squirrel. If the squirrel gets on the ground, no one shoots. Only when it's in the tree, and then only one of you at a time. Now who'll be first?"

Shaun volunteers. Jim points out the squirrel pressed against the bark high overhead, then gives the OK to fire. Shaun bags the bushytail and is congratulated by all.

Six-year-old Zachary gets his chance when the dog next trees. The squirrel runs atop a short snag. With help from Jim, the youngster aims and fires. The squirrel falls. Ranger retrieves it. Zachary beams.

The boys shoot often throughout the day, and a few squirrels are taken for the frying pan. As we return to the truck, the boys are smiling and talking excitedly about the hunt. "When can we go again, Dad?" they ask.

"How 'bout tomorrow?" says Limbgripper Jim, winking at me. "I'm gonna let you boys move in with me, then you and me and ol' Ranger can go huntin' every day."

It is, for all of us, a memorable day.

In the fraternity of treeing dog enthusiasts, Jim Rhea (a.k.a. Limbgripper Jim) is legendary. This fifty-one-year-old businessman owns R & R Kennels in Wynne, Arkansas, where he raises and trains some of the world's finest pedigree squirrel dogs and coon dogs. He's well known in field-trial circuits. Dogs from his Limbgripper line (Limbgripper Buck, Limbgripper Danny, Limbgripper Jack, Limbgripper Ranger and others) have won every major award in the sport, including dozens of state, regional, United States and world championships. Limbgripper Ranger, the dog that treed squirrels for my sons, won world-champion honors in 1995, 1996, 1998, and 1999, and was inducted into the National Treeing Cur Association Hall of Fame.

To say Jim is proud of his dogs' trophies and plaques would be an understatement. He loves bragging on his canine friends and showing his awards to visitors. I learned years ago, however, a competitive nature is only one facet of the rich character that embodies Limbgripper Jim. This red-headed dynamo is generous to a fault, active in community affairs, and totally dedicated to his family. He sings country music, plays a mean guitar, and cooks the best game dinners you ever sat down to. Friends say he works too much, sleeps too little, and "Don't ever get behind him and his hunting dog in the hills; he'll walk your legs off and never break a sweat."

I met Jim in 1988 and was immediately impressed with his accomplishments. More than that, I was impressed by his kindness. On short notice on an icy day in January, at the request of a mutual friend, he took

Limbgripper Jim and friends.

me and two out-of-state visitors on a squirrel hunt with Limbgripper Jack, another of his world-champion dogs. Watching the mountain cur work with his master was better than Super Bowl Sunday. Never had I seen a more flawless performance. In the poorest conditions—high wind, sleet-covered ground—Limbgripper Jack treed more than a dozen squirrels. And while walking the woods together, watching Jack work, Jim and I became friends.

I discovered early on that Jim loves sharing the joys of hunting with children. And that, more than anything, impressed me about my newfound friend. I hunt often at the invitation of friends and business acquaintances, but seldom does the invitation extend to my sons as well. Jim never fails to invite the boys—all six of them.

"My oldest daughter, Sonya has been hunting squirrels with me since she was only six," he told me years ago. "My daughter Sam, too. The time we spend together in the woods watching the dogs work is quality time. It's fun for all of us."

Jim told me about early experiences hunting with his grandfather, who also raised squirrel dogs. Those hunts remain vivid in his mind despite the passage of decades.

"My grandpa started taking me when I was just six," Jim reminisced. "But I can remember those hunts like they were yesterday. They were fun because we didn't have to slip through the woods being quiet. I could talk while I watched the dog work. I didn't have to sit still and keep my mouth shut like I was hunting turkeys or deer. I learned then how thrilling it is to watch your dog operate. And that grew into a lifelong love of treeing dogs."

More importantly, perhaps, those trips with his grandfather instilled in Jim the value of sharing the hunting experience with his own children and with youngsters in his community. In 1997, he helped found the Little World Championship Youth Hunt, a national field-trial event for those eighteen and under. And though his schedule is hectic (he runs three businesses), he frequently takes a young apprentice under his wing and teaches him or her the art of dog training and handling.

My oldest son, Josh, now twenty-four, was one of those apprentices. His experiences working with Jim and his extraordinary dogs taught him valuable life lessons that can't be learned in a classroom or Sunday-school class. The father of another young man who apprenticed with Jim told me that working with Jim had given his son a new sense of confidence and personal value.

"When you and I were kids," the man said, "we had lots of good role models—presidents, sports heroes, teachers, pastors. But look around you now. Good role models are few and far between.

"Good role models are still out there, though," he continued. "And Jim Rhea is one of them. I thank God every day that Jim took an interest in my son, and is teaching him that spending a day hunting with a dog can be just as much fun as playing video games or watching TV. More than that, he's teaching him the importance of working hard, sharing things you love with other people and taking time to help friends and neighbors. Jim spends hundreds of hours teaching good Christian values to the young people in our community, and he does that by taking them hunting. We should all be thankful."

I, too, have learned lessons from Limbgripper Jim. When I started hunting with him a dozen years ago, killing was still important. A day in the field wasn't satisfying unless I blooded game. Then one day Jim called and invited me and my boys for a hunt. When we agreed on a meeting place, he told me, for the first time, "Leave your gun at home. This hunt's for the kids."

I was taken aback by the suggestion, and told him so. "My boys don't have much hunting experience," I said, "and if one of us doesn't carry a gun, we may not kill any squirrels."

"So what?" Jim answered. "We're not gonna starve if we don't kill any game. And if you're carrying a gun and doing all the shooting, how are your boys gonna learn? Tomorrow will be their day to have fun. You and I are just along for the ride."

That night, I thought about what Jim said, and knew he was right. I remembered my own childhood, growing up in a single parent household, and how I became a hunter. Uncles, cousins, school teachers, and neighbors who enjoyed hunting took me to the woods. And thinking back, I realized it wasn't often they carried a gun.

I know now that is why I am a hunter. The men who taught me were hunters, not killers. They watched while my youthful bloodlust was satisfied, and didn't deny me one iota of excitement. Hunting was fun not just because I killed game, though that was a part of it. It was fun because I was out there with good hunters sharing pleasures only hunters can know.

Jim and I leaned against a tree last year, watching the boys as they searched for a squirrel Ranger had treed. He looked at me and smiled a devilish smile.

"What are you grinning about?" I asked.

"I was just watching you and those boys," he said. "And watching you guys have fun makes me happy."

He turned then and headed for the oak where Ranger was treed.

"OK, boys. Now who's turn is it? Remember, safety first. Watch your gun barrels. Keep your safety on until you see the squirrel . . ."

Thank God for hunters like Limbgripper Jim.

Gene Moore

In the world of trophy deer hunting, there are basically two kinds of hunters. First are those whose every waking moment is consumed with the desire to kill a big deer. To them, bagging a wallhanger is an obsession. Nothing counts but records and numbers. A hunting trip without a deer for the wall is a failure.

Then there are the Gene Moores of the world. To them, hunting isn't a competition between hunters. It's a competition between animal and hunter, a matching of wits and senses in which we humans are so woefully inferior. They'll tell you that hunting is for those who don't need to prove anything to anybody. What matters most is that you've gone up the creek and over the rise. Just because you haven't killed an animal doesn't mean you've failed, for the only failures in hunting are those who don't love the outdoors.

Too much is made today, in some circles at least, about the trophies a hunter may have, and how long of antler they are. Don't get me wrong. Big heads are fine as long as we don't let them undermine the real reason we're in the field—hunting—for then our ethics begin to suffer. A hunter may take shortcuts to get the big head, and he may be miserably dissatisfied with anything less than an outstanding specimen.

That's why it was such a pleasure to do this story on Gene Moore. Moore is cut from a different cloth.

Moore has some very good trophy bucks of which he can be rightfully proud. In fact, one buck he harvested was just sixteen points shy of making the Boone and Crockett record books.

But Moore tells about the smaller bucks he's bagged with equal fervor and excitement. You listen to him and know that he's just as fond of his mediocre heads, because no matter how old he gets, those mounted heads will represent the wonder of the day, from sky to smell to breeze. He hadn't merely killed an animal. Rather, the beast became something more, a symbol of that moment. Those are his trophies. Not dead animal heads, but living memories of some of the best days of his life.

Unlike most of us, Moore didn't start deer hunting until he was twenty-seven years old. Work obligations and a hitch in the service kept him out of the field. But what he's learned in the ensuing years has

earned him a place in the ranks of Arkansas's best trophy deer hunters. The advice he offers could help you capture some of the best memories of your own life.

As you read on, however, keep in mind there are more important things to be learned here than just how to bag a trophy deer. This is a story about a hunter and his values. Learn Moore's secrets for successful deer hunting, but learn, too, the importance he places on other, more subtle treasures. Learn to hunt so your memories are right with you in your heart, for therein you'll find the true meaning of being deer hunter.

It's obvious, almost from the first moment you meet Gene Moore, he's a man of the outdoors. His face is etched with wrinkles from too many days in the sun, but his youthful features and blonde hair belie his age. The crow's-feet and cockles simply add character to his tall rugged frame.

He greets me with a firm handshake in the campground at East Moon Lake in White River National Wildlife Refuge. It is here Moore has bagged some of his biggest whitetails, and here he comes with his wife Joan and son Tommy to enjoy another passion, crappie and bream fishing. It's raining too hard now to fish, so we visit in the camping trailer with his brother W. T. and nephew Curt. Almost immediately, Moore starts talking about the family traditions of deer hunting that have been so important in shaping his values.

"My uncle, Jack Scott, is the one who really got me interested in deer hunting," Moore says, trying to speak above the patter of rain beating down outside. "Dad never did deer hunt all that much, and since Uncle Jack was the deer hunter in the family, he's the one I started hunting with. W. T. started hunting with him, too. I'd say he's one of the best deer hunters of his time. He started hunting in the St. Francis bottoms, and he's killed a lot of deer in his time, a lot of good deer. Many things I know about deer hunting I learned from Uncle Jack."

Moore relates with a chuckle the first lesson Uncle Jack taught him. He'd just killed his first deer, a three-point buck, and eager to finish the deer off, he jumped down from his stand to cut the animal's throat

"Uncle Jack heard all the commotion going on out there and here he come out through the woods," Moore says, laughing. "He got to the

---

Gene Moore.

deer just about the time I did. I grabbed the deer by one foot with one hand and started to stick the knife in him with the other, and Uncle Jack hollered 'Don't do that!' When he did, the deer kicked me right across the hand and the knife went flying through the air. He said 'Son, let me tell you something right now. You haven't hunted very much, but when you walk up to a deer and he's laying there with his eyes shut, back off from him, because he's fixin' to hurt you just like he almost hurt you then.'"

"I said, 'Well Uncle Jack, you know I never have deer hunted any.' And he said, 'Well, that's one good lesson you've learned.' That was the first lesson I learned about deer hunting."

Uncle Jack taught Gene Moore a lot of other things that have stuck with him. "He taught me to scout my area, to find fresh rubs and scrapes and to try position my stand where I can see a good-sized area. He taught me to hunt with the wind blowing in my face if possible, and that once I found a stand I liked, to get on it and stay there. Don't move. After you're on a stand a while don't think, well, that looks like a better stand down yonder, I'll move down there. I've had that happen to me a couple of times.

"I was hunting with W. T. one time," he says, "and he put me on a stand I thought was pretty good at the time. But after it got daylight, I kept looking and thinking, that's a real good stand down yonder. So I picked up my gear and walked down to the other place, and just as I threw my gear down, I saw the horns of a whitetail as it left the area by my first stand. So I learned that once you're on a stand, believe in it and stay with it."

Evidently, Moore learned his lessons well. He's bagged twenty bucks in as many years, each one tallied with a notch in the stock of one of his rifles. His largest buck was a massive eight-pointer killed between East Moon and Swan Lakes on White River National Wildlife Refuge. That whitetail weighed 192 pounds field-dressed and had a rack that scored 144 points on the Boone and Crockett scale. He bagged an almost equally impressive eight-point on St. Francis National Forest Wildlife Management Area. That buck weighed in at a hefty 180 field-dressed pounds. And these are just two of many big bucks Moore has taken.

Like so many of us, Moore doesn't hunt nearly as much as he would like. Wife Joan says he'd retire and live in a camper on the bank of East

Moon Lake if he could, but for now he has to settle for hunting weeklong stretches when he has time off from his job as a truck driver in Memphis, Tennessee, where he's now living.

Moore has hunted deer in several states, including Mississippi and Missouri. He and brother W. T. hunted Colorado mule deer in the mountains near Meeker for seven years straight, and Moore bagged some awesome mulies, including trophy six-point and nine-point bucks. Today, however, Moore concentrates his efforts primarily in two Arkansas areas—White River National Wildlife Refuge and, when he can draw a permit, St. Francis National Forest on Crowley's Ridge.

"I especially like St. Francis," he says with conviction. "St. Francis has good deer habitat and produces some big deer. There are plenty of good open places to hunt on the ridges and in the bottomland, but there's also plenty of thick cover where deer can hide and bed down."

Moore also enjoys hunting deer on White River National Wildlife Refuge, mostly, he says, "Because the deer are so big down here." White River, Moore notes, has an abundance of the things deer need—good cover, plenty of mast, and water. Consequently, deer are fairly abundant, and the chances of bagging a big deer, a real trophy, are as good as one can find anywhere in Arkansas.

Regardless of where he's hunting, though, Moore follows the same successful pattern. He hunts with a rifle—either a .308, 30.06, or a .30-caliber carbine—fitted with a breakover scope. He tries to scout his hunting area thoroughly for at least a couple of days before the season, looking for deer trails in areas with abundant acorns and other mast. When possible, he says, he prefers hunting over a fresh scrape or rub.

"During the rutting season," he says, "a buck's going to return some time within twenty-four or forty-eight hours to check his scrape. So when I'm scouting I try to locate fresh scrapes I can hunt over. When I find one, I don't disturb it at all, and I try to place my stand so I don't have to cross that deer's trail when I go to the stand. I set up fifty or a hundred yards from it where I can concentrate on that scrape at all times. Some of the bucks I've killed have been right in the scrape when I shot them.

"There's a lot of luck in deer hunting, no doubt," Moore says seriously. "But you can help put some of the luck in your favor by trying to think like that buck thinks. You have to understand the things the whitetail does and how he acts. That puts you more one on one so you'll be able to outsmart him.

"I try to be in my stand before daylight because deer are most active early in the morning. I try to face the wind so my scent isn't blowing to the deer because his sense of smell is so keen. And I try to remain motionless when I'm on my stand, because a deer is extremely sensitive to movement. He's color blind, I know, but you can bet he'll see you if you move."

Moore tells one especially humorous story about the deer's canny ability to detect a hunter's movements. He and son Tommy had two deer spotted from their stand one morning, and Tommy, still quite young, offered to let Dad take the shot. "I put my rifle up," says Moore, "and just as I pushed the safety off, the deer wheeled and took off. Now I've hunted long enough that I knew the deer couldn't hear the click of that safety, but I knew that was the only movement that deer could see me make. So I turned to Tommy and said 'What did you do, son? You must have done something that scared that deer.' He said 'Daddy, I didn't do anything but put my fingers in my ears.' It was just like he'd waved a red flag," Moore says chuckling.

Moore is especially fond of the times he spends outdoors with Tommy. Tommy's just eleven years old now, and though he hasn't bagged his own deer yet, he's been on the deer stand with his dad since he was three. "He's real interested in deer hunting, and it's very important to me to share my time outdoors with him," Moore says. "I want him to learn the safety aspects of hunting, and how to hunt. He's been handling a gun since he was about five years old, and anytime I'm hunting or fishing and he's out of school, he'll be with me. He loves to fish and he loves to hunt."

When you listen to Moore talk about all the fantastic hunting trips he's made, it's obvious that killing a trophy deer isn't what motivates him to be out in the woods. He hardly talks about the many trophy bucks he's taken, although he has every reason to brag. He talks most about times like these. Sharing the outdoor experience with his son and wife and brother and uncle. Spending quality time in a beautiful setting with people he loves.

Oversize trophies are impressive. But if you want to impress me with the fact that you're a great deer hunter, you'd do well to follow Moore's example. Tell me how you're teaching your son or daughter to shoot and to appreciate the outdoors. Show me your rifle and tell me how you practice with it to make humane kills. Describe to me the prettiest stretch of country you've ever hunted and why you like it. Show me how you hunt the animal with respect and reverence, not with indifference or callous disregard.

Even then you might have trouble explaining "proper hunting ethics," but like Gene Moore, you will know the meaning. It's that knowledge, not how many trophy bucks you have hanging on your wall, that will make you a truly great deer hunter.

Appendix: Arkansas Hunting Information Sources

The following agencies provide information invaluable to all who hunt in Arkansas.

Arkansas Game & Fish Commission
2 Natural Resources Dr.
Little Rock, AR 72205
800-364-GAME
www.agfc.com

    Information available: hunting-regulations guides; maps and information on AG&FC wildlife management areas; free brochures and booklets on Arkansas game animals and hunting; for-sale publications of interest to hunters, including *The Arkansas Outdoor Atlas* (with seventy-five county maps showing the locations of public
hunting lands).

Arkansas Geological Commission
3815 W. Roosevelt Rd.
Little Rock, AR 72204
501-296-1877

    Information available: topographic maps for the state of Arkansas.

Big Lake National Wildlife Refuge
POB 67
Manila, AR 72442
870-564-2429

    Information available: hunting-regulations guide; free brochure with refuge map.

Cache River/Bald Knob National Wildlife Refuges
Rt. 2, Box 126-T
Augusta, AR
501-347-2614

> Information available: hunting-regulations guide; free brochure with refuge map.

Felsenthal/Overflow National Wildlife Refuges
POB 1157
Crossett, AR 71635
870-364-3167

> Information available: hunting-regulations guide; free brochure with refuge map.

Holla Bend National Wildlife Refuge
Rt. 1, Box 59
Dardanelle, AR 72834
501-229-4302

> Information available: hunting-regulations guide; free brochure with refuge map.

Ouachita National Forest
POB 1270
Hot Springs, AR 71902
501-321-5202

> Information available: maps of national forest lands showing lakes, streams, campsites, and more.

Ozark National Forest
POB 1008
Russellville, AR 72801
501-968-2354

> Information available: maps of national forest lands showing lakes, streams, campsites, and more.

St. Francis National Forest
2675 Highway 44
Marianna, AR 72360
870-295-5278

>Information available: maps of national forest lands showing lakes, streams, campsites, and more.

U.S. Army Corps of Engineers
Little Rock District
POB 867
Little Rock, AR 72203
501-324-5551

>Information available: maps and information for all agency lands and state's large navigable waterways.

Wapanocca National Wildlife Refuge
POB 279
Turrell, AR 72384

>Information available: hunting-regulations guide; free brochure with refuge map.

White River National Wildlife Refuge
POB 308
DeWitt, AR 72042
870-946-1468

>Information available: hunting-regulations guide; free brochure with refuge map.

Index

Apple, Bill, 109
Arkansas River, 54, 55, 81, 95, 121, 215
Audubon, John James, 113

Baldwin Creek, 197
Bateman, Dr. Simeon, 4
Bayou Bartholomew, 73, 161
Bayou Des Arc, 73
Bayou de View, 73, 96, 161
Bayou de View Wildlife Management Area. *See* Earl Buss/Bayou de View Wildlife Management Area
Bayou Meto Wildlife Management Area, 21, 35, 65, 73, 82, 161, 193
bear, black, 3–13; basic hunting techniques, 8–10; charged by, 11–12; hunting and use by native Americans, 4; reestablishment by Arkansas Game & Fish Commission, 6–7; use of oil and meat, 4
Bear Creek Lake, 177, 178, 181–82
Bearden, Richard, 103
Big Bayou Meto, 73
Big Creek, 73, 198
Big Lake National Wildlife Refuge, 121
Big Lake Wilderness Area, 206
Big Lake Wildlife Management Area, 36
Big Piney Creek, 198
Billingsley, John, 101
Black Fork Mountain Wilderness Area, 206
Black Mountain Refuge, 102
Black River, 96
Black River Wildlife Management Area. *See* Dave Donaldson/Black River Wildlife Management Area
Black Swamp Wildlife Management Area. *See* Rex Hancock/Black Swamp Wildlife Management Area

Blue Mountain Wildlife Management Area, 149
bobcat, 135–39; calling, 138–39
bobwhite, northern, 147–55; dogs and guns for hunting, 150–51; hunting in small pockets of cover, 153–55
Bodcaw Bayou, 73
Bogardus, Capt. Adam H., 25
Bois d'Arc Wildlife Management Area, 36, 82
Bossu, Jean Bernard, 101
Branscum, Austin, 103
Buffalo National River, 103, 104, 198
Buffalo National River Wilderness Area, 206
Buffalo River Wildlife Management Area. *See* Gene Rush/Buffalo River Wildlife Management Area
Bull Shoals Lake, 82

Cache River, 96, 161
Cache River National Wildlife Refuge, 8, 73, 96
Camp Robinson Wildlife Management Area, 143, 149
canecutter. *See* rabbit, swamp
Caney Creek Wilderness Area, 206, 244
Caney Creek Wildlife Management Area, 197, 199
Combs, Capt. George, Sr., 25
coon. *See* raccoon
coot, American, 32–33
cottontail, eastern. *See* rabbits
coyote, 140–43; calling, 141–42
crow, American, 39–44; calling, 41–42; decoys, 42–43
crow, fish, 40
Cut-off Creek Wildlife Management Area, 21, 161

273

Dagmar Wildlife Management Area, 21, 35, 73, 96, 143, 161
Dave Donaldson/Black River Wildlife Management Area, 36, 73, 82, 96
Deane, Ernie, 114
deer, white-tailed, 205–28; hunting during the rut, 218–24, 265; hunting in farmlands, 211–17; hunting in White River National Wildlife Refuge, 225–28; hunting in wilderness areas, 205–9. *See also* Moore, Gene
Delaney Creek, 197
de Soto, Hernando, 108, 113
Dorcheat Bayou, 73
Doughty, Dan, 214
dove, mourning, 47–59; hunting along rivers, 53–56; hunting around gravel pits, 57–59; paid shoots, 47–48; private lands hunting, 49–50; public lands hunting, 50–51
Dry Creek Wilderness Area, 206
duck, ring-necked, 94
duck, wood, 65, 68–74, 86, 87, 94; basic hunting techniques, 72–74; historical notes, 71–72; life history, 72. *See also* ducks
ducks, 63–97; calling, 65–66, 88, 91; decoys, 74, 81, 88, 91; hunting in green timber, 63–67; hunting on big rivers, 90–97; hunting on small waters, 73–74, 83–89
Dunnahoo, Patrick, 114

Earl Buss/Bayou de View Wildlife Management Area, 73, 96
East Fork Wilderness Area, 200, 206
East Moon Lake, 264
Ed Gordon/Point Remove Wildlife Management Area, 36
elk, 101–4
Elk Festival, 103
Elkhorn Tavern, 102
Ellis, Shelton, 161
Elvas, Gentleman of, 113

Farris, Melvin, 103

Featherstonhaugh, G. W., 102
Felsenthal National Wildlife Refuge, 21, 73, 97, 161, 193
Feral Hog Task Force, 234
Flatside Wilderness Area, 206
Fort Chaffee Wildlife Management Area, 143
Frog's Bayou, 198

gadwall, 65, 83, 86, 91. *See also* ducks
Galla Creek Wildlife Management Area, 142
gallinule, purple, 34–35
Gene Rush/Buffalo River Wildlife Management Area, 7, 103, 243
Gillett Coon Supper, 108
goose, blue. *See* goose, snow
goose, Canada, 94, 119–23; basic hunting techniques, 121–23; restoration program, 120–21
goose, snow, 124–28; basic hunting techniques, 127–28
goose, specklebelly. *See* goose, white-fronted
goose, white-fronted, 129–32; calling, 131–32
Gresham, Grits, 26
Gulf Mountain Wildlife Management Area, 7, 149

Harris Brake Wildlife Management Area, 35
Henry Gray/Hurricane Lake Wildlife Management Area, 21, 35, 73, 82, 93, 160, 193
Heuston, John, 137–39
Hobbs State Management Area, 142
hog, feral. *See* hog, wild
hog, wild, 231–36
Holder, Trusten, 108
Holla Bend National Wildlife Refuge, 121, 215, 243
Holland Bottoms Wildlife Management Area, 36

Honor, Dr. Albert, 5–6
Hope Wildlife Management Area, 149
Horsehead Lake, 197
Huggler, Tom, 148
Hurricane Creek, 197
Hurricane Creek Wilderness Area, 206
Hurricane Lake Wildlife Management Area. *See* Henry Gray/Hurricane Lake Wildlife Management Area

Illinois Bayou, 198, 200
Indian Creek, 198

jacksnipe. *See* snipe, common
Jones, Bill, 207–9

LaGrue Bayou, 161
La Harpe, Bernard de, 4
Lake Greeson, 200, 201
Lake Greeson Wildlife Management Area, 143
L'Anguille River, 22, 69, 73, 82, 161, 178, 249
Leatherwood Wilderness Area, 206
Leopold, Aldo, 128
Little Bayou Meto, 73
Little Missouri River, 200–201
Little Piney Creek, 198
Lynch, Rocky, 109

Madison County Wildlife Management Area, 142
Madson, John, 244
mallard, 63–67, 83, 86, 87, 91, 94, 95. *See also* ducks
marsh hen. *See* coot, American
Maslowski, Karl, 161, 164
Mercer Bayou, 96
merganser, hooded, 94
Middleton, Hugh "Ed," 161, 249–54
Miller, Jim, 240
Millwood Lake, 82
Minton, Jimmy, 104

Mississippi River, 54, 55, 73, 94, 178
Moore, Gene, 261–67
moorhen, common, 34–35
Moro Bayou, 73
Mount Magazine Wildlife Management Area, 243
Muddy Creek Wildlife Management Area, 197, 199
mud hen. *See* coot, American

Nimrod Wildlife Management Area, 82
Noland, Charles Fenton Mercer, 3
Norfork Lake, 82

Olsen, Sigurd, 209
opossum, 111–15
Ouachita National Forest, 195, 205, 215
Ouachita River, 73, 82, 96
Overflow National Wildlife Refuge, 21, 161

Patterson, Gregg, 241
Peeler, Lewis, 57–59, 161, 165–68
Peters, George, 94
Petit Jean Wildlife Management Area, 35
Piney Creeks Wildlife Management Area, 7, 197, 198, 243
pintail, northern, 83, 86, 91. *See also* ducks
Point Remove Wildlife Management Area. *See* Ed Gordon/Point Remove Wildlife Management Area
Poison Springs Wildlife Management Area, 143
possum. *See* opossum
Poteau Mountain Wilderness Area, 206
poule d'eau. *See* coot, American
Pringle, John Julius, 25

quail. *See* bobwhite, northern

rabbit, cottontail. *See* rabbits
rabbit, swamp, 159–64
rabbits, 159–74; hunting with dogs, 165–67; hunting without dogs, 169–74. *See also* rabbit, swamp; Middleton, Hugh "Ed"
raccoon, 107–10
Ragland, Mark, 124
rail, black, 33
rail, clapper, 33
rail, sora. *See* sora
rail, Virginia, 33–34
rail, yellow, 33
Ranjel, Rodrigo, 113
razorback. *See* hog, wild
Red River, 73, 96
Rex Hancock/Black Swamp Wildlife Management Area, 21, 73, 92, 96, 161
Rhea, Jim, 255–60
Robertson, George, 6
Rocky Mountain Elk Foundation, 103
Rue, Leonard Lee, III, 125

Saline River, 96
scaup, 91, 94
Schoolcraft, Henry, 101, 108
Sealander, John, 222
Searles, Leon, 103
Shirey Bay-Rainey Brake Wildlife Management Area, 36, 82, 96
shorebirds, laws protecting, 26
Short, Hunter, 104
shoveler, northern, 83, 86. *See also* ducks
Smith, William, N., 25
snipe, common, 24–29; basic hunting techniques, 27–28; historical notes, 25–26
snipe, Wilson's. *See* snipe, common
sora, 33–34
specklebelly. *See* goose, white-fronted

Spencer, Jim, 66, 91–93, 97, 127, 239, 241–44
squirrel, black. *See* squirrel, fox
squirrel, fox, 190–94. *See also* squirrels
squirrel, gray. *See* squirrels
squirrels, 177–201; early season hunting, 180–81; guns for hunting, 182–83; hunting from a boat, 184–89; hunting in beech trees, 180; hunting in mountains, 195–201; hunting on Crowley's Ridge, 177–83. *See also* squirrel, fox; Rhea, Jim
St. Francis National Forest, 22, 36, 143, 177–78, 244, 265
St. Francis River, 22, 53, 55, 73, 83, 96, 102, 107, 161
St. Francis River Floodway, 54, 55
St. Francis Sunken Lands Wildlife Management Area, 22, 35, 73, 96
Storm Creek Lake, 178, 182
Stough, Mike, 161
Stuttgart, 64, 124
Sulphur River, 73, 96
Sulphur River Wildlife Management Area, 22, 36, 82, 96
swamper. *See* rabbit, swamp
Swan Lake, 264
Sylamore Creek, 198
Sylamore Wildlife Management Area, 142, 197, 243

teal, blue-winged, 65, 75–82; decoys, 81; guns and loads, 80; hunting hotspots, 81–82; identification, 78; scouting, 79–80. *See also* ducks
teal, green-winged, 65, 75–82, 86, 87; decoys, 81; guns and loads, 80; hunting hotspots, 81–82; identification, 79; scouting, 79–80. *See also* ducks
Trusten Holder Wildlife Management Area, 21, 35
turkey, wild, 239–45

Upper Buffalo Wilderness Area, 206

Wapanocca National Wildlife
 Refuge, 121
Wattensaw Bayou, 161
Wattensaw Wildlife Management Area,
 21, 35, 73, 93, 143,
 149, 160
whitebill. *See* coot, American
White River, 54, 55, 73, 93, 108,
 160, 198
White River National Wildlife Refuge,
 6, 21, 65, 73, 93, 121, 161, 193,
 225–28, 263, 264
White Rock Wildlife Management
 Area, 7, 197, 243
wigeon, Amercan, 86. *See also* ducks
Wilderness Act, 205
wilderness areas. *See* Big Lake
 Wilderness Area; Black Fork
 Mountain Wilderness Area;
 Buffalo National River
 Wilderness Area; Caney Creek
 Wilderness Area; Dry Creek
 Wilderness Area; East Fork
 Wilderness Area; Flatside
 Wilderness Area; Hurricane
 Creek Wilderness Area;
 Leatherwood Wilderness
 Area; Poteau Mountain
 Wilderness Area; Upper
 Buffalo Wilderness Area
wild turkey. *See* turkey, wild
Wilson, Steve N., 219–24
Winona Wildlife Management Area,
 143, 149, 243
woodcock, American, 11–23; basic
 hunting techniques, 20–21;
 habitat, 18–19

Young, Kenn, 214